THAT'S ME IN THE CORNER

Andrew Collins

D0784264

EBURY
PRESS

1 3 5 7 9 10 8 6 4 2

Published in 2007 by Ebury Press, an imprint of Ebury Publishing

Ebury Publishing is a division of the Random House Group

The Random House Group Limited Reg. No. 954009

Addresses for companies within the Random House Group can be
found at www.randomhouse.co.uk

A CIP catalogue record for this book is available from the British Library

The Random House Group Limited makes every effort to ensure that
the papers used in our books are made from trees that have been legally
sourced from well-managed and credibly certified forests. Our paper
procurement policy can be found on www.randomhouse.co.uk

Printed and bound by Mackays of Chatham Ltd

Typeset by seagulls.net

Extracts from *EastEnders* reproduced with kind permission of the BBC

Inside back cover photograph copyright © BBC

ISBN 9780091897864

CONTENTS

Prologue: *Jaws* Actor Dies   1

1   Stacking Mandarin Segments for John Sainsbury   8

2   Cursing Porkbeast   18

3   Praising the Lord for Andy Crane   32

4   Standing on the Deck of an Aircraft Carrier with the Soup Dragons   40

5   Redirecting Killing Joke's Stripper   51

6   Marvelling at Andrea Dworkin   73

7   Understanding Lenny Kravitz   92

8   Letting Down Steve Wright   114

9   Keeping the Door Open for Johnny Vaughan   132

10   On a Yacht with Will Smith   160

11   Having My Hair Mocked by Noel Gallagher   179

12   Writing Comedy Gold for Judith Hann   201

13   Having Nothing to Say to Mark Fowler   223

14   Getting Drunk with Doctor Who   242

15   Pissing Off Christina Ricci   260

16   Getting On Famously with Black Rebel Motorcycle Club   277

17   Eating Coronation Chicken with Doctor Who   294

18   Going On after Garry Bushell   306

Epilogue: What *Am* I?   320

'I didn't get where I am today by thinking.'

CJ, *The Fall and Rise of Reginald Perrin*

Acknowledgements

This is not the book I set out to write. It was supposed to be a novel about a teenage love affair at the time of the Falklands War. The very existence of *That's Me in the Corner* is testament to Andrew Goodfellow at Ebury, who knows what's good for me. An inordinately patient man, who introduced me to the word 'solipsistic', he's now the proud editor of a *trilogy*. Imagine that! A long haul, interrupted by the six months it took me to go off and co-write a sitcom, we got there in the end.

The incomparable Kate Haldane continues to help assemble the rough patchwork of my ongoing career into something approaching a wearable garment with warmth and foresight, while the eyrie at Amanda Howard Associates (hello, Annette, Mark, Chloe, Darren, Kirsten, Lucy and Amanda – mine's a cup of boiling water and a fork) provides a constant, Soho-based refuge.

Any trip down memory lane requires verification, hot denial and added colour, and the following players were generous with recollections to add to my own: Stuart Maconie, Andy Rowe, David Quantick, John Harris, Jerry Perkins, Mark Salisbury, Simon Blackwell, Steve Lamacq, Paul Quinn, Jeff Smith and Tania Branigan. Mum and Dad were invaluable on the Sainsbury's period, and showed a keen interest in the later chapters, which, after putting up with some of the rum stuff in *Heaven Knows I'm Miserable Now*, was greatly appreciated. Thanks also to Graham Kibble-White and Ian Jones for honest, discreet and encouraging feedback on the early chapters. Some of the detail in Chapter 17, 'Eating Coronation Chicken with Doctor Who', first appeared in a piece I wrote for impeccable TV criticism website www.offthetelly.co.uk. This material has been borrowed back and remixed with kind permission.

A ripple for the assembled students, parents and staff on graduation day at Northampton University, 11 July 2006, who allowed me to road test the James Bolam anecdote in my acceptance speech. For bestowing upon me an Honorary Fellowship, and all the pomp and circumstance inherent in that, I thank Dean of the School of the Arts Dave Keskeys, Vice Chancellor Anne Tate, Chairman John Castle and the Governing Council and Senate – not forgetting Melva Duley, who held it all together on the day.

The one job I don't write about in this book of jobs is, for fear of disappearing in a puff of solipsistic smoke, writing books. But writing books has opened a lot of doors for me, most of them attached to libraries. After-hours speaking engagements held at council-run lending institutions make it all worthwhile – intimate, lively, good-natured and happy to accommodate a slide show – so rather than getting the threatened tour T-shirt made up, I'd like to thank everybody involved with putting me on at the following venues over the past two memoirs: Kingsthorpe Library, Northampton Central Library, Weston Favell Library, Willesden Green Library, Billericay Library and, most imposingly, the Mitchell Library in Glasgow. I have enjoyed disobeying the notices in all of them. Charlie Harris and Midas PR did a fine job of getting me out there, and the good folk at Ebury deserve appreciative noises from the back for allowing me to appear in my first podcast, filmed at the Ebury comedy night, notably Sarah Bennie and Di Riley. Thanks also to Rachel Leyshon and Verity Willcocks, who were hands-on with the book.

To the likeminded souls who congregate, virtually, around my blog and radio shows, or simply bother to get in touch after reading the books, I offer a humble nod of community.

Julie Quirke continues to operate a keen editorial radar in matters of writing, and sense and stability in the real world, which is where I live, lest we forget. She's in the book without being in it. Eternal peace to Chilli.

And finally, to my mentors. All of these people, in strict

chronological order, taught me important things and helped shape me into whatever I am today: James Brown, Justin Langlands, Alan Lewis, Danny Kelly, David Quantick, John Yorke, Judy Leighton, Matt Hall, Mark Goodier, Jeff Smith, John Sugar, Mark Ellen, Andrew Harrison, David Cavanagh, David Hepworth, Vivienne Clore, Kenton Allen, Johnny Vaughan, Richard Osman, Mark Salisbury, John Leonard, Andy Rowe, Elaine Bedell, Richard Drewett, Clive James, Billy Bragg, Ian Gittins, Mal Young, Keith Temple, Tony Jordan, Faith Penhale, Alix Brennan, Ian Hargreaves, Robert Yates, Adam Smith, Ian Nathan, Mark Lawson, Matthew Dodds, Stephen Hughes, John Goudie, Nicholas Brett, Gill Hudson, Ian Callaghan, Lucy Armitage, Alex Walsh-Taylor, Jon Plowman, Simon Day, Frank Wilson, Miles Mendoza, Leona McCambridge, Jim Moir, Lesley Douglas, Ric Blaxill, Will Saunders, Jon Holmes, Robin Ince, Dawn Ellis, Gary Russell, Richard Grocock, Richard Herring, Francis Welch, Lucy Lumsden and Lee Mack.

Too many to mention at Radio 5 (as was), Radio 1, Radio 4, Radio 2, 6 Music, *Radio Times*, BBC Comedy, BBC Drama, BBC Bristol, BBC Scotland, BBC Local Radio, IPC, Emap, Channel X, Rapido, Watchmaker, Pearson, World, Unique, Smooth Ops, Somethin' Else, AHA, Virgin, Ebury, Fat Bloke, Avalon, TCM and, of course, Sainsbury's in the Grosvenor Centre, Northampton. Thanks to Jon Thoday for allowing me to tell the *Select* story.

A special apology to Stuart Maconie for writing so much about him.

That's enough memoirs. I didn't get where I am today by writing memoirs.

Andrew Collins
London, February 2007
www.wherediditallgoright.com/BLOG

PROLOGUE

Jaws Actor Dies

It's a normal day. I'm at Redhill station, boarding my usual train into town, calling at East Croydon, Clapham Junction and London Victoria. A trolley service of drinks and light refreshments will be available on this train. This train is formed of *eight* coaches. I'm afraid I have become one of those people who stands on the same spot on the platform each morning, knowing that if it's an eight-coach train the second set of doors on the first carriage, my preferred set, will stop *riiiiiight heeeeeere.*

Once settled in my usual seat (window, facing backwards), I take out my book about Stalin and try to remember which of his trusted generals are dead and which are still alive. It's then that I notice a familiar face sitting at a table seat on the other side of the aisle. (I always avoid table seats.) Lurking behind a copy of the *Telegraph* – the third most visible newspaper on this line after the *Mail* and *The Times* – I can confirm with some delight that it's the actor James Bolam. He is largely obscured by his broadsheet but I catch a glimpse of him as he turns the page. He is peering over little oblong glasses and probably hoping that other passengers will recognise him without actually bothering him.

Me and James Bolam in the same carriage. Fancy that.

It makes you wonder, doesn't it? It makes me wonder, anyway. What if there was a fatal train crash on this particular line, on this particular day in history? How would it be if the Chichester to Victoria train was derailed just outside East

Croydon and everyone in our carriage was killed? First of all, it would go down in history as 'the East Croydon rail crash', eventually abbreviated to 'East Croydon' just like 'Potters Bar' or 'Ladbroke Grove'. Secondly, it would be remembered as the one in which *Likely Lads* and *Born and Bred* star James Bolam was killed, aged sixty-six.

My chances of getting a headline would be pretty slim. And how would they sell it?

'DJ KILLED IN EAST CROYDON RAIL CRASH'?

'AUTHOR KILLED IN EAST CROYDON RAIL CRASH'?

'*RADIO TIMES* FILM EDITOR KILLED IN EAST CROYDON RAIL CRASH'?

'DJ-AUTHOR-JOURNALIST KILLED IN—'

Oh, it doesn't matter.

Richard Dreyfuss, a Hollywood star no doubt admired by James Bolam, has achieved so much in his thirty-five-year screen career, and yet he always says he is haunted by the knowledge that when his final headline comes it will read: '*JAWS* ACTOR DIES'.

Perhaps the *Redhill & Reigate Life* would mark the passing of a local resident. Maybe I'd merit a footnote in the nationals, the sort I would customarily read and then pontificate over: 'What about the *ordinary* people who died? Who cares about some DJ? Is a DJ's life worth more than a heating engineer's?'

Bolam's obituary would be huge and glowing – especially in the *Telegraph*, one hopes – and who would begrudge him that? Not me.

I find myself distracted from Stalin's latest purge, instead morbidly calculating comparative posthumous column inches as we pull into East Croydon (our next 'station stop' according to the on-train announcement, a weasel tautology that speaks loudly of the mangled age in which we live, or indeed the age in which we die horribly in a grotesque tableau of twisted metal and corporate livery). At which point, Ainsley Harriott gets on.

Though wearing a woolly hat over his trademark bald head,

his trademark goggly eyes are unmistakable. It's him, the TV chef and bloke off the Fairy Liquid adverts. Two points.

Ainsley sits down across the aisle from Bolam, but Bolam keeps his *Telegraph* guard up, and no eye contact is made between these two unconnected celebrities.

I'm starting to feel quite depressed. My footnote in history is shrinking before my very eyes. Suddenly my carriage is a news editor's dream: TV chef and sitcom star killed in same crash. What use would a little-known DJ-author-journalist be in those unlikely circumstances?

It reminds me of the punchline to an old Jewish joke that Philip Roth quotes in his coming-of-age novel *Portnoy's Complaint*: 'Help! Help! My son – the doctor – is drowning!' I've always loved the economy of that gag. What, I ask myself, would my own mum shout were I to find myself in aquatic peril – and were she suddenly, inexplicably Jewish: 'Help! Help! My son – the writer, DJ and *Radio Times* film editor – is drowning!'

Doesn't have the same ring, does it? Mum might simplify and cry, 'My son – the former *EastEnders* scriptwriter – is drowning!' (Mention of *EastEnders* usually gets people's attention.)

'Really?' my potential rescuers would pipe up, roused from a nearby picnic by a mother's distress. 'Which characters did he write for?'

Then she'd have to explain – as I have patiently done on so many occasions – that individual scriptwriters are given individual episodes to write, like slices cut from the same never-ending dramatic salami.

'Did he do any that I might have seen?'

'The one where Nick Cotton's son died?'

Meanwhile, *I'm* dying, slipping under the surf, gasping for my last breath, wishing someone other than my dad, a lifelong non-swimmer, had taught me to swim as a child, waiting for the *doof doof doof* that comes at the end of *EastEnders* but never in real life.

Why all this unnecessary worry about posterity and death? I'm not normally like this. I'm generally happy with my lot on the fringes of recognition. But then I'm at a funny age and I'm on the Celebrity Express from Chichester.

If only I'd been a doctor. The mother of a doctor never asks, 'When are you going to get a proper job?' If only, in fact, I'd been an insurance man like my non-swimming dad. Something neat and comprehensible. Neat and comprehensive, in fact – third party, fire and theft. Not that folk would be falling over themselves to save an insurance man from drowning – too busy grumbling about their premiums – but at least it's a job that doesn't need annotating. A literal job description.

No matter that Dad, now retired, specialised in pensions, or that when I was growing up his work seemed to me an arcane and remote whirl of 'meetings' with 'clients'; he was *in insurance*. End of discussion.

'Ah, insurance. What car do you drive? Terrible weather we've been having. Did you read about that train crash? James Bolam *and* Ainsley Harriott!'

When I first entered the world of full-time work aged twenty-two, I too had one job – albeit not exactly a proper one. On submitting that inaugural tax return in 1988, after my first year's trading, I entered 'illustrator' in the box marked profession. Despite the initial whiff of pretension, illustration was still a job, a service, a vocation. It was also obligingly literal: I illustrated; I did illustrations; I drew pictures that looked like the thing they were supposed to be, whether it was a panda or a plane, for money.

Self-employed, as respectably and honestly as any heating engineer, the tools of my trade were pens, ink, magic markers, tracing pads and paint. If I was in cavalier mood, I sometimes used masking fluid, a rubber-based liquid gunk you apply to the page with a brush. When it has solidified you may gaily throw coloured ink all over it and, when that's dry, gently rub and peel off the masking fluid in satisfying rubbery strands. This creates pure white space, a virginal oasis amid the coloured ink, as if you have painted with pure nothing.

If I was in a similarly cavalier mood when someone asked me at a party what I did for a job, I would say 'cartoonist' – because this was my chosen area of expertise. I drew cartoons that looked like the thing they were supposed to be, for money. Mickey Mouse money, you might say, if *you* were in a cavalier mood. But at least it was a job that could be summed up in one word and, on the surface at least, seemed quite interesting – albeit never as interesting as partygoers hoped.

They say that when you drown your whole life flashes before you. By the time you reach forty, as I did two weeks ago, at least half of that is likely to be your working life. I'm not drowning, I'm on a train rattling through Purley Oaks, it's merely a hypo-thetical, but since my first tax return in 1988 I've had seventeen jobs. That's roughly one a year, although it was never that neat. There they go, like the Surrey countryside, flashing past, some of them lasting for months, others a couple of weeks, many of them overlapping, one of them earning me some shares, each one for a fleeting moment my amazing Technicolour dream job, until I realised it wasn't.

I've changed offices; I've changed companies; I've changed job titles; I've had the same job title in three different offices at two different companies and found it to mean completely differ-ent things in each one; I've applied for jobs I didn't want because it would 'look good' to the people upstairs; I've been advised *not* to apply for jobs I *did* want by the people upstairs; I've considered becoming one of the people upstairs; I've resigned from jobs, rescinded my resignation and then resigned again; I've been on strike and risked losing my job; I've been promoted, I've been moved sideways, I've been sacked; I've interviewed *other people* for jobs; I've hired and I've fired; I've been on probation; I've been warned; I've been rejected; I've been trained, re-trained and I've trained others; I've brainstormed; I've blue-skied; I've hot-desked; I've been on 'away days', and I've won an engraved pen, presented to me by Ian Hislop at an in-house awards ceremony, months before leaving the job I'd won it for and the company who'd awarded it to me. Can I just quietly drown now, please? I'm getting tired just thinking about it.

I'm forty years old. I sat on this very train on my fortieth birthday in this very seat, facing – aptly enough – backwards. It snowed that day, just as it did on the day I was born. Between those two significant snowfalls, I think it's fair to say I've worked my arse off trying to decide how best to work my arse off.

This does not make me special. Most people work their arses off, often at the same job, thereby getting better at it and even becoming experts in their field. Heating engineers work their arses off, with mended radiators to show for it each day. James Bolam works his arse off and he's sixty-seven in June with no retirement in sight. Many people switch jobs, even careers, and some of them win engraved pens. Like it or not, work defines us. It defines us if we don't do it. My ongoing search for a definitive job defines me.

At school we're asked what we want to do when we grow up, but the joke is that when we do grow up, we still don't know what it is we want to do. Even my brother Simon, aged thirty-eight, who'd wanted to join the army as soon as he'd removed his first Action Man uniform from the backing card, and did so at the age of sixteen, eventually left the job of his dreams. True, he left the army to join the prison service, and then the prison service to join the police, thus revealing himself to be addicted to hats, but he switched jobs when not switching jobs would have been the easy option.

So work, and an imagined search for stability within the world of work, has defined me since 1988 – since 1981 if you count my first Saturday job at Sainsbury's, and I intend to – yet it has constantly failed to define me in any useful way. I certainly could have made the past seventeen years easier by sticking to one job, but that appears not to be in my blood. Maybe in my forties a change will come. Would that not be an apt time to settle into a single furrow? Some people are driven by material gain, or status, or financial security, or the need to belong. Am I really only driven by indecision? I'm not sure (obviously).

Work has certainly paid my rent. It has introduced me to my friends and my wife, made me ill, dressed me in a suit and cut my hair, made my parents proud and got me on the telly. And if I've learned one thing over those seventeen years it's this: don't personalise your desk. Don't arrange a Gonk or family photographs, put a sticker on your PC, save anything personal on your desktop or stash anything important in the lockable drawer. It may be your desk today but it won't be your desk tomorrow.

I've never been anything respectable or honest like a docker, nor a miner, nor a railwayman. I can't mend radiators. And today I'm a forty-year-old DJ, author and film editor of the *Radio Times*, wondering if essential engineering works at Thornton Heath will slow the trains down and make a fatal crash less fatal, thus postponing the unlikely death of a Likely Lad and a TV chef.

I don't intend to die today, or for another forty years. But one question hangs over me at this momentous railway junction in my life, and it was put to me at Christmas by Harry, the nine-year-old son of my brother-in-law's sister. Having seen me on a clips show on television the night before, he fixed me with his unselfconscious, exploring child's eyes at the buffet table and asked:

'What *are* you?'

Not *who* am I, but *what* am I.

It's the best question anyone has ever asked me and I didn't have an answer. But I'd like to find one.

1

Stacking Mandarin Segments for John Sainsbury

I hope all job interviews go like this:

'So, you're Janice Cave's nephew, are you?'

'Yes.'

'Welcome to Sainsbury's.'

It's May 1981. Hello. I'm sixteen and it's the summer term: my last as a fifth-former. Hooray. Spotty chin (cheers, Biactol). 'Heavy fringe' (that's what Carol who cuts it says). Blue plasticky-looking shoes (which I love). Virgin (most kids in my year still are, except maybe Neil). I'm into girls, Rubik's Cubes and *The Hitchhiker's Guide to the Galaxy,* and I'm too small to get into *Kentucky Fried Movie* at the ABC, about which I am *vaguely* bugged, in the same way that I am *vaguely* excited about malt loaf, finishing my CSEs and O-levels, and the new Simple Minds twelve-inch. (It's called 'The American'.)

So a schoolboy, yes, but don't be fooled by my appearance. I am growing up fast. After all, I have a job. My first job. Friday nights and all day Saturday at Sainsbury's in town. Hooray.

It all started with a small ad in the paper in February, when I was still only fifteen. I stuck it in my diary: '*PREMIER drum kit. Six months old. £225 ono. Telephone Northampton 58438942 after 6pm.*'

It was in a block of flats down Jimmy's End. Dad knocked the weary old mum down to a 'nearest offer' of £200. We loaded it into the back of the Cavalier, piece by piece. I had a drum kit. Ace!

Spanking white Premier job – 22-inch bass, snare, hi-hat, two toms (one mounted, one floor) and two cymbals (one ride, one splash). Mum and Dad occasionally let me set it up in the extension downstairs as long as I don't hit it too hard. But there's a catch. I've had to promise to pay them the £200 back. For the first time in my life I owe money. Grown-up or what?

Auntie Janice has worked at Sainsbury's for about twelve years, she's something of a fixture round here. I'm in. I hope it doesn't interfere with my exams.

Here's my plan. Pass my CSEs and O-levels. Go to the sixth form. Pass my A-levels. Go to college. I don't really know which one, or where, or what I'll do at this place called a college, but it's a plan. Then I'll get a job. I'd like to be a drummer or an artist or Gene Hackman's assistant, but I don't know if I'll be allowed to. I might work at Sainsbury's.

You get £1.17 an hour, which is a load when you add it up. That's over £14 a week and it comes in an actual wage packet, in cash. The payroll lady gives them out each Saturday lunchtime. I give some of it to Mum and Dad, which goes towards the drum kit. The rest I can spend on luxuries, like the new Clive James book or the new Cure album *Faith*. It's got a song on it called 'Doubt'. I'm doing a module called 'Poems of Faith and Doubt' for O-level English.

Funny how it sums up the way I feel. Grey and gloomy. It feels like the elephant that gradually presses down on my chest as the school week moves towards the dreaded Friday.

All roads lead to the Grosvenor Centre; more specifically to the dark, grimy underbelly of Northampton's modern shopping arcade: the service entrance.

I've seen parts of Sainsbury's that the public doesn't see. I'm getting the behind-the-scenes induction tour with fat, jolly store instructor Mrs Ewins. Total old Northampton. She sits me down in front of the Sainsbury's instructional films on a big telly and lets me try out my box-opening utensils and price-label gun under her supervision. She even fetches me a cuppa from the canteen.

There is tons to learn. For a start, 'grocery' doesn't mean apples and potatoes and cabbages – that's 'produce'; it means everything else you can buy in Sainsbury's, like tinned peas and washing powder and jam. Shelves don't magically stack themselves. Tins don't magically appear in cardboard display palettes with the Heinz label facing front. Nor do they come with sticky price tags already on them. This is your job.

I'm learning a skill. It's better than learning about Chaucer and canals and the cross-section of a testicle.

The rule of Sainsbury's is this: a tidy display is good, an untidy one is *bad*. Customers like tidy displays; it makes it easier for them to see things on the shelves and buy them. If a customer can't see something on the shelves to buy it, your job is to find it for them. And fetch it. And be polite to them. This comes handed down from John Sainsbury himself, who is not called John Sainsbury's, so don't call him it.

My uniform is a grey overall, the colour of *Faith*, which is all right, but it's too big, even with the sleeves turned up. It makes me look small. Maybe that's the idea. Mind you, my plastic, pin-on orange name-tag is cool: A. Collins.

Mrs Ewins, who speaks in proverbs ('I can resist anything but temptation!'), says I will get a snug-fit overall when the new uniforms are introduced in two weeks' time.

My job here is to be on 'grocery' (in other words, not on fruit and veg – special workers do that). I am a shelf-stacker and a Saturday boy. A. Collins.

And this is what being a shelf-stacker entails:

Put your civilian clothes into a locker. Change into your grey overall. Pin on your name badge. Find your name on the rota and see what duty you're down for ('grocery' – there's also 'checkout' but mostly girls get that). Then you take the big, metal staff-only lift with the pull-open gate down to the warehouse where you report for duty. Here, you learn Sainsbury's backroom hierarchy.

Boys who look like they shave have probably been here longer than you: they know stuff and command instant respect.

Men are probably supervisors and they are your senior. They are to be respected and obeyed. They get pissed on Friday nights and talk about it the next day.

Old men are senior again; they swear like mad and smoke roll-up fags.

And if you see anyone in a dark-blue pinstriped suit, look busy.

I've eased into Sainsbury's life. As long as you remember that you're the bottom of the food chain, you'll get on fine. If your label gun is sticking, ask a shaver, and if you can't find one, ask a lady – they take pity on schoolboys.

After my first full day at work, which seemed to last a hundred hours, Dad asked me all about it in the car. In a man-to-man way, he said, 'Are there any decent birds there?' (This question keeps repeating in my head as I do my repetitive work.) I had no answer. Are there? I haven't once thought to gaze upon the girls working here in *that* way. Not in my baggy overall and with a constant film of sweat across my brow. They're not going to fancy me, so there's no point fancying them.

I just get on with my job and keep an eye on the clock for tea breaks and lunch hour. It's a bit like putting the cups and plates away after washing up in the kitchen, except it takes all day and you're constantly interrupted by old ladies asking where the jam is.

It's as well to establish early on where the jam is.

A couple of Saturdays in, and I am officially a worker. An employee with my own number (RM46635) and my own pay scale (grade 1). I work in *retail*, that's the word for it. Harder than working in an office like Dad, I bet. And it's actually quite varied – one minute you're stacking Whiskas, the next, Mah Ling mandarin segments, or even tin foil.

During tea breaks I sit on my own in the canteen sort of wishing I smoked because everybody else does. At lunchtime I eat on my own in the canteen, then cover up my stupid white shirt with my baseball jacket and venture out into the centre to buy something like *Smash Hits* or *New Sounds, New Styles*. Then I'll go back and sit in the communal smoking bit to read it. Then it's overall on and back to wheeling and stacking and replenishing and stacking and pricing and stacking. It reminds me a bit of Sisyphus and his rock.

I am earning every penny of that £14, I'm telling you. Sainsbury's is a parallel universe to school. I haven't really made any friends here. I say hello and nod to some of the other Saturday boys, but that's it.

We all bond when the new, brown uniforms arrive. The women look good in theirs but the men and boys have been made to suffer.

Previously allowed to wear our *own* dark trousers under the grey overall, now we have standard-issue brown flares. Big, wide, uncool, flapping flares, about which I am *vaguely* bugged. Even in Northampton flares are only worn by dads and hippies. Some of the London dandies in *New Sounds, New Styles* are wearing jodhpurs! At the very least, pegs. Flares tell the world you are dead from the waist down: a relic, a dinosaur, a square, a policeman, a tramp, a nutter, an outcast, someone who owns *Brain Salad Surgery*. The real horror is the clip-on tie. A fake, ready-knotted tie, a bit like the one on elastic I wore as a toddler, the idea being that you're forced to fasten your top shirt button for it to clip on properly. We can wear our own shoes, as long as they're brown.

We look like shit. Are we shit?

*

I am the master of my domain. I know where the jam is. I know how to unstick a label gun. I've worked out how to hide. You go down the toiletries aisle, which is dead quiet, and make it your business to sort out the toothbrush display, which is always a mess, as each individual toothbrush has to be placed in a slotted stand, and customers rifle through them, searching for the ideal combination of colour and bristle type and leaving the stand looking like a bomb has hit it.

No decent bird action as yet, but I have seen a couple of new boys start work, which automatically nudges me up the chain. One has New Romantic hair like me.

Bad news today, though. I consult the rota sheet. Instead of 'grocery', they have put me down for 'service'.

'What's *that*?' I ask one of the Jack-the-lads.

'Trolleys,' he says, adding, 'Top dog!'

It means collecting up the shopping trolleys and delivering them back to the front of the store. It means … being outside.

Dressed like a cross-section of a testicle in flares and clip-on tie, I am about to be shoved, blinking, into the outside world: the concourse, the centre, the bus station, the walkways, the subways, the car parks, the open air.

Somebody might see me.

The lion's share of the top dog job is spent in the multi-storey, purpose-built to serve the Grosvenor and situated above it. You work in pairs, which is a plus, although you have to split up to cover more ground. There are designated trolley parks on each floor of the car park but not every customer bothers to use them, leaving the trolleys in the middle of a parking bay or just up against a wall. Lazy twats.

You get used to the rattle of wheel on concrete as you gather up the strays, slot them into each other from behind and drive them home to the 'front of store' using the force of your body. High point is servicing the top floor, for obvious reasons –

daylight and air; low point is having to fill one of the two lifts with trolleys, because members of the public who've called the lift tut at you and give you dirty looks because you're in it, filling it up.

'Sorry! Service lift!'

The people hate you for it. Your name (A. Collins) is, like your uniform, mud.

I hate being *out here* in my uniform, with my John Keeble fringe all greasy from always pushing my dirty hands through it. What if I see a nice girl from school? I feel so exposed, especially when I have to venture out to the further-away car parks, the Mayor Hold, and the bombsite, in my wide trousers. And we have to trawl every inch of the bombsite. Two Saturdays ago Mr Engels called the trolley boys into his office and gave us a stern warning. A tall, dark ogre with a heavy brow, sunken eyes and a moustache that overhangs his top lip, he bollocked us for not rounding up every single trolley the week before, and ordered us to search more thoroughly from now on – no dark alley is to be left uninvestigated. This wasn't an official warning, just a shot across our bows, but it did the trick.

Engels went straight in at number two in that week's Wanker Charts in my diary, above the barmaid at the Sturtridge Pavilion who refused to serve me at a sixth-form induction party.

There is tension in the air. I'm picking my way through the bus station, head down. As we speak, they're still putting out fires in Toxteth (which is in Liverpool). Copycat riots have broken out in London, Reading, Hull, Preston, Chester and – nearer to us still – Luton, Wolverhampton and Birmingham.

A rumour has been spread around town that Northampton is going off, too. Today! Saturday, 11 July 1981. The big day.

It's been appreciably quiet. People seem to have stayed away from the town centre. This town – *aaaah-ah!* – is coming like a ghost town. Sorties into the bus station are eerie, as if perhaps at any moment violence might break out. But I have a plan and it might just work.

If civil unrest flares up while I'm out here I'm going to climb inside one of my trolleys for protection and curl up into a brown ball. If it kicks off, I'm convinced I'll be free from harm inside my cage.

Freeze. What's that noise? Coming from the escalators? It's the unmistakable murmur of *lads*. I clutch the bar of my trolley as a small gang of kids – and they are kids – starts to charge through the bus station towards the main concourse. There must be about seven or eight of them. They're making a lot of noise, shouting in their deepest voices. But it's not a riot.

Their disobedience fizzles out before they reach C&A, and I remain on the outside of my trolley.

The weeks pass and the old grey Cure blanket of work-doom that used to block out the light lifts now that I'm off the shop floor. I almost look forward to trolley duty and being outside. My own man. Last week, after another gruff warning from Mr Engels at 8.20 a.m. during which he controversially advised us to forgo our tea breaks for more efficient turnover, he actually had us back in his office at the end of the day to shower us with praise for bringing them all back in on time: 'Well done, lads. Excellent job.'

It made me feel good. Most of your work at Sainsbury's goes unnoticed. You're only picked off from the herd if you've done something wrong like stack a new tray of tinned soup on top of one with a can missing, thus creating an untidy display.

I found an extra 50p in my wage packet today (don't know why – staying late for stocktaking perhaps?) and treated myself to a can of Britvic 55 with my lunch. Cheers! It's all right here. I am apparently capable of doing 'an excellent job'. I'm king of the bus station, and my drum kit is gradually being paid for – in sweat.

The party's over. Mrs Ewins is back, and she's turned my life upside-down again. Cashier training. Checkout!

I should be flattered. Selected for advancement. Moving up the ladder. And it's mostly girls who do tills. There's no extra Britvic money, but it is seen as a more responsible duty. I'm not sure I want responsibility. I'm only sixteen. I'm still at school.

The mechanics of the till are easy enough (giant calculator!) and it's nice to sit down, but the mental pressure is *pain*. Grocery and produce now come at you all at once:

Peaches, washing-up liquid, eggs, yoghurt (put those in a separate bag), toilet rolls, biscuits, nail brush, wine (have to call a supervisor to ring that up as I'm not eighteen, don't rub it in), peas, marmalade, Mah Ling mandarin segments (aaah!), Special K, honeydew melon … a carnival of different products to be processed and pushed down the chute, blurring into one long, multi-coloured retail smear until you mis-punch a price and have to call up a 'void' (*vaguely* bugged by that word), which again involves ringing your bell for a supervisor, the equivalent of admitting defeat and calling for your mum.

I've got a headache. I never get headaches at home or at school, even during Chaucer revision or canals.

I may only work Fridays and Saturdays but the elephant starts to sit on my chest from around Wednesday afternoon – unless there's a party on Thursday night at the Willow Tree, and a couple of illegal Pernod and oranges to take my mind off the looming twelve hours of retail misery.

The problem is compounded by the fact that I am now a sixth-former. I've started my A-levels: English, Biology and Art. Microscopes, dissection, mitochondria, T.S. Eliot, *Hard Times* … never mind that we're grown-up enough to have Study Periods – you're supposed to *study* in them. I've got a headache. Void.

Last night, it happened. Someone from school came through the till. Paul Bush. I went red. First time I've been seen in my uniform by someone from outside. He went red, too. After all, he was the one out shopping with his mum on a Friday night!

*

I broach the unthinkable with Mum and Dad at breakfast and they're really cool about it. I'm packing in my job. I write my letter to the store manager Mr Ormes, who I don't think I've seen since my interview ('Welcome to Sainsbury's'). I tell him, with my hand on my heart, that work is impairing my ability to study for A-levels.

No more £14.04 a week, no more top dog, but in exchange for my overall and flares, I've got my life back. I've already volunteered to do the posters and the programmes for the sixth-form pantomime.

Cheers, John Sainsbury, whoever you are, for teaching me responsibility, respect and how to open a cardboard box of cat food with a special tool. It's nearly the end of 1981, I'll be seventeen next year, and I know the price of everything.

I can sum up the awkward transition from boy to bigger boy in one Sainsbury's incident. It was when the first new Saturday kid started. We met out by the jams. Though I was only a few weeks into the job, to him on his first day I must have seemed a wise old sage, maybe even a shaver. It was a good feeling.

We introduced ourselves, and he offered me his right hand in a manly but unexpected fashion. Though I understood the ritual, I'd never shaken another boy's hand before and in the heat of the moment I offered him my left hand. I don't know what came over me – I'd seen it done enough times on telly. The pair of us were left in that instance with no escape option. We momentarily just held hands, right there, in the middle of Sainsbury's. And then let go.

If that ever happens again, I'll be ready. Because I've now *been to work.*

2

Cursing Porkbeast

Ow! Fucking Porkbeast with his stupid name. I've just taken the top off my finger with a scalpel blade. Straight through. Like cheese. There's blood on the layout. With almost tortured symbolism, I am bleeding for the *NME*.

There was no mention of this in the job interview: 'Are you prepared to spill blood for the *NME*?' I would have said yes, without hesitation, though not expecting actually to have to prove it.

It's 1988 and heady being back at work after such a long interval. Seven years have passed since packing in Sainsbury's, during which time I got myself further-educated: two A-levels out of three, and one Bachelor of Arts – not that anybody here asked to see my certificates. This is rock'n'roll.

The interview was held in what I presumed to be a storeroom, with back issues of my beloved music weekly stacked all around us. James Brown, features editor, asked the questions; I felt like a band being interviewed for the paper.

'What was the last LP you bought?'

I found myself perched upon the knife's edge of credibility with this innocuous enquiry, selecting *Surfer Rosa* by the Pixies over the more truthful *Raintown* by Deacon Blue. It was risky – James would have known that the Pixies came out three months ago. Perhaps he'd think I hadn't bought an LP since March.

Quickly, I threw in the *Full Metal Jacket* soundtrack. Vietnam scores points at the *NME*.

'Who are your favourite bands?'

The Fall – obviously! – The Jesus and Mary Chain, Cocteau Twins … I also boldly confessed to a liking for the great *toons* of George Gershwin. (It's a Woody Allen thing.)

James raised his eyebrows ambiguously. Good? Bad? Had I blown it?

'How often do you go to gigs?'

I swallowed hard and considered massaging the figures, but instead recklessly gave him the truth: about once a month.

'Good. We want someone who's mature.'

James Brown is twenty-two. A year younger than me.

That was four eventful weeks ago. I didn't even know what job I was being interviewed for. Certainly not for this job: design assistant. Assistant to the art editor. Boy with a scalpel in the art room. Boy sizing up a photograph of Crazyhead, the much-fancied Leicester Grebo band. A new job always shrinks you back to boyhood. It did in 1981, aged sixteen, just as I was starting to feel grown up; it did every time I walked into the office of a new client as a postgraduate freelance illustrator, and it has at the *NME*. But you'd better believe it, this is my calling.

For the uninitiated – and there'll be a test at the end – 'sizing up' involves reducing a pic on the photocopier until it aligns perfectly to the width of one, two, three, four or five columns on the five-column grid, then cutting it out (careful!) and spray-mounting it onto the layout sheet with carcinogenic aerosol glue. Does that sound mundane? Does that sound boring? Does that sound workaday? It bloody isn't any of those things. Not when it's a page of the *NME*. Not when it's a page feature about Crazyhead and their fat, beardy-faced bassist Porkbeast on a rollercoaster. (Sometimes you have to take a band to a funfair to make the feature more interesting and visually arresting – I understand this now, from the inside.) Not when it's sprayed with the blood of a boy from Northampton who can't believe his luck.

*

I feel a bit dizzy actually. Darting lights in my peripheral vision. Justin takes charge. He's a man. He's about twenty-eight. He's the art editor. He calmly advises me to go and run it under a cold tap in the bogs while he fetches the first-aid box.

Off I trot, past Karen, the editor's mod-skirted secretary, who makes sympathetic noises. My finger's wrapped in hard, blue paper towel, darkening through multiple layers.

The top of my left forefinger is gone, but I am still here, fourth week in the job, Thursdays and Fridays only, although there is tantalising talk of Wednesday. I have to tell you, I'm head over heels with my new job: being a part of this messy, LP-envelope-filled, beautifully chaotic office in Central London, putting together the very newspaper I have worshipped since the summer of 1979 when I was fourteen and started having it delivered every Thursday.

I remember the first issue I ever looked through. Paul Bush came round during the summer holidays and we wandered up to the newsagent in Weston Favell village. I looked in vain for the new *Mad* magazine and he bought the latest *NME*.

I'd never really looked inside one before – it seemed too grown-up and severe for my tastes (I had only just discovered *Smash Hits*). You'll be ahead of me here, but it was an epiphany. I was instantly besotted. All that densely packed information and slangy invective in inky black-and-white about all the punk and post-punk bands that now had their hooks in my fourteen-year-old soul. I think it was the vast acreage of adverts at the back that truly snared me – the 'Sid Lives' T-shirts and the endless mail-order singles from exotic places like Rough Trade and Adrian's. I used to pore over these like other boys did the football league tables. I knew which side my cultural bread was buttered.

And, not to labour the point, but here I am. Hanging on to the sink in underwhelming workplace toilets, mainlining Kimberly-Clark paper towels, having performed live surgery on my left forefinger in the name of Grebo. The bleeding's slowing down. No it isn't. I'm having an out-of-body experience – as if this is somebody else's finger I'm tending to. I don't wish to make a fuss.

Back in the art room, Justin hands me a number of plasters. I half-expect him to unpeel one and put it on my finger for me, then perhaps kiss it better. No! I'm twenty-three. I live in a flat by myself and everything. The first plaster does the trick of masking the sight of my dissected digit, but the blood soaks immediately through and a second is applied. The third plaster just about wraps it up, for now. Ever since I first stepped over its hallowed threshold a month ago, the *NME* has stopped being a moon of Jupiter from which arcane intelligence about That Petrol Emotion, Jim Foetus and the Cookie Crew is beamed down to earth once a week. Instead, it has turned into an address in Holborn: bricks and mortar, with fire regulations and lockable cupboards and window latches and first aid.

Into the art room bursts Steven Wells, legendary *NME* writer and former ranting poet. Swells, as they all call him, is one of my journalistic heroes. He was, up until a month ago, a spec-tral, unknowable force; a byline on a page. Now he is the red-faced bloke in stained tracksuit bottoms. I remain in awe of him and find myself tongue-tied in his presence.

'Eh-up!' he shouts. 'Have you laid out Crazyhead?'

Swells wrote the Crazyhead piece. I've quickly learned that writers are only interested in the design of a page if they've writ-ten the piece, because they want to see how much of their copy has made the cut. As such, a writer always thinks the pictures are too big, while a designer always thinks the copy is too long.

'Andrew's doing it,' replies Justin, balefully. (He says every-thing balefully – I think it must be quite depressing being twenty-eight. He also DJs, which means late nights. He's not cut out for the nine-to-five.)

'I just sliced off my finger doing it,' I inject, waving my plasters in the air.

'That's brilliant!' Swells yells, not about my layout, but the fact that I've harmed myself. I can't think of anything funny to say back.

'Is this yours?' he carries on, plucking my Age of Chance baseball cap from the desk. It is. I'm rather proud of it, as a purchase, because I'm still at the stage where I need to summon extra hiphop chutzpah to wear one in public, and I deliberated for ages at the Town & Country before even approaching the merchandise stall. Typically for the band, it's a great design: the 'A' and the 'C' are separated by a star, which stands for and replaces the 'of'. My initials.

Swells puts the cap on his shaven head. It suits him better than it suits me, as indeed does being in the *NME* office in the first instance. It's as if he owns the place, yet he's only a freelancer. He doesn't have a desk or anything.

'What's it stand for?'

'Age of Chance.'

'Oh, I thought it stood for A Cunt.'

I walked into that. Cackling to expose his missing tooth, Swells takes the cap off by the brim and Frisbees it back at me. I still can't think of anything funny to say so I just snort my self-effacing amusement and busy myself re-sizing the pic of Porkbeast. Fucking Porkbeast. I love Porkbeast and I love Swells and I love Justin and I love James and I love Karen and I love this darkening plaster because it's an *NME* plaster and I don't even mind being A Cunt because I love this job.

It's August. Justin is on holiday and I've been left in charge of the shop. Two whole issues of the paper under my design jurisdiction. I've only been here since the middle of June and now I'm laying out the entire paper, unassisted. This means something really heavy: it means that Justin trusts me. I must therefore make it my job to abuse that trust and muck about with all the logos while he's on a Greek island.

I know he thinks of me as a 'lackey', as that's the very word he used to describe himself when he was design assistant to the previous art editor. But lackeys have their day, as long as they're patient. Justin is living proof. And I intend to follow his example.

It's bloody hard work laying out this many pages by yourself. The in-tray piles up. Yesterday I missed lunch. Not having a watch, I phoned the speaking clock and it was four o'clock! Too late to go out, I worked right through until 6.30 p.m. This is, after all, my big break; a chance to prove myself to Alan Lewis, the editor – for it is he who controls my destiny, not Justin. Alan is Justin's boss as much as he is mine, and it was Alan who gave me the job, not James. You have to understand the hierarchy when you work in an office. It's all fun and games and arguing over the office stereo until something goes wrong, then the pecking order becomes apparent.

In my first week, still very much on probation, I designed a new logo for the *NME* crossword. Justin didn't like it, said it was 'too sublime', whatever that meant. Then Alan happened to see it as he passed through the art room. After a moment's beard-rubbing rumination he uttered the magic words: 'Let's run it.' He had overruled Justin, which pissed Justin off. I had to keep my head down for a few days to compensate for upsetting the hierarchical applecart. I didn't mean to. I'm just keen. I'm from Northampton. I sort of shouldn't be here. I own *Raintown* by Deacon Blue.

Previous art editor Joe Ewart left under something of a cloud, I'm discovering. There was a kind of Stalinist purge (I learned the word Stalinist from reading the *NME*), which saw off the previous editor and a whole chunk of the senior staff, including one of my favourite writers, Stuart Cosgrove, whom I shall now never meet. It was the end of an orgy of aesthetic and ideological self-indulgence that had caused the circulation to plummet to an all-time low. They parachuted Alan in from *Sounds* to pull the *NME* back from the brink. He's a no-nonsense, no-airs, no-graces sort of editor, with his beard and his shirtsleeves. Although he meddles in the art room and has no artistic sensibilities, I like him. Mainly because he likes me and I don't think he likes Justin. He certainly didn't like Justin's Psychedelic Furs cover – a blow-up of their singer's face lit only by a psychedelic slide projector. Well, it looked psychedelic when we examined the contact strips on the light box and it looked psychedelic on the chromalin, the shiny, full-colour proof of the page they send back for checking. But reproduced on Izal toilet paper, like the rest of the *NME*, it looked at best psychosomatic.

'You can't tell what it is,' Alan complained, when the new issues arrived from the printers that Tuesday, tied up with string just like in the movies. 'Nobody's going to buy that.'

He's quite ruddy anyway, but he had reddened further at the obscure sight of the Psychedelic Furs singer. He seemed genuinely cross, unless it was genuine fear. If an issue doesn't sell, and Alan isn't seen to be reversing the *NME*'s circulation tailspin, his head may roll. These are the harsh realities of retail that I first experienced at Sainsbury's, although in fairness, as a Saturday boy I was far away from the decisions that affected profit and loss. Here, they happen right in front of me. As acting art editor I can actually affect them. My first cover will be a really clear photo of Nick Cave. Let's hope, as I often hear Alan and Danny Kelly say, it will 'fly off the shelves'.

I must go to lunch today though. Justin always goes for lunch. When I first started working here I went with him, trailing him around Soho like a puppy, not knowing what to order in Italian cafés and in awe as he bought authentic salami over the counter in a deli that came wrapped in paper (I'd never even been in a deli) or squeezed avocados at Berwick Street market. He's Professor Higgins to my Eliza Doolittle, although he's making *me* into a cockney. Once, at a tiny café alive with the sound of hissing, steaming machinery, he bumped into Neville Brody. Neville Brody! I have no idea how he knew this design god, but he did. And he introduced me to him. Believe it: I have met the bloke who designed *The Face*.

Perhaps one day Justin will balefully leave the *NME* and become a full-time DJ, and then I can apply for his job. Imagine me as the art editor of the *NME*. I could take my own lackey out to Soho and manhandle some exotic fruits in front of him.

'The music certainly improves in here when you're in charge!' chirps Danny, the deputy editor with the big glasses. (I am playing the House of Love on the cassette player.) I know it's not a popularity contest, but Danny and I have more in common than he and Justin. For one thing, we both love the *NME*. Justin just works here. He never comes out to the Falkland Arms after work. I do. I can't get enough of the people who work here. Just to move among them and breathe in their air makes me more confident.

Danny's a big bloke, gregarious and funny, older than me, and he uses up a lot of available air. Put it this way: you know when Danny's in the room. He becomes the room. You could sit and listen to his stories all day. He worked for British Rail before this. That's a proper job.

While Justin is away I am expected in the office four days a week – that's tantamount to a proper job. I have realised I love working in an office. I love the cut and thrust, the camaraderie, the politics, the rank-pulling, the banter, the piss-taking, the in-jokes, the community spirit and the pub. I love *all that*.

James is the one who called me up on the strength of my fanzine and got me in here. James was my point of contact on that first day, my passport to enter Commonwealth House and travel up in the lift to the fourth floor, as instructed. Staff writer Paolo Hewitt, whom I recognised from a picture byline in the paper, asked me who I was looking for.

'James Brown,' I replied.

'He's the little runt that sits there,' he replied, pointing at an empty desk piled high with press releases, fanzines and half-opened mail. Silently relishing my first taste of inter-office tension, I perched on the edge of the desk and waited.

Danny came past, again looking just like his picture byline, and also asked me who I was waiting for.

I said, 'James Brown.'

'Do you know what he looks like?' he asked. And before I could answer, he produced a life-size cardboard cut-out of James Brown the Godfather of Soul. I walked into that.

It was the other James Brown who introduced me to Justin and Alan, and tipped me off about the design assistant's vacancy.

I used to dream about being an *NME* writer, but that was an insane fantasy, and now I'm an *NME* designer, which is just as good, if not better, as I get to hang around the office all week, the master of my own domain. At Sainsbury's I was weekend shift, and I used to look up to those who worked full-time; I envied their easy manner, their nonchalance, the way their uniforms seemed to fit properly. Here, I'm the one who's full-time. I have a claim. The freelance writers – John Tague, Stuart Maconie, Stuart Bailie, Barry Egan, Jack Barron, Barbara Ellen, Ben Thompson – they're the casual labour who pop in and loiter and sometimes venture into the art room to be shown how to use the photocopier (they never know how to use the photocopier), stopping to have a subtle nose at the layout of their feature. And then they must leave, while we get on with the actual running of the place. I like that. I may be tongue-tied and awestruck and crippled by hero worship, but I have my own desk.

'Yeah, it looks great,' says Gavin, the media editor, handing back the new two-tone film section logo I have designed for him. He's got a desk – the media desk – and I've had to venture out into the main office to present the work to him, standing there like a lemon while he finishes an important phonecall, but he is gracious enough to hurry the person off the phone and is appreciative of my work.

'Right, we'll run it this week then,' I say, already turning to walk away, having invaded his editorial space for quite long enough with my lowly designer's query. I wouldn't feel quite so self-conscious crossing the office in my art-school dungarees if Swells hadn't so mercilessly mocked them earlier today. Gavin is kind enough to ignore them. I make it back to the art room without arousing any further comment. Back here, I am king, and Gavin's signed off my logo. Time to get back to work again. Once I've phoned the speaking clock.

Well, Justin's none too pleased. Bronzed and seemingly even more placid than before he went, he's none the less systematically going through the new issue with headmasterly severity: my second as acting art editor, this one with the Proclaimers on the cover.

'Cover looks OK,' he concedes, flicking on past news, which the news desk throw together. 'Not sure about "Thrills".'

'Thrills' is the double-page section between news and features for smaller pieces and amusing oddities, overseen by a different freelancer every week – this week John Tague, a writer with a big chin and quiet demeanour whom I never quite cracked, but nevertheless waved through my wacky, hand-drawn new logo.

'I think we'll stick with the old one,' announces Justin.

Why not just stick a scalpel through my heart, you miserable old square.

'This My Bloody Valentine picture has a lot of white space around it. Did you mark it up properly?'

Now he's nitpicking. Of course I marked it up properly. If I'd made it any bigger, the subs would've had to cut five hundred words out of the piece and Ben, who wrote it, would have been *crestfallen*. But Justin cares not for the lavender sensibilities of the writer, only for the purity of page design. And yes, there is too much white space around the picture, but I quite like the way it's floating. It's very My Bloody Valentine. Not that Justin is big on My Bloody Valentine. He prefers the Brand New Heavies.

'I don't like the Singles logo at all.'

And so it goes. We're changing all my logos back next week, when I will be design assistant once again. Lackey.

Had a dream last night in which I was shot. It was as vivid as anything. I was standing next to Mrs Thatcher, believe it or not. This sniper called out from the top of a high building, something about one of her policies, then shot her. She fell to the ground, presumably dead. He fired again, this time clipping me in the shoulder. It wasn't fatal, but the possibility was there: I faced death in the split-second that the sniper's gun went off. I staggered to the hospital, unassisted, and along the way I developed a tight, almost bloodless stab wound in my chest – where did *that* come from? I recall negotiating the barrier at a Tube station, but then I woke up.

Tonight I find myself in the Falkland Arms with perhaps the most illustrious *NME* roll call imaginable: James, Danny, news editor Terry Staunton, Jack Barron, live editor Helen Mead, Barbara Ellen, Mark Sinker (highbrow writer of the old school; mostly covers world music with Jonathan Romney) and legendary photographer Kevin Cummins. Bit unfair of me to drop my old college pal Rob into a works do, but he's gregarious enough to cope, and they don't bite. James and Kevin have been exceptionally welcoming to this extra stranger in their midst, albeit extracting great merriment from the fact that he looks like Mick Hucknall with his curly red hair. Rob can handle it.

I'm pissed, there's no better way of putting it. Well, it is Friday night. Justin's not with us, but then when is he? You have to admire the way he clocks off and gets the hell out of Holborn. I warmed to him today. I like to think he warmed to me, too, now that I've stopped trying to topple him in a bloodless coup with my sublime logos. (I've stuck to boring layouts since he came back; toeing the line, keeping my head down, knowing my place.) I accompanied him to the New Era café, like the old days when I needed my hand holding, and he revealed that he's having a mid-life crisis. He's the first person I've ever met who's having one. And guess what? He's not twenty-eight at all. He's twenty-nine! He turns thirty in four months' time. And it turns out he's got a five-month-old son from a previous relationship. No wonder he's so serious and far away. What a sack of responsibility he's carrying round with him the whole time. I'm flattered that he confided in me and it brought us closer together. His life does not begin and end at the *NME*.

Private lives very rarely intrude here. It turns out from dropped hints that Danny has a girlfriend. So does James. You never hear about them round the pub table. You certainly never see them. It's all office talk and music and piss-taking. Even by bringing Rob here I feel I may have broken the circle.

We drink until last orders. James admits his lust for glory, saying that he doesn't care whether anybody likes him or not – 'as long as I get what I want'. Our number fritters away to a hard core of me, Rob, James, Terry and Barbara, and come last orders, we're in no mood to end the evening. Terry, something of a ligger, reckons he can get us into Emma 'Wild Child' Ridley's birthday party at the Hippodrome, so off we trot in the drizzle. Rob and I feel very much like stowaways, but it's exciting. Barbara borrows my Breton cap to stay dry. She's like one of the Goth girls I used to like in Northampton: sultry, pale, interesting. I bet everybody in the office fancies her.

Arriving, damp but unbowed, at the Hippodrome in Leicester Square, I witness Terry doing his best to bullshit our way into a party we have no invites for. He explains that we are from the *NME* – even though Rob isn't – and that somebody called Mel should have put us on the guest list. The bouncer isn't having any of it.

Giving up, Terry takes us to a bar in Charing Cross that seems not to close when other bars do. There's barely room to stand up and we all smell of rain but it doesn't matter. I'm on a night out with the *NME* and I have a witness. I can't wait to casually drop this into conversation with Justin. The next thing I know, we are outside a porno cinema in Soho.

'Anyone fancy it?' asks Terry.

'I'm up for it if you are,' says James.

'Go on then,' says Barbara.

It's just like a normal cinema, only smaller and darker. We each buy a ticket for *French Erotic Fantasies* (not a film I've seen recommended in *Time Out*) and load up on popcorn. Well, I could do with some solids. The film's already started as we drunkenly bumble our way in, giggling behind our fingers. Barbara walks out after five minutes, offended not by how dirty it is, but how dull, whispering her goodbyes and leaving behind her popcorn. This must really be annoying for the men who are already in here to see the film.

The film *is* terrible – dubbed, slow, hammy, only fleetingly erotic – it's a perfect end to a crazy night. We last a further ten minutes then head for the exit light. My head is spinning as Rob and I get the night bus home.

These mornings really stabilise my life. I get up sometime between 7.30 a.m. and 8.00 a.m., clean my teeth, wander round in my boxer shorts for a bit, turn on *TV-am* to see how many people have been killed, make a cup of tea, eat a bowl of Start, write my diary for the day before and listen to a bit of select music: Eric B, Pop Will Eat Itself, House of Love. I usually leave for the bus stop at around 9.00 a.m., really *prepared* for the day. I can't believe I survived a whole year as a freelance illustrator with no job to go to. A proper job is so much more disciplined.

I love living alone. I don't even say a word until I'm at work.

Imagine that. Most people christen each morning with some form of mumbled contact. Not me.

I really am part of the furniture now. We moved offices in September to King's Reach Tower in Waterloo where *NME*'s owner, IPC, is based, and it was character-building to be part of the team, packing everything away in green crates and labelling them, going through James's throw-out pile and taking home armfuls of advance cassettes and twelve-inches. We're now on the twenty-fifth floor, overlooking the Thames as it sweeps east towards London Bridge and Docklands, and there's a clock on the side of the building next to the Savoy across the river so I don't need to phone up for the time any more. It's all very clean, spacious and modern in here, with partitions and air conditioning and an electric filter in the art room to suck up our carcinogenic spray mount, and I even have my own corner. There are coinless drinks machines on every other floor and a canteen, too, which is just as well, as there are no trendy Italian cafés in Waterloo.

Justin's not happy here. Unless it's the fact that his thirtieth birthday is almost upon him. He moaned yesterday when there was a fire drill because we had loads of layouts to do and it took about fifteen minutes to shuffle down twenty-five flights of stairs. It took so long that a collective decision was taken to repair to the Stamford Arms while everybody else in the building made their way back in. That's what they'd expect the staff of the *NME* to do, surely? It was fantastic! Like being naughty at school except with the teacher's blessing, as Alan came, too. The entire staff in the pub in the middle of the day. What could be better? I love this place. I love the new office because I am no longer at a disadvantage – nobody has any history here. We've all been here for six weeks, starting from scratch together.

Justin's probably fed up because the design assistant's job is advertised in this week's paper. My job. It's official. *I'm* official.

3

Praising the Lord for Andy Crane

Typical. I scan the room. I'm getting quite practised at scanning. Bollocks. Not even a member of Whitesnake and it's their party. There are free sea breezes and finger food, granted, and it's yet another posh club in Central London to cross off my list – that is, the list of posh clubs in Central London I never wanted to frequent in the first instance – but without a single celebrity guest my evening's wasted. I'm living off a diet of tiny French toasts, a little blob of taramasalata and a sprig of dill.

It's 1989 and yes, I'm getting used to the high life. I never thought I'd find myself a seasoned partygoer but when it's your job, you can't help but grow blasé about peering into the dark for celebrities in clubs and bars and the occasional function room at the Natural History Museum. Last month I found myself at a huge church in Vauxhall which had been tastefully draped and dressed and fitted out with a thumping sound system for the occasion of the release of Terence Trent D'Arby's second album, *Neither Fish Nor Flesh* (which didn't augur well for the finger food). There were scores of good-looking people there – the sort that don't normally find themselves in Vauxhall – but if Terence was among them, he was keeping a low profile, which is pretty stupid when the party's being thrown solely to raise that very profile. This is a man who recently got stopped for an autograph on his way into Capital Radio by a fan who had mistaken him for one of Milli Vanilli. True.

I say 'true' – it was printed in the *NME* gossip page so it must be. I should know, I put it there.

Oh, come on. We've got a photographer here and everything. Where's David Coverdale, snake-hipped, poodle-haired lead singer? It's getting late – I'll settle for Steve Vai, Whitesnake's poodle-hipped, snake-haired new guitarist. But all I'm looking at are record company personnel and other journalists. The sea breezes are going down nicely and we're listening to a loop of Whitesnake's new album *Slip of the Tongue* (whose title is at least an ideological improvement on their last one, *Slide It In*). The Thompson Twins turned up to *their* album launch party in Ladbroke Grove. I was too timid to go up and speak to them, but it gave me a couple of inches of copy: 'Thompson Twins turn up to Thompson Twins party.'

Gossip columnist is a dirty job and someone's got to do it. Actually, it turns out I've got to do it.

It would be melodramatic to say that I recklessly left my part-time gig in the art room to become the *NME*'s gossip columnist. I didn't. I left to become a full-time sub-editor, prompted into applying for this new post by Alan. But then I changed my mind and didn't become one. Justin was relieved, because, for all the friction and power games, we had become a good layout team, and were less likely to get cancer now that we had an electric spray mount filter. I don't know how we survived without one. I made my decision to stay but only on the tacit understanding that I would seek out writing work at the paper to assuage my literary urges. I wanted to work with words, not just pictures.

Justin soon wearied of this arrangement. Once I'd manoeuvred myself into the eyeline of all the section editors through repeated Falkland duty and blatant office badgering, and had a few tryout reviews commissioned and accepted, staffers started coming into the art room, bypassing Justin and seeking me out. Our power base was all out of whack again.

I was living out the old handyman joke. A man applies for the job of handyman at a big house. The lady who lives there, his potential employer, interviews him.

'Can you fix doors?' she asks.

'No,' he answers.

'All right,' she says. 'Are you any good around the garden?'

'No.'

'What about changing a plug?' She is becoming exasperated.

'No, can't change a plug.'

'Plumbing?'

'No.'

'Decorating?'

'No.'

'What kind of handyman *are* you?' she asks.

'Well,' he says. 'I only live round the corner.'

Geddit? That was me. I had a unique head start on all the other wannabe *NME* writers: I was stationed in the office. I only lived round the corner. My sheer proximity to the beating heart of the paper led to sporadic writing assignments: a comics round-up for Sean O'Hagan's books section, a Wire gig for Helen Mead, a two-hundred-word 'Thrills' piece on The Wolfgang Press for Stuart Bailie. If an Ozzy Osbourne solo album arrived at five o'clock and needed reviewing for the next day and nobody on the writing staff fancied it, how much easier for albums editor Alan Jackson to wander down the corridor to the art room and give it to me than call up a stringer and wait for them to travel into town. Now I know what a stringer is: someone on the end of a piece of string. And how long is a piece of string? Longer than the walk from the main office to the art room.

Clearly, if my reviews were unreadable or without any literary merit, the work would have quickly dried up, but having read the 'bible' for nine years, I found I was pretty good at approximating its house style. Steven Wells once playfully described me as 'an *NME* reader with a typewriter'. But aren't we all? I think it was playful.

So in the summer of 1989 the moment of truth came. The commissions were piling up, and I was having to ask Justin for time off in which to conduct my very first interviews with lesser-known bands. Did I want to be a designer who did 'a bit of writing' or did I want to be a writer? I chose the latter.

It was my first big career decision, and I experienced that lightheaded feeling you get when you jump off a high diving board, which, as an aquaphobe, I have never done. But I've jumped off things in my dreams and it felt like that. Bracing, liberating, but a bit stupid, and difficult to square with my mum and dad, who'd grown used to having a son with a job. (It kept Nan Mabel off their backs.) There were money implications, too. In the art room I was on Grade 8 when I started in June 1988; that's £49.08 a day. They upgraded me to Grade 7 in October – without fanfare or flypast – after which I was paid £55.95 a day. That's £167.85 for a three-day week. A lot of Findus meals-for-one. If I was to keep myself in the manner to which I had become accustomed, I would have to pull in some decent writing work. Or even some indecent writing work.

James Brown, somewhere between kingmaker, patron and charity worker, threw me a rope ladder: the offer of taking over 'Public *NME*', the gossip column. I leaped at it, even though this wasn't the kind of writing I had in mind. For one thing it's anonymous, a conceit designed to conjure mystery and danger out of what is a light-comic register of minor misdemeanours by members of Wolfsbane and the Darling Buds with the names picked out in **bold type**. The kind of writing I had in mind included a byline. Perhaps even a picture byline.

I'm not complaining. Not only do I now have a weekly stake in the paper, my own section and a guaranteed income, I warrant my own desk *in the main office*. All right, a desk-share, with Fred Dellar, the oldest swinger at the *NME*, but he only comes down to London once a week to put through his 'Fred Fact' page and make really quiet phonecalls, and we work happily around each other. There's something poetic about the paper's longest-serving veteran and its youngest buck sharing the same desk. We're like Kirk Douglas and Emilio Estevez. In the same film. Or something. The important thing is that I have access to an electric typewriter, or half an electric typewriter. And half a phone extension. I owe James big time – after all, the *main office* is where I'd always dreamed of being whilst doing my previous dream job.

Gossip columnist is not my dream job. I have never been a natural fishwife (I was the last to know when Neil and Lis had it off in the sixth form) and the idea of attending every record company launch, every after-show party, every pre-show party and every opening of a case of promotional lager brings on a leaden pall. But hey, it's a responsibility, there might be a dream job at the end of it and I wasn't about to turn it down. Necessity is after all the mother of invention and I'm growing into the part, like the new President Bush or The Cult's latest drummer Matt Sorum.

Steve Vai used to be in the Mothers of Invention. Where is he?

The launches and aftershows themselves may have become routine, but I don't think I'll ever tire of getting into things for free. Once you've tasted that privilege it's hard to go back to being a paying punter.

My first experience of life as a freeloader went badly. I asked a girl I'd just met if she wanted to accompany me to a Wedding Present gig at the Town & Country. I know – high roller! I was on the guest list, plus one, my first such freebie since crossing the *NME* threshold. I'd wangled it because my first ever interview for the paper had been with a rising Rough Trade boy-girl guitar band called the Heart Throbs. They were supporting the Wedding Present that night, and their manager kindly put my name down. How confidently I ushered my expectant date past the Wedding Present fans in the queue and presented myself at the guest-list window. And how crushed I was when neither my name nor that of my plus-one turned out to be on the guest list. We were in fact minus two, forced to buy overpriced tickets from a loveless Cockney tout on the street instead. A healthy first lesson in the art of freeloading: don't rely on managers – certainly not managers of indie bands, who tend to be the friend of a friend of the bass player.

I convinced her that, as gossip columnist, I could get her into any party she fancied. We'd have some star-spangled fun together. And we did, the first couple of times. But then it became a job, a chore, and she stopped coming with me. After all, when you've been to one record company party you've been to them all, and don't be flattered by the invite: you're only on the list because the record company have reasoned that they can get some acreage out of it. Hence the maxim: there's no such thing as a free launch.

A 'free bar' is always advertised on the ticket, but this means if you want something *other* than a sea breeze made with a new Kazakh vodka currently being promoted you have to pay club prices. (I have never been a club person. I learned in Northampton never to drink anywhere with a doorman.) I've perched on the leather stools and gazed into the mirrored walls of a whole host of London's bars and discos, but I haven't seen a lot of celebrities in them. Unless you count someone who used to be in Dream Academy. And believe me, I have to.

Wait a minute. Who's this coming through the door and handing their invite to the muscleman in the overcoat? David Coverdale? No. Praise the lord, it's Andy Crane! From Children's BBC! The Broom Cupboard! Took over from Philip Schofield! Edd the Duck? Come on.

Even I'm not too timid to talk to Andy Crane. Hey, I spoke to Billy Duffy from The Cult at a launch in Westbourne Grove, and tipsily danced with Andrea out of the Darling Buds. I can do this. I hop off the leather stool and approach him. He's wearing a black leather jacket, very much off-duty.

'Andy? Hi. Andrew from the *NME*.'

'The *NME*? Ah, brilliant!'

He's as pleased to see me as I am to see him. I've got some-one famous to write about, and he's going to get in the *NME*. Hark! That is the sound of the well-lubricated wheels going round in the Wankel Rotary engine of public relations. We approach the bar together.

'Another one of those, please.'

James looked after 'Public *NME*' before I took it over and he was a natural at it, afraid of no one, embarrassed by nothing, adept at barging. I'm not one of life's doorsteppers and he knows it, but he needs me to succeed at this to vindicate putting me forward for the job. I've just handed in my typewritten copy and I can see him from my own half-desk as he red-pens it.

'Why didn't you go to the Iron Maiden party?' he shouts over, having reached the end.

'I didn't get an invite,' I explain, by way of an excuse. It's a pretty poor excuse for a gossip columnist, but then I *am* a pretty poor excuse for a gossip columnist.

'I had one – you could've gone as me!' (This is new: only in showbiz, and perhaps Shakespeare, do people pose as one another at parties.)

I have no comeback. 'It's only Iron Maiden.'

'I know,' he concedes. 'But Clint Poppie was there.'

Clint Poppie from Pop Will Eat Itself? He's at everything. It's hardly news.

'And the bloke out of Aswad. And Ringo Starr's son. Ask Terry – he went.'

'All right, I'll add a paragraph.'

I dutifully consult Terry, who's busy letting Steve put the news pages through, it being a Friday. He gives me the goss. The party was held at the Dorchester Hotel to mark the release of a concert video called *Maiden England*, hence there were

Union Jacks everywhere (ah, the English flag!), and the finger food was fish, chips and pickled eggs. For a start, Iron Maiden were actually there. All five of them. That, in itself, is worth putting down. Also on the guest list: Brinsley Forde out of Aswad (who used to be in *The Double Deckers*!), Zak Starkey and – according to Terry, whose enthusiastic appreciation of record company hospitality never impairs his newshound's memory – the singer from Wasted Youth, a Goth troupe who disbanded years ago. But hey, it's **another name in bold**. (Neither of us can actually *remember* his name and I haven't time to look it up, so he goes in as 'the bloke out of Wasted Youth'.) Gossip round here is measured by the yard. I'll insert the Maiden item after the story about Marti Pellow being booed offstage at a Memphis Soul Revue and before the one about Then Jerico's Mark Shaw being beaten up, both of which must be true as people from record companies told me them over the phone. There's also a press shot of Maiden posing on a British-made motorbike in Terry's in-tray. I type up the new item and a picture caption (something about 'Hardly Davidson') and pass the extra sheet to James, who gives it to the subs.

A gossip columnist is someone like Nigel Dempster or John Blake or J.J. Hunsecker, a social butterfly gathering titbits and whispers, flitting from exclusive engagement to high-society ball, and filing explosive copy at four in the morning from a payphone in the kitchens of some St Tropez restaurant. I'm cock-a-hoop if I bump into Andy Crane. I *was* cock-a-hoop when I bumped into Andy Crane. (So was Andy Crane.)

Incidentally, David Coverdale did eventually breeze into the Whitesnake party later on that evening. He breezed right past me with my free sea breeze while I was talking to Andy Crane about his desire to break out of children's TV. Luckily, our photographer got a picture of him. Guess who was in the background looking like a social butterfly? Terry.

4

Standing on the Deck of an Aircraft Carrier with the Soup Dragons

So, it's now October 1990, two months after President Bush drew his 'line in the sand'. I find myself watching CNN in a New York bar, imagining I'm P.J. O'Rourke and taking great fistfuls of complimentary rice crackers. All the talk is of UN resolutions, a threatened air embargo and yet more US 'hardware' being shipped out to the Gulf for the big showdown. (Actually, if I was P.J. O'Rourke, I wouldn't be in a New York bar; I'd be in Riyadh taking great fistfuls of complimentary Saudi Arabian rice crackers, wouldn't I?) They're showing a televised message from Saddam Hussein. It has those of us sipping Budweiser on barstools in rapt attention. He's basically sending a direct, grim-faced warning to President Bush: mess with me in Kuwait and you will kick-start a new Vietnam. This is good stuff.

A couple of power-dressed Wall Street boys exchange words accordingly: Saddam is stopping them from enjoying their metaphorical apple pie, one says. He's just a guy selling a *product*, says another.

I discreetly jot down their words in my notepad under the bar. A good journalist always carries a notepad. I may not yet be a good journalist but I carry one anyway. Advisable to get a bit of local colour: the time, the place, background chatter. After all, I am on a foreign trip, I'm a fully fledged features writer from the *NME* and I can't *just* write about the Soup Dragons.

The next morning, I find myself standing on the deck of an aircraft carrier, feeling windswept and psychedelic in my James logo top and oversized trainers. A pretty cool place to be in these times of military build-up, it's overcast (always worth specifying the weather) and I'm prepared to call those 'war clouds' in the Manhattan sky above us, even though they're just 'clouds'.

I'm not too good on boats, but the USS *Intrepid* isn't sailing anywhere. Permanently docked in New York, an 872-ft floating museum, she saw plenty of action during the Second World War, helping to capture the Marshall Islands in 1944 (this kind of stuff always looks good on the page). She spent much of the fifties and sixties in the Mediterranean (is that interesting?), then joined the Pacific Fleet in 1966 off the coast of Vietnam (that's more like it: Vietnam!), finally being decommissioned in 1974. The *Intrepid* was opened to the public in 1982. And here come the Soup Dragons, who didn't have to pay to come up the gangplank, thanks to some top wrangling by Ed the photographer. I love coming on trips with Ed. He's old enough to have a family, carries himself like a grizzled war photographer who's seen it all, travels with one change of T-shirt and makes vapour trails with the coloured lights in live shots.

It's the band's first visit to the Big Apple and my second. This means I get to play the old veteran and watch the four of them hyperventilate over the most basic things: fire hydrants, yellow cabs, steam rising from the sidewalk, the fact that it's *called* a sidewalk, really big slices of pizza, all the things I hyperventilated over on my first New York trip in May. On that occasion, which dramatically coincided with the deaths of Sammy Davis Jr *and* Jim Henson, I found myself cycling around Brooklyn with They Might Be Giants and eating the biggest salad I've ever seen, enough for a whole family. They Might Be Giants called it an 'industrial salad'.

Sinatra was playing the Radio City Music Hall in May. This time round, it's the Teenage Mutant Ninja Turtles. I'm sure I can make something out of that in my copy. On this trip, far from going anywhere by bicycle, PolyGram have laid on a stretch limo for the entire three days, because the Soup Dragons are visiting ambassadors of England's famous 'Manchester Scene'. They're from Bellshill in Glasgow, but don't ruin it. They're also the proud bearers of a bona fide Top Five hit, 'I'm Free', and a gold-selling UK album, *Lovegod*. And as we all know from *Spinal Tap*, money talks and bullshit walks.

We're not walking anywhere. Since hooking up with the ascendant, chauffeur-driven, indie-dance next-big-things, our feet have barely touched the ground. The record company hopes to repeat the Soup Dragons' crossover UK success over here. Meanwhile, the Soup Dragons, like every other visiting British band ever to marvel at the really big slices of pizza, hope to crack America; to 'slay the States' as *NME* headlines always used to say in the sixties.

It's a bunch of guys selling a *product*.

Ed arranges the foursome in front of a military helicopter and a fighter jet for the cover shot while I silently ruminate over possible headlines ('ALL BANDS ON DECK'? 'YOU AIN'T SEEN NOTHIN', JET'? 'MILITARY SOUPER-POWER'?). Frontman Sean looks exceptionally cool in white jeans, white top, shades and dyed black hair. It's as if the other three have agreed never to look as cool as him in photographs.

Sean says that the worst part of making records is when other people hear them and make comments. He talks of building an immune system to 'the crazy world of the music biz.'

Snaps taken, we pile back into the limo and head for Westwood One, which syndicates interviews across the country and whose inclusion on the Soup Dragons' packed itinerary is designed to help build on their college radio success and move them to pop radio. Sean's still buzzing about having spotted John Cale coming out of Coliseum Books. Drummer Paul, who likes butter, has already decided that American toast is 'too buttery'.

Usually, on a foreign trip, which is paid for by the record company and not the *NME*, journalist and photographer are chaperoned by a press officer from the London end. But ours, Chris, has food poisoning, so Ed and I made our way to New York unaccompanied. If Chris were here, that would bring the total of press officers in the radio booth to *three*: there's the clean-cut Marty from PolyGram New York, who keeps saying 'Aces!', and the strident Barbara, from Westwood One, who actually uses the word 'fabuloid' in a built-up area.

Chuck is the DJ who's currently interviewing Sean and guitarist Jim on the other side of the glass. He asks them about Manchester and where they got their crazy name, which, being a reference to *The Clangers*, is tough to translate into American. Sean says 'knickers' at one point, which causes a minor flap, as nobody here is sure if he's allowed to say that or not in a syndicated radio interview.

The interviews continue on the cellphone in the limo – 'important fanzines', apparently. We visit MTV for a gentle grilling on uncomfortably high metal stools by a VJ called Dave for *120 Minutes* and then enter the hallowed portals of the PolyGram building for a further conveyor belt of promo in a vast conference room around a black conference table you could play five-a-side football on. Beer and pizza is provided, although Paul is convinced that the company who make this particular brand of beer pay their black workers *half* what they pay their white workers ('It's a racist brew!') and it's sent back. The Soup Dragons are in a position to do this. Heineken is the replacement.

The interview questions blur into one another: the Acid

House scene … Jim Kerr … Scottish Eggs … even: 'If you could be any vegetable, which would it be?'

It's a cheap shot, as a journalist, to write down the questions of other journalists but when they're as vacant and pretentious as American journalists, resistance is futile. It's also a low trick to quote press officers, who are only doing their job, but hey, it all helps to convey the 'crazy world of the music biz' and I'm only doing my job. I am a journalist. That is my job. Yes, yes, a music journalist, a *rock* journalist, but these are all branches of the same noble profession. I've got a notepad.

The big joke is when I went into the sixth form in 1981, a Sainsbury's trolley-boy with his heart set on being an artist or Gene Hackman's assistant, Mum and Dad impressed upon me how important it was to get my English A-level. 'If it doesn't work out, you can always fall back on journalism,' they used to say.

Journalism? This, to me, was more remote and foreign-seeming than becoming an artist when I was sixteen. Something to do with wearing a trilby and having a pencil behind your ear. So I assured them that I would indeed pass English and hoped in my heart of hearts that I would never need to 'fall back' on it. Nine years later and here we are. I am a journalist and if it doesn't work out I can always fall back on being an artist.

So when did I actually become a journalist? Let's say the first week of October 1988. That was when my very first reviews appeared in the *NME,* and when I still worked for Justin. It was quite an auspicious *entrée:* three in the same issue. Two album reviews – *Blow* by Butterfield 8 (Go! Discs) and *Indestructible* by the Four Tops (Arista) – and one film review – *Masquerade,* the yachting thriller starring Rob Lowe. Don't think me a bread-head, but the film was worth £23, the albums £17 apiece. That week I earned a staggering £57 for typing, which was more than a day's pay in the art room and yet posed no immediate physical danger to the top of my left forefinger. But was I really a journalist that week? Or a designer with dreams?

You might in fact say that I became a journalist when I conducted my first interview with a band. That was way back in July 1988, when I was still under James's wing, staking my claim in the art room and yet still keen to pop my cherry. I was dispatched to interview the Heart Throbs – whose manager would later embarrass me in front of my date outside the Town & Country. They were signed to Rough Trade, previously home of The Smiths and one of those mail-order names in the back of the *NME* that so intoxicated me in my provincial teens. I was ordered to telephone Rough Trade and ask for my first record company press officer, a man called Chris Stone, who turned out to be a woman called Chris Stone. Dialing the Rough Trade number was in itself a thrill. Maybe Morrissey would pick up.

'Are you a new writer?' Chris asked, before we arranged the meet-up.

'Yes,' I replied, for I was precisely that.

She sent over three Heart Throbs twelve-inches – and not in the post but by courier. A motorcycle rider made me sign for them. As he left, I don't mind admitting I fondled them. I was getting used to free records knocking about the office, but these were the first that had arrived in a square cardboard envelope with my name on it.

I met Chris and three-quarters of the band at the Rough Trade office in King's Cross one balmy evening. I remember being quite sweaty and smelly, but the band's nerves matched my own – they were, after all, going to be in the *NME* – and we conducted the interview in the garden of a pub called the Waterside Inn, for maximum ventilation.

As if following some kind of first-time journalist's code of practice, and foreign to the functional concept of Dictaphones, I took along a huge ghetto blaster upon which to record the interview, removing it from a holdall and plonking it on the pub table without a trace of self-consciousness. At least I saved myself the trouble of wearing a large top hat with the words 'THIS IS MY FIRST INTERVIEW' picked out in flashing lights. We got on famously, the Heart Throbs and I – they even gave me a lift home in the singer's clapped-out Mini – and though little more than indie clichés were committed to two sides of a brand-new TDK C90, I managed to carefully transcribe and embroider them into my first eight-hundred-word piece, which read, if nothing else, like an interview with a band in the *NME*. Result. I even gave it a meaningless *NME*-style pun headline: 'THROB'S YOUR UNCLE'.

In the true spirit of Fleet Street, the piece never ran, shunted to the back of the queue and carried over for reasons of space every week for the next month until it was finally out of date. I had let the band down. I had let Chris at Rough Trade down. But most of all, I had let myself down. I see now from my lofty position of multiple passport stamps and cover stories that it was a rite of passage. In *not* getting something published I had in fact become a journalist. The day after King's Cross I invested in a hand-held tape recorder from an electrical shop on Tottenham Court Road.

And here it is, wheels still turning and red battery light still blinking, two years later, nowadays used just as often to surreptitiously record 'local colour' while secreted in my army surplus bag as it is placed on the table for the official sit-down interview. It has never let me down. Once, I was sent, on a whim, to interview Mike McShane, roly-poly star of *Whose Line Is It Anyway?* for Gavin's media section. Unprepared, I was forced to borrow Danny's tape machine, which looked as if it had been around the world a couple of times. Insulating tape was involved.

The wheels kept stopping of their own volition and we kept having to recommence the interview. After three false starts I gave up and stressfully dictated the actor's answers into my notepad at the dining table of his rented North London flat. I think it's fair to say that I was sweating more than Mike McShane, which is an achievement. It would have been less hassle if I could do shorthand, but even though I'm a journalist, I can't. Terry and Steve are the only writers at the *NME* who can do shorthand, and that's because they both came up through local papers (Wolverhampton's *Express & Star* and the *Harlow Gazette* respectively).

I can't touch-type or do shorthand, nor do I have a trilby or a pencil behind my ear but hear this: I am a journalist.

Sean orders our driver to stop the car. The driver, who's called Kern, and once had Madonna, Grace Jones and Kid 'N Play in the back of his limo, pulls over. We're en route to the Hard Rock Café for a press conference, but Sean's seen a Superman logo T-shirt in the window of a clothes shop that he's simply *got* to have. Being driven around in a limo for three days can turn a young Glaswegian's head.

He climbs back in with his spoils five minutes later, talking about how he likes Pop Art because it takes ordinary things out of context. He could be describing himself.

At the Hard Rock, whose wall-mounted rock memorabilia gives Sean the creeps by putting extraordinary things, like Jimi Hendrix's guitar and John Lennon's cracked assassination specs, out of context, we bump into the band James, or 'the original Manchester band' as they are introduced at their meet-and-greet. The Soup Dragons and James are both signed to PolyGram in America. It's burgers and guacamole dip and more stupid questions. I chat cordially to singer Tim Booth beneath the Blues Brothers' original hats, because British bands on tour are always glad to see a face from home – and I am wearing a James logo top. I ask Tim if he minds *all this.* He says he doesn't, that it comes with the territory. James want to slay the States, too.

Sean's keeping his head by affecting a pose of grudging compliance and snooty disdain in the face of all the record company hoops. He is *appalled* when I relay Tim's circumspect attitude to the guacamole dip. Mind you, he's *appalled* that the Hard Rock have mounted a *Never Mind the Bollocks* T-shirt behind glass and taped out the word *Bollocks*.

There is much to love and hate about this country. I've been here once before. I know what I'm talking about.

That night Kern drives us out to Long Island, where's it's all very *Great Gatsby*, except where we're going, a remote and ugly nightclub called the Malibu. Why are we going there? Because it's WDRE Day!

WDRE is a reasonably hip local station. They've laid on a gig for air-punching competition winners with a bill that comprises alternative bands championed by the station. It's a gossip columnist's wet dream backstage, and I will be sure to give all these names to Terry for 'Public *NME*' when I get home. Terry was a natural to take over the gossip column when I gave it up.

The bill includes They Might Be Giants, Something Happens and forgotten ex-4AD art-rockers Modern English, and among the VIP guests, here to introduce the bands and have their photo taken in front of WDRE branding, are Adam Ant, Curt Smith of Tears For Fears, Neil Tennant of the Pet Shop Boys and Seymour Stein, legendary boss of Sire records, to whom James and the Soup Dragons were both briefly signed due to an administrative error. This doesn't stop the DJ who introduces Stein onto the stage describing him as 'the guy who discovered the Soup Dragons!' Guess how Sean feels about *that*? In fairness, he did discover Madonna.

Now that I'm no longer gossip columnist, I find it easier to buttonhole stars out of context. I chat to the manager of Modern English and to my old pals John and John out of They Might Be Giants, who seem pretty bored to be here. I then introduce myself to Neil Tennant.

'Hi, I'm Andrew from the *NME*.'

'Hellooo. What are you doing here?'

'I'm with the Soup Dragons,' I reply, with a degree of pride. They are, after all, very hip.

He witheringly describes them as one of those *opportunist* bands, meaning one of those rock bands who have adopted post-acid house dance beats and reaped the rewards. I think a man who is prepared to come all the way out to the Malibu Club just to stand on stage and introduce somebody else should watch who he's calling opportunist. I make a stout defence of my new favourite band, naturally, before Neil is called away to make his personal appearance. In fact, I love the Pet Shop Boys, as they helped, in 1987, to wean me off Gothic rock and onto dance music. I bought a stripy T-shirt just to be like them. I also love the Soup Dragons because I first interviewed them in 1989 before they were famous, and then again just as they were getting famous. This is my third interview with them for the paper, and I'm starting to feel like the fifth Soup Dragon. We have a relationship. Even their manager knows who I am. Perhaps they'll thank me on the sleeve of their next gold-selling album.

The band and I make our own entertainment backstage sucking the helium out of WDRE balloons. Bassist Sushil's voice is so high anyway that it sounds exactly the same after the helium. Great merriment ensues. Between me and the Soup Dragons. The Soup Dragons plus one. The five Soup Dragons.

The gig itself is frustrating, in that it's only half an hour long, meaning the band peak about ten minutes after they've left the stage. Plus, they are introduced by Curt Smith, for whom they have no respect.

The gig seems, however, to have worked its marketing magic. At the record company office the next day, an enthusiast called Dennis is buzzing about the *phenomenal* sales in New York and how Tower can't keep 'I'm Free' in the store.

Sean is preoccupied with a US copy of the twelve-inch. He's checking that they haven't interfered with the artwork. Dennis weighs in with the assurance that he will not *fuck with their shit.*

In response to what Neil Tennant said about them last night, Sean admits he's trying to sell records, but how can he be an *opportunist* if what the band really want is twenty years of fame, not six months' worth?

There is a measure of irony here. Sean is surrounded by people like Dennis ('Phenomenal!'), Marty ('Aces!') and Barbara ('Fabuloid!') whose every fibre is devoted to selling a few more records, and yet Sean feels sullied by the very Faustian pact that will grant him and his band the next twenty years of fame.

The important thing is that I am now officially blasé about the steam coming out of the sidewalk and the big slices of pizza. I didn't even have a passport two years ago. But thanks to the *NME,* I have become a trainee man of the world. I've been to Lisbon with Bon Jovi, Dusseldorf with The Wonder Stuff, Prague with Carter the Unstoppable Sex Machine, Hultsfred with The Charlatans and Cheltenham with The House Of Love. I've cycled in Brooklyn with They Might Be Giants. I've been on an aircraft hanger in Manhattan with the Soup Dragons. I've confidently chatted to James, who I'm not even here to inter-view, under the Blues Brothers' hats, and my tape recorder's still working. This is what being a music journalist is all about: foreign travel, limo drivers called Kern, access all areas and watching a band crack America at close range. The Soup Dragons are going to slay the States with me by their side, and this time next year we could all be millionaires.

If Sean could be any vegetable it would be a cucumber. Paul would be a carrot. Why? Because he doesn't *like* carrots.

5

Redirecting Killing Joke's Stripper

My phone rings. Perhaps it's Lawrence at Creation about the My Bloody Valentine cover story. No, it's reception. My phone sits on my desk, next to my computer and my Sellotape dispenser.

'Andrew?'

'Yes.'

'We've got your dad down here.'

'OK, I'll come down.'

November 1991. Dad has come to see my desk. Having spent much of the last couple of years globetrotting – eating an awful lot of cheese after the Velvet Revolution in Prague with Carter the Unstoppable Sex Machine, sitting in a broken-down van on the Dutch border with Soundgarden, falling asleep under a table in a bar with The Wonder Stuff in Dusseldorf – I now have a desk job, just like my dad. Insurance, rock'n'roll, what's the difference? We all get desk jobs in the end, even in the crazy world of the music biz. My stapler sits next to my phone book and my mouse mat, under my lockable cupboard. It amuses me, sitting here at my desk answering my phone, to think that I once had designs on Justin's job. I ended up getting James's job.

James got Danny's. Danny got Alan's. A woman called Pru, who plays women's rugby and protests about Red Routes, got Justin's. Steve got Helen's. Iestyn got Steve's. The merry-go-round never stops. In the words of Billy Bragg, whom I was recently flown to Amsterdam to see by his record company, the world falls apart and some things stay in place. Gavin stays in place. He will be media editor long after the rest of us are dead, and Karen will be the editor's secretary. Never mind her sexist job title, it's clear to anyone that Karen runs this office. Without her, we would all be wandering about, lost, including the editor.

James, ever-impatient, hoped that *he* would get Karen when Alan was promoted upstairs, but it wasn't his time. Danny got Karen, they made James assistant editor and I moved into the vacuum at the features desk.

'You're a can-do sort of bloke,' Danny informed me, when offering me the job. (I'm still not sure how flattering that is.) Anyhow, he assured me that even though it was a sit-down commissioning job I could still write features and travel the world. I wasn't worried; the way James had run it, being features editor meant mostly commissioning yourself. The *NME*'s most frequent flyer, he was rarely in the country. If Happy Mondays whistled, his desk was unmanned.

But I've actually grown jaded about travel; world-weary, even. This from a boy who didn't even have a passport when he arrived here.

I have commissioned myself to do the occasional plum job as features editor but they've tended to be in this country – the Manic Street Preachers in Ripley, the Charlatans in Northwich, the Farm in Liverpool, the Cocteau Twins in Teddington, Pop Will Eat Itself in Shepherd's Bush. Trains and cabs and company cars of press officers.

I've had enough of Germany. I've had enough of the Netherlands. And I've had enough of New York. Oh yes, the shine even comes off Manhattan after the third and fourth time. I've been up the Empire State Building and seen the polar bear in Central Park and gazed at the entrance to the Dakota and eaten sufficient tuna on rye to sink a ship at Katz's delicatessen where they filmed *When Harry Met Sally* and I've pissed in the disgusting toilets at CBGB and driven through

Harlem to see the black people sitting on the steps and felt paranoid in Times Square and bought some Twinkies and seen a bum selling his shoes and I've done New York.

I am twenty-six years old and I tut and say, 'Oh, not New York again.' Those words actually come out of my Northampton mouth. I fill in the green and white visa waiver forms with my eyes closed. I stand in line at check-in and say, 'Of course, I can remember when it was just *one* hour.' I am such a seasoned transatlantic traveller I no longer even get stressed by US Immigration. It's going to take ages and you'll be kicking your bag along the floor until you reach the yellow line and then an officious black woman with things on her belt will say, 'Step up, please!' or 'Step down, please!' and mean different things and the man at the desk will ask you the purpose of your visit, and you'll say you're a journalist and you'll tell him who you're in New York to interview and he won't have heard of them and you'll tell him they're the next big thing and he'll stamp your passport even though he suspects from the length of your hair that you take drugs and he'll say have a nice day and you'll do your best, even though you don't like the photographer James has sent you with, or the press officer, but you can't always have it your way. It is, after all, your job, not a holiday.

I emerge from the lifts and there he is. In reception, my dad: suit, tie, overcoat, briefcase in hand, down in London on business. What a heartwarmingly normal sight he is in the middle of all this madness, bearing an IPC guest pass. A rock amid all this rock'n'roll. I raise my hand to him manfully as I approach the security barriers and he nods paternally back.

Most of Dad's clients are in the Northampton, Wellingborough and Rushden area, but occasionally his work takes him on the train to London, just as mine occasionally takes me on the plane to Utrecht. It seemed mad not to meet up, even though neither of us has anything like the time for lunch or anything formal. I would take him to the canteen but he's understandably keen to see the inside of the *NME* office on the twenty-fifth floor and I'm happy to oblige, being proud on two fronts – of my dad and of my desk.

'All right, Dad.'

'Sorry I'm a bit late, but my meeting overran.'

'That's OK, I wasn't going anywhere.'

We still conspicuously don't shake hands. That's funny, isn't it? I'm twenty-six and he's fifty-one – for the first time in our lives I am over half his age – and we don't shake hands. He shakes the hands of his clients but I don't shake the hands of mine. I didn't shake the Manic Street Preachers' hands in Ripley, for example. Actually, thinking about it, Bob Geldof offered his hand when I met him at Phonogram's office in Hammersmith last November and I shook it, but he's thirty-six, older than me, and older than most of the people I interview. He's a KBE.

Interviewing Geldof was something of a move up the league tables, too. Having had my fill of indie bands my parents had never heard of, I actually asked James if I could interview some-one a bit more *interesting*, by which I meant someone *older*, someone more *famous*, and Geldof had a new single out. Never mind Mum and Dad, my Nan had heard of Bob Geldof. (She had a bit of a thing for him, in actual fact. 'Such a nice boy,' she would say, 'despite his hair.') So, after I'd met him and inter-viewed him over food at a Christian vegetarian café, I asked him to write a personal message to my Nan, which I then glued inside her Christmas card. It made her cry on Christmas Day. At last, my job had intersected with the real world occupied by my family.

He nicked my dessert, too. Just stuck his fork into my apple pie and ate half of it, without even asking. I expect when you're a knight of the realm who's fed the world you can do this.

Dad pats the top of my arm and it means the same thing as shaking my hand. We head for the lifts together, the pride percolating up inside.

*

I am a desk jockey. A commissioning features editor. On the staff. No longer paid piecemeal on a weekly basis – £17 for a review here, £104 for a feature there – I am now salaried. I receive a payslip, in an internal envelope, once a month, telling me how much I have earned after tax and the money goes automatically into my bank account. I no longer have to queue up at Lloyds to pay my cheques in. I am PAYE.

I'm sufficiently *in the system* that I am entitled to claim expenses, which involves carefully filling out a form, stapling the relevant receipts to it and taking the paperwork to accounts, where, at a window similar to that of a bank, a nice middle-aged lady stamps my form, signs it off and counts out the cash. It's a nerve-racking moment – what if she queries anything?

Expenses have become second nature; now, each time I take a taxi, I ask for a receipt, ensuring the driver makes it out for the full amount, including the tip. Some cab drivers ask, 'Shall I leave it blank?' with a conspiratorial wink. This is no doubt unethical, if not illegal, but it's the black-cab economy, isn't it? We're all in it together, us and cab drivers, trying to squeeze a few extra bob out of our greedy paymasters by seasonally adjusting a few figures.

Terry is the master of expenses. When I was put on the staff and handed the metaphorical key to the non-existent executive washroom, I asked Danny how to fill in an expenses form – indeed where to go about getting one from – and he said two words: 'Ask Terry.'

Terry's been on the staff for years. I bet he was on the staff of the *Express & Star*. He probably claimed expenses at school. The expenses form is his symphony and he is the conductor. He's a model of fiscal and administrative efficiency, clothed from head to toe in promotional items sent over by record companies and able to arrange his social calendar around free bars, complimentary nibbles and meals on *other* people's expenses. Terry claims for everything. Terry claims for *drinks*. I haven't worked up the confidence yet to claim for drinks. I haven't entertained filling in the column marked 'entertaining' on my expenses form. I mean, who asks for a receipt in a pub? Terry. Terry asks for a receipt if he buys a newspaper or tips a doorman, or gives spare change to a tramp.

He occupies the moral high ground. Why should Terry pay for anything out of his own pocket? This is not a charity. The *NME* is owned by IPC, which is part of the mighty, American-owned Reed International empire, and Terry, like the rest of us, contributes to their profit margin. Working for the *NME* is not a nine-to-five. It's a dawn-till-dusk.

I enjoy the legitimacy of being on the staff of the *NME*, though it's not something I dreamed of as a freelance. What the freelance lacks in security, he makes back in certain liberties. The freedom to take the afternoon off. The freedom to wander about in your dressing gown. The freedom, in journalistic terms, to hop on a plane at short notice and head off to Utrecht or Chicago or Glasgow with no need to arrange cover. You're freelance; free to do what you want, any old time.

The main drawback with freelancing is that you never book a holiday. Because if you go on holiday you're not working, and if you're not working you're not being paid. So you don't go on holiday. Who can afford to miss out on freelance work? While you're lazing around by a pool in Dubrovnik, features are coming in and going out again. James is commissioning other writers: your workload is being nonchalantly absorbed by Swells and Quantick and Dele and Simon and Barbara and Roger and Keith and Ian and Mary Anne. Also, who needs to book a holiday when record companies are prepared to act as your travel agent and do it for you? 'Roger? It's Andrew. Fancy going to Barcelona with Adamski? It's a video shoot. Page-and-a-half. Great. Give MCA a call. They'll sort you out.'

I didn't think I would, but I relish this role. It's like being the controller of a minicab firm: jobs come in, you farm them out. The writers love you (except when they don't), as you give them work (except when you don't), and the record companies love you (except when they don't), because you put their bands in the paper (except when you don't).

Dad and I emerge from the lifts. Not quite the top, as *Melody Maker* are above us on the twenty-sixth and above them it's management. This is our corridor, I tell him. Drinks machine to the right – that's free. I recommend the fizzy orange. Never have the soup.

Shoot! magazine is through there, and *Mizz* is through there. I tell Dad the story about Killing Joke, who once sent a stripper to the *NME* to promote their new single. She found a space in the middle of the main office, pressed 'play' on a ghetto blaster and started to disrobe, at which all the new men made a run for it, leaving her with no audience, and if a stripper strips and nobody sees, has she really helped promote Killing Joke at all? We gathered, giggling like schoolboys, in the subs room, where the no-nonsense Antipodeans among the senior subbing staff wondered what all the ideological fuss was about. And James had a bright idea. He went back, rescued her from her own ennui and escorted her to *Shoot!*, who don't get many strippers. Her work was duly appreciated and they even gave the Killing Joke single a plug in their next issue, which is not bad for a football magazine whose usual musical currency is Alexander O'Neal.

I show Dad through into the *NME* office.

'This is Karen, she runs the office.'

Karen doesn't actually *say*, 'You must be very proud,' but she implies it. I wonder if he is proud? I hope so.

Danny looms out of his office and greets Dad with his usual ebullience. 'Hello, Andrew's dad!'

There is patter about how well I'm doing, as if perhaps Danny is my headmaster. That's exactly how it feels. I'm at boarding school and Dad's come to pick me up at the end of term and take me home.

We enter the equivalent of the bridge of the *Starship Enterprise* and turn sharp left, into the cluster of desks that houses features, 'Thrills' and 'Fred Fact'. No further introductions; I allow the rest of them to get on with their work, heads down, putting through their sections, fielding calls, signing for packages, unfolding promotional T-shirts that have just arrived and sending copy through to the subs.

This used to involve walking down the corridor to the subs room waving typewritten copy, Neville Chamberlain style, but in these computerised days it means saving it in the shared folder on the network. Having said that, we all still walk down there to tell the subs we've saved it in the shared folder. Belt and braces, as Danny would say.

Parents are rarely, if ever, invited into the *NME* office. I don't know if it's because the others are too cool and wouldn't want their parents to embarrass them on consecrated ground, or because their parents aren't that interested in what goes on. But I'm happy to have my dad here.

The office was invaded by outsiders in May. That separated the cool from the uncool. They were making a documentary about a week in the life of the *NME* office for BBC Radio 5, the new youth and current affairs station. Danny announced it on Monday morning and asked us to be accommodating. Most people grumbled into their coffee. I thought it sounded really exciting and decided to be really accommodating.

It was just two of them: presenter Mark Thomas, the firebrand stand-up comedian, and a young producer called John, whose job it was to hold the microphone.

(I'd already met Mark as I'd interviewed him for the paper. Comedy is the new rock'n'roll, or so Janet Street Porter apparently says. Certainly since the Vic Reeves cover, the *NME* had been doing more of it, and as I was one of the few writers who actually went to comedy gigs I was empowered by James to seek out rising stars. You get a lot more sense out of comedians than you do bands, but less laughs.)

It was just a normal week – Pet Shop Boys cover, Bob Dylan's fiftieth birthday, Thousand Yard Stare exclusive – but that's what Radio 5 were after. As the week wore on, Stuart Maconie and I emerged as the paper's self-styled friendly ambassadors, always ready with the lowdown and a quip. By Wednesday, we had become unashamedly indispensable to our BBC visitors, something of an *ad hoc* double act in fact, while all around our contemporaries scowled at the outsiders and busied themselves with nothing. Then on Thursday it all went off.

Mark Thomas does a quick piece to mic, which is held under his nose by John. 'Oh, here we are, just walked into the *NME*, Thursday morning, and immediately, big buzz going round, Andrew Collins sitting here, saying, "Ooh, something's happened!" What is it?'

I'm sat on the edge of my desk, relishing my role as the documentary crew's first point of contact, and also trying to play the mayhem down in my Northampton drawl: 'The thing that's happened, right, is that last night, Steve Lamacq went up …' I call over to a shellshocked Steve at the live desk. 'Where did you go?'

'Norwich.'

He's just returned from interviewing the Manic Street Preachers in Norwich where, in a fit of disturbing pique, guitarist Richey cut his own arm to prove how serious he was about the band. Richey felt a bit woozy. Steve felt a bit woozy. Now he's reported back to the office.

'It certainly wasn't what I was expecting to happen,' Steve tells Mark and John, who are beginning to realise they're in the right place at the right time. A genuine scoop. 'You won't get much coherent sense out of me, I'm afraid.'

'Do you want to tell them or shall I?'

'No, you tell them,' says Steve.

So I take up the story. 'Steve's a bit suspicious of them so it was going to be this sort of, not a *backlash*, but he was going to suggest that they're not all they're cracked up to be. Anyway, went up there, saw the gig, and you know what they're like, they're just these young punks basically, the return of punk, and a lot of people are very suspicious of them, think they're just sort of faking it, and trying to get rich and famous, and they're not really being serious. So Steve did half an hour of chat with – which one was it?'

Steve takes over: 'Richey said, "Have you got a minute to come backstage? There's one last thing I've got to say." So we went backstage and I just said, "I don't think a lot of people will think you're for real." And I don't know where he got it from, but he got a razor blade and wrote "4 REAL" on his arm, down the side of his arm, while I was standing there watching him. And, er, that's about it really.'

'This is good,' I add. 'This is a good story. Everyone will have a reaction to this story. Unfortunately, Ed Sirrs didn't get any pictures of it.'

At which, word goes round the office that Ed Sirrs has arrived, and he *did* get pictures of it. Colour pictures.

Action moves to the light box outside the art room, where photographers display their transparencies for art editor Pru and assistant Marc. Not usually with this kind of audience though. The whole office is down here. Mark and John buttonhole Ed, who tells the tale with his trademark war-photographer's insouciance.

'A roadie rushed out and lashed some bandages around him. And I whipped the camera out and he took the bandages off for me, and I looked, very quickly—'

'He actually said, "Here, do you want to photograph this?"' establishes Mark.

'Yeah,' nods Ed, unflustered by all the attention. 'He said, "I'd better take the bandages off." Which had just been put on, so it was mint.'

'So he's got a *mint wound?*'

'Oh yes.'

Back to me, official spokesperson for the *mint wound*: 'And, er, question is: can we print this picture? 'Cos it is really 'orrible. I find it extremely 'orrible. He's upset. People down there are upset. Grown people are upset by this picture. It is an 'orrible picture. Danny's in a meeting and he hasn't seen it yet. He's going to be jumping around. You could say it's trivial. I say, within our little world, it is not trivial.'

Mark interrogates Steve. 'How do you feel about all this?'

'I don't really think I've quite got over the shock of it really.'

'Do you in any way regard it that you may be responsible for it, because he did it for you, almost?'

'Nah,' shrugs Steve, with a slight quaver in his car dealer's voice. 'Not really. He chose to do it. He chose to make his point in that way. I don't think, you know, I don't kind of, I don't feel guilty about the fact that he's done it. [Deep sigh] Dunno. It's been one hell of a week now.'

At which, a forewarned Danny arrives back from his meeting. He explodes through the door and is immediately pounced upon by staffers and documentary-makers.

'Danny,' I say, with some urgency. 'Get down there. We've got bloody colour pictures of the mutilation. It's just too 'orrible to look at. You'll faint.'

Karen throws in her tuppence: 'The guy's sick.'

'I know,' he replies, unflappable. 'But I'm in the publishing caper, aren't I?'

'There's no way you can print that,' she insists. 'You'll get all their fans doing the same thing.'

'Rubbish, Karen!'

As Danny approaches the light box, Steve announces, 'More people to see gore, Ed.'

'Well, I'm in charge of gore,' proclaims Danny, bullish. 'I am in fact Gore Editor.'

'Have you had anything to eat this morning?' Ed asks, as the crowd parts for the editor.

'Yes thanks.'

Danny is genuinely taken aback: 'Oh my *God.*'

In the most lurid shot, in living colour, the slashes in Richey's arm gape. His face is a mixture of fierce situationist pride and blank, vandalised numbness.

Instinctively aware that this is radio, I take the mic: 'That's Danny Kelly that just said that.'

'That's the R and the E of "4 REAL",' explains Steve.

I ask Danny if he considers the picture a problem. He doesn't. 'These things happen, Andrew, it's a newspaper.'

'Print them, Danny!' calls out Brendan, no-nonsense Australian production editor.

Pru is still ranting. 'What's he gonna do next? Slit his throat?'

'Hopefully,' says Danny, getting wound up by all the moral indignation. 'Maybe they'll all cut each other's heads off! And that'll be an end to it.'

Over at the preternaturally tidy news desk, preternaturally tidy news editor Iestyn is making 'that call' to the band's PR, Philip Hall.

'Hi, Philip. You know about last night and all that? Obviously everything's going berserk here, you know, I mean we're gonna do a news story on it, so have you got any details about—?'

Back at the light box, James arrives, demanding, 'Where are these photographs?' He grabs the spyglass used to inspect transparencies and bends over the offending frame. With predictable bravado and to amused noises from various onlookers, he declares, 'That's nothing!'

'We were expecting that,' grumbles Marc the fiery Frenchman.

'That's my man!' shouts Ed, resisting a high five. 'Come and stand in this corner.'

Battle lines are drawn now. I can't imagine this much excitement when the picture of the flag being raised at Iwo Jima went round the wires in 1945. James seems to think that it says 'T REX' on Richey's arm.

'He's spelled it wrong,' he says. 'It looks more like "TREAT" or something.'

Someone explains that it's '4 REAL'. He starts to froth, like a kid in a toy shop.

'You've gotta print that! It's rock'n'roll, innit? I think it's an excellent photograph. Good one, Ed. I think more bands should do that sort of thing.'

'Oh yeah, very clever,' says Marc, witheringly.

'Don't come on with the moral stuff,' James counters. 'Because we have people smoking in the paper every week, we have people like Jack, who used to work here, glorifying drugs for weeks on end—'

'Yeah, but all you need—' butts in Pru.

'We had a letter E on the cover—' continues James, on a roll now.

'All you need— '

'When E was the national symbol for Ecstasy—'

'— is one kid, one child, to copy that—'

'Come on!'

'— and kill themselves, and you'd be …' Pru mimes cutting her throat.

James is having none of this. The floor is his. 'You couldn't kill yourself cutting yourself on the forearm.'

'You could if you missed.'

There is further heated debate about Sid Vicious and Iggy Pop and what James calls 'a fine tradition of self-expression' and Marc throws his hands up in the air in Gallic fashion with the declaration, 'He is a dickhead.'

'But,' says Danny, keen to move on, 'we are entitled to report it.'

James loses it. 'If he burned himself in Tiananmen Square, we'd print it. It's artistic expression, innit?'

'You're more of an asshole than I am,' adds Marc, going back to his Thousand Yard Stare layout. 'Artistic expression? Do me a favour.'

The whole furore feels historic in its own way, certainly loaded with portent about the crazy world of the publishing caper. As we return to Thursday morning mundanities, I am struck by how potentially alive and stimulating this job is. OK, maybe Richey is a dickhead, and maybe Marc is too, and maybe Iestyn shouldn't tidy his desk to that degree, but all human life is here. At that moment, gathered around the light box like the scientists circling the UFO in *Close Encounters*, gazing upon that act of self-harm in Norwich, nothing else in the universe mattered to any of us more than Richey's arm.

You do feel as if you're married to the paper; devotion and fidelity come with the territory. You might work here, but you don't just work here. It's more of a calling. That's why writers gravitate here from Belfast and Wigan and Northampton and Wolverhampton and Harlow, and why designers come here from France: the *NME* is like our mothership. I'm reminded of the ship's purser in *The Poseidon Adventure* who reveals at the captain's table that he has a mistress.

Cue sharp intake of breath from other diners.

Then the punchline: 'The sea.'

I flirted with another publication but it didn't work out. Towards the end of 1990, after much secrecy and planning, during which Alan spent less and less time in the *NME* office, IPC launched a glossy music monthly to compete with rivals *Q* (owned by Emap) and *Select* (owned by United). Ours is called *Vox* and models itself, at least in terms of size and pomposity, on

Rolling Stone. Alan oversaw the launch, but its day-to-day editor is Roy – the longest-serving staffer after Fred, a squat, wizardly man with a comb-over who, after running out of journalistic credit, made himself indispensable by curating and producing the *NME*'s famed mail-order albums and cassettes. (He has an amazing photo of himself on his office wall with his arm round Bruce Springsteen, and they're wearing *kimono*s!)

When, in the summer of 1990, certain among the *NME* team were approached by Alan to 'straddle' both titles it seemed very exciting: in addition to bringing down the monthly competition, *Vox* would test new desktop publishing technology, being produced entirely on computer. This really was boldly going where no mag had gone before. I jumped at the chance of getting involved with *Vox* – strapline: 'From the makers of *NME*' – partly because it was *more work* and a freelancer, as I still was then, can always fit in *more work*, but also because it offered the chance to see my words printed on glossy paper. You've no idea how enticing that is when you're used to communicating your thoughts on the new Thee Hypnotics single on toilet tissue.

So it was that I typed up my first ever feature – an interview with the group James – on an Apple Mac Classic II. Actually, I believe it's called 'inputting' not typing. Then I watched as pugnacious designer Paul turned my copy into a full-colour layout before my very eyes, moving the headline around with a mouse and sizing up photos not on the photocopier but on a telly. It was cosmic.

We all wanted a piece of the *Vox* action when it started; half the magazine was written by the makers of *NME*, freelancers and staffers, either for extra money or extra kudos. But the sheen soon came off.

For all its noble intentions, it was a magazine without a soul, unsure whether to go after the elderly, pipe-smoking readers of *Q* or the Madchester-style whippersnappers of *Select*. It fell down a hole in the middle. How we all laughed at the *Vox*

'Encyclopedia of Rock', which began at the back of the magazine and was designed for readers to cut out and keep, building
month by month into an Aladdin's cave of musical knowledge
that you will treasure for ever. What must have seemed like a
top idea at the meeting actually turned out to be the magazine's albatross. The encyclopedia had only just reached the
letter B by issue three. *Vox* would have been going for six years
before reaching the end of the alphabet, by which time all the
preceding entries would be out of date and would have to be
rewritten. One can only assume that Sisyphus was at those early
meetings. And the name of this never-ending encyclopedia?
'It's Too Late To Stop Now'.

They eventually did stop it, and not before time. A new era
dawned. They installed a features editor from 'outside' (cue
crash of thunder, sustained chord, horses whinnying). His
name was Mal. He understandably wished to stamp his own
signature on the magazine and duly phased out the commissioning of mercenary *NME* refugees.

Alan and Roy had put me in charge of *Vox*'s comedy section.
It was largely a case of sending myself to interview comedians I
liked and reviewing comedy videos I wished to blag. It was fun
to do, and it broadened my freelance portfolio. However, Mal
had other ideas. But he couldn't exactly sack me, as I was not
on his staff. This is how our introductory meeting went:

Knock on office door.

'Come in.'

'Hi. I'm Andrew Collins.'

'Ah yes, hi. Take a seat.'

Don't like the look of him much.

'I've been going over the comedy section.'

Going over?

'What have you got coming up for the next issue?'

'Er, Skint Video, and an interview with Clive Anderson, the
bloke who presents *Whose Line Is It Anyway*?'

'Mmmmmm,' he replies, his *mmmmmm* loaded with meaning. 'It's all very left-wing, isn't it?'

'What do you mean?'

'If you look back at previous sections, it's all left-wing, alternative comedy. *The Mary Whitehouse Experience*, Paul Merton, Denis Leary – it lacks balance.'

I am actually flabbergasted by what I'm hearing. I'm used to criticism from James and Danny and Alan and Justin, but not this. 'What do you mean, balance?'

'Some right-wing comedians.'

'But all the best comedy is left-wing.'

'What about Bernard Manning? He's still very popular.'

I am almost speechless now. He's serious. It's 1990. The comedy wars have been won. Alternative comedy has become the establishment. Bernard Manning has been consigned to the dustbin of history. Should I go over Mal's head to Roy or Alan? I'm certainly not commissioning a piece on Bernard Manning.

'I don't get paid for putting this section together, you know.'

'I appreciate your enthusiasm. It's just that it's all one-sided.'

'Well, perhaps you should take it in-house. Get someone else to do it.'

'If that's the way you feel about it.'

The conversation had been civil enough. I wasn't on the staff of *Vox*. I was commissioning myself to write the comedy section out of love. If I resigned my post there would be no paperwork, no redundancy package, no leaving do. I had met my first nemesis.

Mal ran my Clive Anderson piece in the next issue, but opposite an interview with Bernard Manning for balance. I kid you not. I never went back.

So, aside from some basic computer training, my affair with *Vox* left me with little more than confirmation that I was married to the *NME*. Most of us came back from the twenty-sixth floor, where *Vox* was based, feeling dirty. Like a glossy siren, it tried to lure us onto the rocks, but, for the most part, it failed.

'From the makers of *NME*' disappeared from under the logo.

In October 1991 the Levellers sent me shit in a box. They did so because they disagreed with the mark out of ten I gave their album *Levelling the Land*. I gave it three out of ten, an honest reflection of the fact that I didn't like it very much. I don't make a habit of slagging things off for sport. If anything, my default critical setting is way too kind. I once gave an album by little-known Liverpool group Benny Profane nine out of ten. It's an extreme case, but it illustrates my lenience. To make matters worse, albums editor Stuart Bailie gave me the opportunity to reconsider my nine before he put the section through, and I stood by it. Did I ever listen to Benny Profane's classic album again? I think you know the answer.

I'm pretty free and easy with my marks. I gave The Mission's *Carved in Sand* eight out of ten. I gave The Charlatans' *Between 10th and 11th* eight out of ten. I gave U2's *Achtung Baby* nine out of ten. But it's not just about the marks out of ten, that idiot shorthand for people with such busy lives they haven't time to read the prose we've lovingly drawn from the literary fountain. In a just world it would be what's written in the review that matters – that's where the nuance and the subtlety lie.

In my now locally infamous review of *Levelling the Land* I wrote that the Levellers were 'art-hippy poshos … using river metaphors and bad grammar to convince us that Tom and Barbara Good had it right and The Man is someone who oppresses us by building houses for us to live in.' And then I gave it three out of ten. Not two, or one, or nought, but three. It could, in other words, have come off a lot worse.

With the benefit of hindsight, I'm neither especially proud of the writing, nor the sentiment, nor the mark. But I did think the record was horrible. And I did listen to it, something the Levellers subsequently accused me in print of not doing. I have a witness. Stuart was round the flat the night I listened to *Levelling the Land*, and he will attest that I listened to it more attentively and at greater length than the *Konami Track & Field* enthusiast within me would have liked, but hey, I'm a professional, with a job to do. It should also be added that even though the Levellers had developed a substantial live following without once being featured in the *NME* – in other words, they were making it big *without our permission* – I had no axe to grind.

I didn't like the look of them in their bush hats, gardening jumpers and half-beards, I detected pretence in their wood-cut logo, and I suspected, rightly or wrongly, that their alternative lifestyle was something to do in their gap year, but I listened to their folksy music with an open mind. And I thought it was horrible. Which is why I gave it three out of ten. And why they sent me some shit in a box.

The *NME* mail sack is a poisoned chalice. It contains free records. It also contains readers' letters. And it sometimes contains a giftwrapped present postmarked 'Norwich'. Each morning, one enterprising hack upends the sack onto the floor in the bit by Karen's desk and sorts through it looking for anything addressed to them. It was Barbara who came across the giftwrapped present with my name on it.

'Andrew,' she called over the partition. 'Somebody's sent you a present.'

Fool that I am, I joined her at the post mountain; I was filled with childish, Christmas morning excitement.

'A present? Top!' (We all said, 'Top!' in 1991.)

And there it was, sitting to one side of the avalanche. The description 'giftwrapped' flatters it somewhat. It was a cardboard box around which cheap decorative paper had been slung, Sellotaped in place without care or finesse. The patterned membrane had torn in transit and the whole thing

looked rather sorry for itself. The address label had been written in a remedial scrawl. I smelled a rat.

Something made me pick the package up at arm's length. I
shook it in the spirit of Christmas morning. It gave a dull rattle.
Perhaps it was a rat. Or a rattle. Either way, I instinctively knew
it was a gift I did not wish to receive, one that would go on
giving in all the wrong ways. I ceremonially escorted my present
from *NME* soil and dumped it in one of the big bins by the lifts
– if there had been a pair of *NME* tongs, I would have used
them. I have embroidered the story in subsequent retellings, so
that the suspect package was taken outside the building by security and destroyed in a controlled explosion. This never
happened, but the outcome is the same: I never opened or
looked inside that box. Satisfaction had been demanded in a
scatological duel but none was gained.

I had written a piece in the paper provocatively entitled
'Why Football Is Shite', commissioned in a fit of balance by
James to counterpoint the terrace-anthem tone of a special
beautiful-game issue, and death threats from hooligans had
ensued. One among them cautioned against me ever visiting
Bolton again, which wasn't quite the inconvenience imagined
by the letter-writer. I presumed the rat-in-a-box was from a football fan, and vowed not to let it impinge upon my life.

Then the real culprit owned up to *Melody Maker*, presumably
of a mind that if a band defecates in a box as a statement backstage at the Norwich Waterfront, sends it to a journalist by
Royal Mail and the journalist doesn't open it, have they really
made a statement at all? It turned out that dreadlocked
convent-boy bassist Jeremy had exercised his right to reply, but
unilaterally. This was not, to be fair, a band shit, but it played
into the hands of those who sought to dismiss the Levellers as
crusty guttersnipes who gave the New Age Traveller movement
a bad name. At least the Travellers buried theirs in a field.

All hell broke lose at the *NME* after Jeremy had put his

head above the parapet, as it were. We closed ranks against the Levellers and vowed never to put their name in the paper again, a boycott that was fairly easy to maintain, as we never put their name in the paper anyway. They could continue building a powerful fanbase through their live gigs and we would ignore them.

The boycott stood until May 1992 when they had their first hit and we felt they'd suffered enough.

I show Dad my desk and point out with a sweep of the hand the view across the Thames. You can't buy a view like that, I say, like an estate agent. I show him my lockable cupboard, which I never lock, even though we're convinced the cleaners steal our records. Maybe it serves us right for having so many free records; maybe it's redistribution of vinyl wealth. This is my phone. I'm expecting a call from a record company about a band I'm meant to be interviewing next week for a cover story and I don't know where the interview's going to be yet. Berlin? Manchester? Stockholm? (To be honest, of the three, I hope it's Manchester.) Dad and Mum must have entertained doubts that I would ever amount to anything, even when in my own mind I *was* amounting to something. But this, they can understand. An office job. A stapler and a Sellotape dispenser.

When I was a boy, I visited Dad's office in Wellingborough. It was exciting because it was where my dad worked, but, at the end of the day, it was an office. There's not much to do in an office, except steal stationery or look out of the window. So even though this is a momentous occasion, an historic father-son summit, there's not much to do here either. But hey, it's only a flying visit, an affirmation that I really am doing something useful for a living, if not a proper job *per se*, certainly one that looks proper, that has all the proper accessories. And Dad's got a train to catch.

He hands over the ceremonial cuttings from the *Daily*

Telegraph about things he and Mum think might interest me, thus saving on stamps, and we drain our plastic cups of fizzy orange. It's time for me to walk him back down to reception.

'Nice to meet you!' trills Karen, as we leave.

Would it be melodramatic to say that something has changed for ever as Dad and I travel back down to the ground floor, facing forward, watching the descending numbers? That in turning the tables and inviting him into my office I have taken possession of a generational baton? Certainly something unspoken has passed between us, something significant, something profound. Perhaps I have come of age in my dad's eyes. Getting a degree didn't count – partly because there was no ceremony with gowns and scrolls, and partly because it was only a degree in drawing pictures. My first *NME* layout didn't count, because although they dutifully went out and bought that issue and held it in their hands, there was no proof that I'd sized up that Roddy Frame photo and spray-mounted a photocopy of it onto a grid. There was no credit. It was only casual work. But this, features editor, on the staff, salary, expenses, laminated ID, this is 4 REAL. This is Bob Geldof's autograph. This is a Sellotape dispenser. And Dad's seen it. I'm a man now. Maybe I'll get married and raise a family. And maybe not.

'Lawrence from Creation phoned,' Stuart tells me when I get back to my desk.

I call back. It is about My Bloody Valentine and the cover feature. I'm to meet and interview the band on Monday. Where? At their manager's house. In Streatham, about ten minutes from my flat if I take the 133 bus. No flights, no cabs, no hotel. I'll be back at my desk by 10.30 a.m. All the plum jobs.

6

Marvelling at Andrea Dworkin

Well, this is a first. As we enter the already-crowded champagne reception, a footman announces our names.

'Andrew *Collins*! Stuart *Maconie*! John *Yorke*! And Judy *Leighton*!'

It's like walking into a ball at Mansfield Park, and not something I've planned for. Fortunately ours are names of little or no consequence to the great and the good, so we barely merit a glance upwards from the you-were-*marvellous*-darling chitchat. We none the less descend the steps, as is our entitlement, into this ornate, mirrored-and-marbled chamber with apologetic humility, blushing at the formality of the occasion and the fact that we don't need a booming, uniformed servant to draw attention to us.

It's clear that we've made a terrible *faux pas*. Perhaps we should just cut our reddening losses and leave. Does a footman call your names out when you leave, as if perhaps to alert the outside world that important showbiz people are re-entering it?

I'm sweating already. Damn this top button. Doing my best to carry myself like an important showbiz person, I take a glance around the room. It's like the deck of the *Titanic*: every woman is in a ball gown and every man is in a dinner suit and bow-tie, some with piping and cummerbund. Every man except for us three. Judy's in a smart print dress and little black cardy and looks as if she's meant to be here, but blushes anyway, on our collective behalf. It's a costume tragedy. We may as well have come dressed as chimney sweeps.

Welcome to the Writers' Guild of Great Britain Awards 1993, the reason we find ourselves at the Dorchester Hotel on Park Lane in London's famous Mayfair, the two most expensive streets on the Monopoly board – although one of them isn't a street. It's evidently a much more formal bash than any of us had anticipated, and a new frontier for Stuart and me, now joined at the ampersand by burgeoning double-act status.

It stated quite clearly 'black tie' on the invites. With neither of us exactly versed in going-out etiquette, we deferred to John – who, after all, works for the BBC. He confidently assured us that 'black tie' was not binding, merely a euphemistic term that meant any kind of smart suit, as long as you wore a tie with it. Didn't even have to be black. Black was itself a euphemism: any tie would do.

No problem. From my impressive collection of two suits, I chose the bottle-green Top Man I bought for Melissa and Graham's wedding, slightly more formal-looking than the light-grey Top Man with the electric blue Duran Duran lining I bought for Simon and Lesley's wedding. To this I added the smartest white shirt in my wardrobe – which, if I'm honest, is the *only* white shirt in my wardrobe – and the black tie I bought for Pap Collins's funeral. If I was being hyper-critical, I'd say that the white shirt is too soft and cottony for the job, as the tie knot makes the collar poke outside the jacket, but this is the least of my sartorial worries.

Stuart has on a dark suit and a stiff-collared white shirt, but offset with a very colourful tie made of diamond shapes. John also has a dark suit, but offset with a stripy tie, as if he is perhaps at a regimental reunion. In deference to the fact that this is a bit of a do, I have neatly scraped back my long grunge bob into a ponytail.

The problem is not so much that we look *different* from everybody else (God, when are they going to let us go in and sit down?), more that they'll think we dressed this way to cock a revolutionary snook at convention. Look at us! We're rockabilly rebels! We're smashing the system with our different-coloured suits and our non-bow-ties! In the stirring words of Rage Against the Machine: 'Fuck you, I won't do what you tell me on your invite!' It's the rebellious equivalent of wearing your top button undone at school, just to prove you're hard. Perhaps we should have worn trainers. Perhaps we'll be kept behind afterwards. I'm sure the board of the Writers' Guild have plenty of marking they can be getting on with.

Waiters circulate with silver trays of champagne and bucks fizz. We take one each and sip it too fast. Gritted-teeth recriminations won't ease the situation – although it is obviously *John's fault*. Let's just stand against this gilt-etched wall and feign invisibility, while Lesley Joseph talks to Jack Tinker, theatre critic of the *Daily Mail*. There's Alan Yentob. And Denis Norden. And Tony Robinson of *Who Dares Wins*. One of these elderly gents in a cummerbund must be Alan Plater as he's the president of the Guild. He wrote *A Very British Coup*. We wrote a six-part radio comedy about two ex-hospital-radio DJs being shrunk to microscopic size and injected into the bloodstream of Richard Whiteley.

Even though we don't look like we have any right to be here, we actually do. We are nominees. We are nominated for a Writers' Guild Award for Best Radio Programme (Comedy/Light Entertainment). Me and him. For writing Radio 5's *Fantastic Voyage*, a very silly spoof of youth television about a Saturday morning TV show whose unique pitch to a commissioning editor called Janet Street-Preacher is that the entire show, presented from a bespoke submarine, is shrunk to microscopic size and injected into the bloodstream of a different celebrity every week.

The footman speaks: 'My lords, ladies and gentlemen, would you kindly take your seats in the *ball*room!'

Bloody hell, are there lords here as well?

*

The first episode of *Fantastic Voyage* – ahem, the Writers' Guild Award-nominated *Fantastic Voyage* – was, thanks to the do-anything potential of a proper doorknobs-and-gravel BBC radio drama studio and a vast library of sound effects discs, presented from within the bloodstream of Richard Whiteley. The humorous idea was that the programme's first choice, Sigourney Weaver, had pulled out and we had to go for the next best thing.

John, our producer, keen to do things by the book, insisted we seek the chuckling *Countdown* presenter's permission to exploit his image and his name. Being journalists John felt that this was our territory. He obviously forgot for a moment there that we are *music* journalists and thus, our idea of 'a story' is one faxed to us on a press release from Polydor. Nevertheless, in a fit of what-could-possibly-go-wrong abandon, I just phoned Yorkshire TV one day from the *NME* office.

'Hello,' came the reply. 'Yorkshire Television.'

'Hi, I'm calling from the BBC [white lie], I wonder if you could put me through to *Countdown*.'

'One moment, please.'

Blimey, this is easy. I could be anybody. I *am* anybody.

'Hello,' came the next reply. '*Countdown*.'

'Hi, I'm calling from the BBC [I'm starting to believe this]. Is it possible to speak to Richard Whiteley?'

'Yes, hang on a minute.'

Voices in the background. One of them shouts, 'Richard!' then a familiar Yorkshire voice comes on the line.

'Hello, Richard Whiteley here.'

Bloody hell!

'Hi. Er, my name's Andrew Collins. We're making a comedy series for Radio 5—'

'Oh yes?'

'It's called *Fantastic Voyage* and well … [may as well just come right out with it] the idea is, it's a spoof youth TV show and each week, as a gimmick, the programme is shrunk to microscopic size and injected into the bloodstream of a different celebrity.'

MARVELLING AT ANDREA DWORKIN

Richard begins chuckling. It's definitely him anyway.

'And the first show is presented from *your* bloodstream. Would you have any problem with that?'

'No, not at all. I'm flattered.'

'That's brilliant. It's going to be on Radio 5 next year, April sort of time.'

'*Fantastic Voyage*, you say?'

'Yeah.'

'Well, good luck with it!'

'Thanks.'

One of the more surreal conversations of my career, and a clue that we were not in Kansas any more.

So here we are in the cavernous ballroom at the Dorchester Hotel, at the high-rolling end of the Monopoly board, loitering by our table until ordered to sit down by a servant. How, in the name of Lesley Joseph, did we *get* here?

To trace it to the source and gain an illuminating insight into the way the media works, the fuse was lit in May 1991, two years previously, that week Radio 5 came to the *NME*. The lime-light-hogging architects of our own destiny, Stuart and I were all over the finished documentary, *Sleeping With the NME*, when it finally went out at the end of December. It so happened that John the producer – John *Yorke*! – also worked on a youthful Monday night Radio 5 magazine show called *The Mix*. The pluralistic BBC notion is that in the 10.10 p.m. to midnight slot, each weekday's magazine show comes from a different region: Monday, London; Tuesday, Glasgow; Wednesday, Manchester; Thursday, Birmingham; and Friday, Cardiff.

We knew about *The Mix* because one sociable evening in the Stamford, as a gang of us were putting the world to rights – i.e. the world of Birdland, Thousand Yard Stare and Bang Bang Machine – Terry and Quantick refused a drink because they had to hop in a cab and tear across London in time to record their slot on a youthful Radio 5 magazine show. It was a satiri-cal music-based slot that had turned into a regular gig for this frankly unlikely double act. (I think they wrote it in the cab.) I remember thinking they were cutting it a bit fine. But then, they were Terry and Quantick. They were old school.

As an *NME* writer, you are occasionally asked to break free of the printed page and appear on the radio or television to offer what is laughingly referred to as your expertise. It's taken me long enough to get used to calling myself a journalist; 'expert' will require more advanced mental contortion. My first experience of this was when, as features editor, I appeared in an ambassadorial capacity on Jeff Graham's show on Radio Luxembourg, basically there to plug what was in that week's *NME* and help fill a bit of spare air. As a can-do sort of bloke, this did not reduce me to jelly. It's just talking, but talking to order. I performed this extra-curricular task every week until the week I went directly to the studio from the *NME* Christmas lunch. Forgivably refreshed, I accidentally used the word 'poof' on-air and the cloak of irony offered no protection.

The most instructive thing I took away from the Luxembourg gig was how self-sufficient radio stations are. Barely any staff, everybody doing three jobs, Jeff seemed to be his own producer. The second most instructive thing was that drinking does not enhance live radio.

Stuart trumped my brief run on a moribund AM radio station by appearing on national telly: firstly as a pundit on Channel 4's impossibly awful *Club X*, from which he manfully emerged with his dignity; and secondly as a sort of cultural travel guide alongside James Brown on Granada's timely Madchester documentary *Celebration: The Sound of the North*, to which he brought a touch of class, pointing out the 'witty' use of a red girder in the toilets of Manchester's Dry bar. Not being from The North, I was of no use to the programme, but the eagle-eyed may have glimpsed me briefly in a sequence shot in the *NME* office. This was 1990, and, as Stuart sweeps past, delivering a cheery link to camera, that's me in the corner, banging theatrically away at the old typewriter I used to share with Fred. (I'm not actually typing anything, just banging the keys to get noticed. Television cameras have that hello-mum effect.)

As a full-time music journalist I had never considered myself part of the media. I barely considered myself part of journalism. Music journalist was enough of a dream job on its own. I was happy in 'our little world'. 'They' were over there with their boom mics, their headphones and their clipboards; we were over here with our typewriters, our well-thumbed copies of *Psychotic Reactions and Carburetor Dung*, and our tape recorders held together with insulating tape. Television, radio, print; pictures, sound, words. Three separate industries linked only by the fact that they're all better than working in Sainsbury's and are the last to shed jobs in a recession.

The cameras came and went, some people from the *NME* got on Channel 4, and we all returned to our desks and got on with our actual typewriting. In the same fashion, Mark Thomas and John Yorke came and went, some of us got on Radio 5, then we returned to our desks and got on with our work again. Except for me and Stuart, who landed Terry and Quantick's slot on *The Mix* because they had become unreliable.

And so it was, in the windowless mezzanine-floor studios of Radio 5 in Broadcasting House, that the notion of the media became concrete. Indeed, walking for the first time through those heavy wooden doors was nothing short of Narnian.

Back in my previous life as a freelance cartoonist, I was occasionally plucked from my drawing desk and called upon to enter imposing buildings. I once attended a meeting at the Mirror Group near Fleet Street, which struck me as exciting on a very shallow level, even though it was nothing to do with the *Mirror* newspaper; they also publish the *Puzzled* magazine range, for whose covers I drew cartoon animals. I was also summoned to the headquarters of the First National Bank of Chicago in Covent Garden for a job that involved drawing animal-based caricatures of the senior staff and meeting a man who really was called Earl Glazier, and to the home of ICI on Millbank, by the Thames, who required a humorous leaflet about the benevolence of petrochemicals for schools.

These buildings made me feel small and scruffy, and had the effect of making me want to get out of them as rapidly as possible, back into breathable air. Walking into Broadcasting House for the first time in 1992 was different. I felt welcome there. I wanted to stay and explore.

It really is one of the most amazing buildings in London, right up there with Battersea Power Station and the Natural History Museum, but it's not just about the creamy Portland stone and the Eric Gill statues of Prospero and Ariel that watch over you as you cross the threshold, it's about what goes on within these walls and has done for a large chunk of a century. Entering the Art Deco entrance hall for the first time in 1992, I was immediately struck by the Latin inscription, which you usually have time to read while you wait for somebody to come and collect you from reception. (It's either that or read *Ariel*, the BBC's parish newspaper, which always turns out to be less interesting than you think it will be, and last week's.)

*TEMPLUM HOC ARTIUM ET MUSARUM ANNO
DOMINI MCMXXXI RECTORE JOHANNI REITH PRIMI
DEDICANT GUBERNATORES PRECANTES UT MESSEM
BONAM BONA PROFERAT SEMENTIS UT IMMUNDA
OMNIA ET INIMICA PACI EXPELLANTUR UT QUAE-
CUNQUE PULCHRA SUNT ET SINCERA QUACUNQUE
BONAE FAMAE AD HAEC AVREM INCLINANS POPULUS
VIRTUTIS ET SAPIENTIAE SEMITAM INSISTAT.*

Translation: *This Temple of the Arts and Muses is dedicated to Almighty God by the first Governors of Broadcasting in the year 1931, Sir John Reith being Director General. It is their prayer that good seed sown may bring forth a good harvest, that all things hostile to peace or purity may be banished from this house, and that the people, inclining their ear to whatsoever things are beautiful and honest and of good report, may tread the path of wisdom, and here comes someone who looks like they work on the programme – I hope they don't banish us from this house.*

Fuck the First National Bank of Chicago! I don't believe *their* building was dedicated to Almighty God so that good seed may bring forth anything other than bank charges. I don't even believe in Almighty God, but I do believe in John Reith.

More people seemed to work on *The Mix* than at the whole of Radio Luxembourg: a self-sufficient unit of enthusiastic, youthful people, some of whom pressed buttons in the 'cubicle' and wore 'cans'; others seemed to just collect people from reception, which was more time-consuming. Many of them wore Kangol hats.

I remember the first time Stuart and I were taken to the Radio 5 studios. It's an odyssey of which Homer would have been proud. We were picked up from reception, ushered past the gatekeeper, known as a security guard, taken up two floors in one of the main lifts, escorted along a seemingly endless corridor that burrowed through the middle of the *Woman's Hour* offices, then *down* one floor in another set of lifts on the other side of the building. Was this to confuse us? We followed our Kangol sherpa, known in the trade as a 'broadcast assistant' or 'BA', out of the second set of lifts, past the five monitors that quaintly display the Teletext listings for the five BBC radio stations, and into the studio area, which was kind of down half a floor, and whose modern glass door opened with a *Star Trek* swoosh and only by the swipe of a small, black electronic BBC key-pass called a 'dongle'. (Don't ask me why a dongle – some media jargon you just accept unless you want to look like a tourist.) I dreamed of the day that I would have my own dongle. BBC staff move about John Reith's big house with casual authority, whereas contributors must be escorted, even to the toilets. This is a symbolic door: lying at the end of your quest, it is the gateway – swoosh – to the media. Here be radio producers.

Each week on *The Mix*, Stuart and I were given a topical theme upon which to tangentially pontificate – Valentine's Day, General Election, Christmas number ones. During *NME* downtime, we'd sit at Stuart's computer in the office and knock up a two-way script with room for music clips or 'grams', as they're called (something to do with the Gramophone Library). We'd go in to Broadcasting House and record it on a Monday afternoon, so that John or Matt or whoever was producing that particular day's show could edit it together in time for broadcast that night. Just going into the BBC by day to record an item was exciting enough for two young men from Northampton and Wigan, but we were also asked to return at night and indulge in some preparatory live on-air banter with the host, Richard Coles, before our item went out.

Yes, *the* Richard Coles, beaky, classically trained former Communard turned radio presenter. Richard was the gayest man we had ever met. Much gayer than the blokes who used to hang around Alan's flat when I was a teenager on the cusp of sexual enlightenment. Richard was also born in Northampton, so despite our divergent sexual paths we have something geographically profound in common. A well-spoken and eminently lovable man with a vast knowledge of the arts, he wears his lifestyle on his sleeve. It informs his banter, and he invites you to play up to it.

The one-minute live preamble was the cherry on the cake of this plum job, if you'll allow me to mix fruit metaphors. While the taped item played out, exquisitely edited on a machine from the war using razor blade and sticky tape – which is how all radio editing is done in Broadcasting House – we would sit in the studio with Richard, smirking at our own jokes under the pretence of admiring the edit, then go live again for a final bit of repartee and a withering *bon mot* from our host. Mocked on live radio by an ex-pop star who last appeared in the *NME* when we were still readers. It's as heavy with symbolism as the swooshing glass door.

What's great about being involved, even peripherally, in a radio programme is the gang mentality, the Blitz spirit, the let's-do-the-magazine-show-right-here resourcefulness. Whether you're presenting it, producing it, timing it, cutting it up with razor blades or fetching Andrea Dworkin from reception to appear on it, everyone plays a part. The other great thing is that you find yourself sitting around in the green room with biscuits, kiwi fruit, alcohol and Andrea Dworkin.

If anyone emblemised this brave and rarified new mezzanine world, it was the mighty Andrea Dworkin, world-famous radical-feminist author and thinker. The night she was ferried through from reception as a special guest, up two floors in one lift, along the endless corridor, through *Woman's Hour* (she'd have liked that) and down one floor in another lift, I must confess I fell into a state of open-mouthed wonder. Every inch the archetypal, man-hating radical-feminist with her functional dungarees, her unapologetic bulk and her unbleached moustache, she was, on her own terms and answerable to no one, *magnificent* to behold. And I must admit I beheld her, all the while trying to look like I wasn't, absentmindedly fiddling with a banana and probably making some kind of figurative *faux pas*. Typical man. I hated being a man in her presence.

You don't get to bask in the presence of world-famous radical-feminist authors and thinkers when you work for the *NME*. Unless you count Ben Elton. I'd certainly never met anyone who thinks that all heterosexual sex is rape. And when I say *met*, we were introduced to Ms Dworkin in the green room: 'This is Andrew and Stuart, they do a regular comedy item on the programme.' Like *that's* going to impress her and stop her thinking of us as rapists.

We ate star fruit and biscuits from the same BBC-catering platter. Although when I say *ate star fruit and biscuits*, she didn't eat anything. She just sat there, like some venerable, all-knowing lady Buddha with slightly laboured breathing. Like all visiting American luminaries on the promo trail, she will have been aware of the meaning and importance of the BBC, but a little vague on the subtle differences between, say, Radio 4 and Radio 5. You can persuade visiting American luminaries to appear on anything if it's prefixed by the letters B, B and C.

Raddled and refreshed old comedian Arthur Smith, something of a cabaret-circuit hero of mine from his days in the double act Fiasco Job Job, methodically asked everybody on the *Mix* team if he could smoke. Having been repeatedly told no, he rolled up a big roll-up and just smoked it with fellow humorist Tony Hawks – right there, inside the Temple of the Arts and Muses, which is a strictly non-smoking Temple. And then ate all the biscuits.

The Mix became a regular Monday fixture. Although the *NME* remained resolutely our day job, it was a happy and manageable excursion into broadcasting. A bit on the side. We could even claim expenses, as it was, in effect, promo for the paper.

In September last year, for two weeks on the trot while Richard was on some kind of gay holiday, Stuart and I got to host *The Mix*, live, which was a seat-of-the-pants thrill. On the second of these, after a rather worthy debate about the future of independent record labels, we had in the studio P.J. O'Rourke, a personal hero of both of ours. I asked him to sign the sleeve of the new Manic Street Preachers single, their cover of 'The Theme From *M*A*S*H* (Suicide Is Painless)'. It bore an American flag, which seemed apt. Across it, he wrote: 'To

Andrew – Don't burn this! P.J. O'Rourke, Radio 5, London, Sept 1992.'

Thanks to John and to Radio 5, Stuart and I now had a foot in the *Star Trek* door of another world. If not a dongle.

'I'd like to thank John, and I'd like to thank Radio 5, and I'd like to thank Drama, Features and Youth Programmes Editor Caroline Raphael for commissioning it, and I'd like to thank Andrea Dworkin for inspiration ...'

I'd *like* to thank those people, I really would, but it's academic at this stage. We may yet not win this Writers' Guild award for Best Radio Programme (Comedy/Light Entertainment). If we do it will be my first significant prize since the Carol Barratt Art Cup at Abington Vale Middle School, which sits tinily atop the bookcase on the landing at Mum and Dad's. We're up against something called *Rent* by Lucy Flannery, *The Nick Revell Show* by Nick Revell, and *The Mark Steel Solution* by Mark Steel and Pete Sinclair, but it's not the winning, it's the taking part, as they always tell you if you've just taken part.

I want this award. I was happy enough with the nomination until I sat down at the table; now I want the glass inkwell with the inscription. It must *not* go to Nick Revell.

This is no time for being philosophical but if it were, you might say that we've already had our award. *Fantastic Voyage* was on the radio! It was on the BBC! It went out, every week, for six weeks in May and June at 9.30 p.m., after *Fanshawe On Five*. We wrote it, and we were in it. What's more, we had our very own publicity photos taken for the occasion, one of which appeared in the *Radio Times* – the one against a yellow background in which, apropos of nothing, I am sucking on a plastic cigar, making Stuart look eminently sensible in his striped jersey.

In deference to the sub-aquatic theme of *Fantastic Voyage*, publicity whizz Judy had resourcefully rustled up a prop periscope for us to hold, reason enough to thank her in our acceptance speech.

Something like, 'I'd like to thank Judy for the periscope.'

There is something surreal about having your face in the *Radio Times*. This is the only magazine I can truthfully say I've read since childhood. One of my earliest boyish scrapbooks is full of grimy black-and-white photos of *Carry On Screaming* and *My Wife Next Door*, scissored from the family copy of *Radio Times* and fixed in place with Gloy. Other people get their faces in the *Radio Times*, not us: Wendy Richard; Delia Smith; Barry Norman; Lesley Garrett; Jesse Birdsall; Sue Cook; Philippa Forrester; Alan Hansen; Laurie Pike.

The most instructive thing about the process of landing our first six-part comedy/light entertainment radio series was how casual and back-of-a-napkin it all was. One minute we were having a pint with John in the Polar Bear, 'bouncing ideas around' and writing things on the back of a napkin, the next we were recording a pilot in a BBC radio drama studio, which led – within *days*, or so it seemed – to a six-part commission. Three hours of national radio were ours to muck about with. I'm not saying it's easy, writing and producing a six-part comedy/light entertainment radio programme, but it's more doable than we might have imagined.

Stuart lives in Birmingham. It's a defiant gesture against the Londoncentric pull of the media, and it's also convenient as it's where his and his girlfriend's lovely house is. This meant he often stayed over at my tiny single-person's flat in London, and, between doner kebabs and frustrating attempts at the triple jump on *Konami Track & Field*, that was when we did our writing. I like to think it's how Galton and Simpson started. In a writing partnership – which, let's not be coy, this now very much is – one person types, the other marches up and down. As a general rule, I typed and Stuart marched up and down. It seemed to work.

Because *Fantastic Voyage* was essentially sketch-based, we just threw in everything we could think of that made us laugh. It was like putting all your best songs on your first album. There was no great plan, no story arc and certainly no whiteboard with Post-It notes being constantly moved around. It went: intro, injection into host body, banter, a spoof report about roofing contractors being treated like supermodels, a parody of *Watchdog*, an interview with the editor of the made-up *Crazy Golf Monthly*, a musical guest, a parody of *London's Burning*, and so on, until it was time to repeatedly pump the Turbo button on *Konami Track & Field* and try to make the man hop, skip and jump, which was actually much trickier than writing three hours of comedy/light entertainment for national radio. I suspect Lucy Flannery applied a lot more craft to *Rent*.

With scripts all typed up to look like scripts, we then took the week off work at the *NME* and holed ourselves up in a studio for six days, with our own bearded, jumper-wearing studio manager, also called John, two younger, slightly cooler and unbearded studio managers, Giles and Andy, Jenny the BA and three professional actor-comedians who played the other parts: Geoff Boyz, Alan Francis – both Scottish and liable to slip into a Sean Connery impression at any given moment – and Debra Stephenson, a bubbly northerner who'd won *Opportunity Knocks* at the age of fourteen and coped admirably with being the token woman.

Thrown together like survivors in a disaster movie – albeit not a very exciting one, as we were only thrown together in a BBC studio and got biscuit breaks – we quickly developed the necessary cocktail of siege mentality and light hysteria brought on by hangovers and the intensity of the work. We were bonded for ever by the end of it, like the crew of a submarine, you might say.

None of us went to Footlights College Oxford and yet here we are, proud nominees at a posh awards ceremony in our wrong attire, sucked into the twin worlds of radio comedy and light entertainment and force-fed rich food like geese to the slaughter.

The posh nosh starts to arrive at 7.15 p.m., by which time the champagne has taken the edge off our self-consciousness. For starters, we are served halibut mousse with a rosette of Scottish smoked salmon and *neige raifort*, followed by the main course: a small pie containing *asperges et champignons sauvages*. Very nice. However, it turns out not to be the main course but a buffer between the starter and the actual main course: what looks like a miniature chicken but is, according to the menu, a guinea fowl – a bird I can't actually picture in its natural state, but it must get picked on by the bigger birds. This comes with glazed baby onions, *pommes sables* and gratinated spinach, at which I fold up a menu and tuck it inside my jacket as a souvenir – not a dignified act, but I think Mum and Dad will be impressed by it, and there's no point in stowing away at a fancy dinner with Denis Norden and Lesley Joseph if you can't impress your parents at a later date.

For afters it's fruit: seasonal berries in a raspberry sauce with vanilla *sabayon* – whipped egg custard with booze. Feeling considerably rounder than when I bought this suit in Top Man, I greedily scoff more than my share of the sweet, crunchy *mignardises* that come with the coffee. Now I know what it's like to eat as if there's no tomorrow. This French banquet, whose menu descriptions deserve a Writers' Guild nomination of their own, is all topped off with a glass of Macallan whisky, because the awards are sponsored by Macallan whisky – commerce. It's disgusting, but then it is whisky, the most unpleasant member of the spirit family. Mine goes to Stuart. Even though he's only a couple of years my senior, he has a much more mature palate. I expect he likes Stilton, too. He certainly likes classical music and fell-walking in the Lakes. I probably shouldn't look up to him – we are a double act, after all.

Hold on. Someone's up at the podium.

'My lords, ladies and gentlemen. Would you please charge your glasses and stand for the toast.'

We all do.

'The Queen.'

I feel no urge to toast the Queen – she ain't no human being, after all, indeed, she is a complete waste of money and an anachronism – so I stand and mime the words. It is a pathetic act of rebellion, but assuages my conscience as a Billy Bragg fan. If I was a real republican seditionary, I'd remain seated, but I'm overcompensating for the suit.

To make the situation worse, the surly-looking Mark Steel and Pete Sinclair, seated next to us, have actually left their top buttons undone and loosened their ties, just to prove that they're hard. It makes me wish even more fervently that we'd worn the correct prizegiving uniform. Haven't they heard of subversion from within? Alan Plater will think people who write comedy/light entertainment for radio are all riff-raff.

Time's marching on. We've had the cigars, though I gave mine to Stuart. We've had the speech by Alan Yentob. We've had the 'reply' by Guild chairman Gerald Kelsey. Come on! When do the awards get handed out?

At last! To a generous ripple, Denis Norden and *Dad's Army* creator Jimmy Perry take the stage at 9.30 p.m., our hosts for the rest of the show. At least the radio awards come first, as the evening builds in reverse order of sexiness through theatre, books, film and television. Ending with a lifetime's achievement award for Alan Ayckbourn.

'If we don't win, the table's going over,' jokes Stuart, ironically pugnacious on single malt highland whisky.

We don't win. The table stays where it is and we all magnanimously applaud – including Steel and Sinclair, who would otherwise be cruising for a detention – while deserving winner Lucy Flannery goes up to collect her glass inkwell and, being a woman, looks perfectly presentable in a dress. But it's not the winning, it's the taking part. And fuck it, after Alan Ayckbourn, there's dancing to Laurie Holloway and His Orchestra. If Northampton could see me now.

*

It's the end of an era. So soon. It's a lesson I learned during my first bout of desk-hopping at the *NME*: don't get too comfy, as the media-go-round has a habit of starting up when you least expect it.

Upheaval one: John Yorke's leaving Radio 5 to go and work as a script editor on *EastEnders*, which strikes us as something of a comedown after producing award-nominated radio but it's something he feels he must do – perhaps they have their own dongles up there.

Upheaval two: *The Mix* – the programme that put us on the road to radio legitimacy – has been axed. It's been replaced by near-identical magazine show *Fabulous!*, whose chief difference is that it's produced by Jonathan Ross's production company Channel X, presumably to meet some new BBC quota for independent production. *Fabulous!* is presented by the professionally grumpy Mark Lamarr, with whom there is no camp repartee. Yes, as luck or lack of imagination would have it, Stuart and I survived the cull, and now present a weekly satirical slot on the new programme just as we did on the old programme, now formalised as *Collins & Maconie's Hipster's Guide*, covering anything from Frank Sinatra to the Bosnian airlift.

Because it's produced 'out of house', as they say at the Beeb, *Fabulous!* represents another step deeper into the media jungle. We go for script meetings at the luxuriously appointed open-plan offices of Channel X, where you might see Rowland Rivron sprawled on an ideas sofa, or even the towering Jonathan himself, wandering through like a media Caesar. We are now looked after by boyish, chipmunk-faced producer Andy Rowe, with whom we clicked instantly. I think he might be younger than me. He's certainly younger than Stuart. If ever I harboured images of radio producers being old men with briar pipes and white coats, the illusion is shattered. They are boys.

We record our slot in studios away from the whole fandango of Broadcasting House, which I must admit takes some of the grandeur and gravitas out of the job. At first, we recorded them at Capital Radio, meeting Andy every Monday in the same lobby where Tracey Corkhill famously bumped into Morrissey in the *Brookside* spin-off *South* ('You're Morrissey.' 'I know.'). Now we record them at a much more plush suite of studios called Pelican round the back of Theatreland's Drury Lane, under the aegis of Ray Stiles, whose name used to be Mud, when he was in the hit seventies group of that name. It's cool just to be in his presence, and he sometimes tells scurrilous stories about other seventies glam rockers. The booth we record in is lined with pink soundproofing material and it's like doing it inside Mr Blobby, a joke we never fail to repeat every Monday, and one Andy never fails loyally to laugh at.

Andy does things like make us record the whole thing twice because the first one sounded flat and 'Christmas-holiday'. He's always right. We like to call ourselves 'one-take' performers, but a third party like Andy behind the glass is essential if we're going to play the professional card.

One week, when Mark Lamarr was away on a not-gay holiday, the fey-voiced *Time Out* columnist Jon Ronson took his place at the helm, and back-announced our *Hipster's Guide* thus:

'And Collins and Maconie will be back next week with more of their scatological humour.'

Which was odd, as if there's one thing our humour isn't, it's scatological. However, I like the idea that we *have* a humour. And the idea that there'll be more of it next week.

Did I mention we've left the *NME*? Upheaval three. Take one.

7

Understanding Lenny Kravitz

I suspect I've made a grave tactical error. I don't like this toilet. I don't like this toilet at all. Perhaps I should never have taken the job. It's so cold and small and grubby in here, conducive only to rapid turnover, and nothing like the palatial conveniences at IPC, where one could comfortably tarry awhile, get some thinking done, perhaps come up with a funny headline. Never mind gents and ladies, there's one toilet here – unisex, pan-gender, sit-down – and it serves the whole floor. To make matters worse, I came in this morning to discover that the bulb's gone, leaving the occupant in a half-light of soul-sapping gloom.

I haven't been at *Select* long enough to know who to ask about bulbs. The office itself may be situated on London's trendy, pedestrianised Carnaby Street, with a Dunkin Donuts a few doors along and any number of adjacent boutiques selling acid-house-style bandanas and blue Doctor Martens to Dutch tourists, but once you're inside the functional building, past the service lift, up the stairs and into the bit where *Select* is made, the shine comes off.

I've started buying the *Big Issue* because there's a young homeless man selling it outside and it feels like a very Central London thing to do. I'd read it if it wasn't so dark in here. It's amazing how important toilets are in a job.

*

It's 3.15 a.m. and I'm still at work. My new job is no longer new but six months old, and I'm not in the office. It's either very late or very early, depending on which way you look at it. I'm looking at it from the end of a very long Saturday night that began at about half past four in the afternoon, when John Peel played a record by Polvo over the PA, saying, 'That was Polvo. They may not show their dicks but they're very good. I was toying with the idea of showing you mine. It'd certainly be the oldest thing you'd see at the festival.'

I find myself in the Glastonbury medical centre where I have joined the festival's walking wounded. Inside the Portakabin there's a post-curfew urban raver in an acid-house-style bandana staring into the middle distance, probably lured here from the dying embers of the Stone Circle Rave by the too-bright fluorescent strip lights; a pale teenage girl in monkey boots and an ironic feather boa, sprawled over two plastic chairs, asleep, perchance to dream of facilities, comfort and order; and a pair of his-and-hers sixth-form scrumpy casualties, one in a 'Hear No Bullshit; See No Bullshit; Say No Bullshit' long-sleeved top, the other in this year's *de rigueur* Back to the Planet T-shirt, whereupon the band illiterately enquire, 'Whos Fucking Planet?' (They've dropped an E. Insert your own joke here.)

It's past their bedtime. It's certainly past mine, although time is an amorphous concept at Glastonbury, whether you're at work or play. It reminds me of Charlton Heston's speech in *Planet of the Apes.* Seen from out here everything seems different. Time bends. Space is boundless. It squashes a man's ego. There is no clocking on here, just tuning in, turning up and dropping off. I'm not ill. Just ill-inclined to call it a day, and very keen to use the flushing toilets available to accredited medical staff.

It was a bit of luck that I met an accredited nurse on the hay bales outside Steve's Wine Bar, a lorry serving hot, spicy mulled wine which stays open late for intense conversation and internally heated night-sky inspection. Steve has spelled spicy with an errant E on his sign. Perhaps it's the E missing from the Back to the Planet slogan. I'm sure the nurse told me her name, but I can't remember it and it would be rude to ask again now. Names are an amorphous concept at Glastonbury. Names bend. It's about the *vibes*, man, not names and numbers. I am not a number. It's about staying up past your bedtime, wearing the same pants you woke up in yesterday, gradually untying the various layers lashed around your waist and putting them on in defence of the cold. Although it's not that cold, not with the 'spicey' mulled wine and the wartime *camaraderie*.

Flushing toilets! Meet you back here.

The nurse with no name bids me goodnight outside the Portakabin. She's got a shift. She's part of the secret infrastructure of the Glastonbury festival; the stewards and Samaritans and litter-picking volunteers who keep it ticking over while the rest of us treat it like a great big grass hotel. The spices are wearing off and reality's setting in. I wander back to the hire car to get some propped-up sleep.

Whose Fucking Planet?

Over at the *NME* stage earlier in the evening, Rob C, cod-Jamaican scarecrow and singer with the Stereo MCs, urged all *politician*, all *racist*, all *policeman*, all *industrialist* to come to Glastonbury. Is he out of his mind? We come here to get away from those people.

I was, of course, filled with a certain melancholy as I took in the giant *NME* logos at either side of the stage. That used to be my playground. But midway through our life-changing stint on *The Mix*, Richard Coles stopped describing Stuart and I as '*NME* journalists'. Because we had stopped being *NME* journalists.

We had become *Select* journalists. Richard never described us as that. Partly because I crossed the floor before Stuart, so the transfer wasn't synchronised, and partly because '*Select* journalists' doesn't have the same ring, the same sense of history or cultural heft. It sounds as if we are *select* journalists. But get used to it: *Select* magazine – monthly, glossy, colourful, post-'baggy', self-conscious – is where we now ply our trade.

I'll be honest, when I was *in*, I never thought I'd be *out*. I never thought the day would come when I didn't have those particular letters after my name: Andrew Collins, *NME*. They were a badge of honour. A qualification from the University of Life (formerly Life Polytechnic). The *NME* gave me a passport and taught me how to use a computer. It initiated me in the way of print jargon (dog-legs, kerning, going to bed) and put the days back in my week. It got me into places on the strength of the name. (I really did once talk my way past the bit where you pay at Camden Dingwalls by saying, 'I'm from the *NME*.' I was, but I could have been anybody.) It introduced me to a number of my heroes, including Ben Elton, Robert Smith and Alan Moore. It flew me to Utrecht so many times I started to get recognised by the airport cab drivers. It taught me page layout, rudimentary sub-editing, commissioning, delegation and expenses. It also taught me that having a job wasn't necessarily a kind of death. It terminated a long-term relationship, in a roundabout sort of way, which really did almost boil down to that ultimatum: the *NME* or me. Guess which way I jumped? And now my relationship with *it* has been terminated.

This is my first ever Glastonbury as an ex-*NME* writer. Actually, it's my first ever anything as an ex-anything, unless you count ex-Chelsea or ex-boyfriend.

My first ever Glastonbury came in 1989, before I was an ex-boyfriend. Indeed, it was my future ex-girlfriend of the time, more attuned than I to ley-lines, nuclear disarmament and the disapproval of animal testing, who talked me into going, even though open-air discomfort was anathema to me, my only camping experience a night in the back garden at Winsford Way with Simon.

I was but a junior freeloader at the time, only just making the heady transition from art room to main office, and as such saw nothing weird about *buying tickets*. While assembled for the big Glastonbury staff meeting in Alan's office, it emerged that I had *bought tickets* for £28 apiece and was planning to camp, like a member of the public. This novelty approach was greeted with genuine amazement by the more seasoned hacks, and I was immediately charged with going undercover to write a piece about what it was like to be a punter, *Road to Wigan Pier* style. My naivety had landed me a plum feature-writing job. The piece ran over two dog-legs. They even photographed me, sitting cross-legged on the parched grass in a vest, eating some chips from a polystyrene tray. Did that make me a 'personality journalist'? I'd better start working on a personality, I thought.

Sleeping in a tent with my future ex-girlfriend and two of her friends from Wales by night, I hung out with the other *NME* freeloaders by day at the inaugural *NME* stall, selling branded baseball caps, T-shirts, 'Feed Your Head' boxer shorts and left-over *NME* tapes. It was heartening to see our boss Alan mucking in and manning the trestle tables in his denim shirt and shades, as I soaked up the atmosphere, ate plentiful vege-tarian biryani and posed as a member of the public.

The horror stories that filtered through to us from the fabled backstage paddock – one *NME* staffer wigging out on acid while the Waterboys were on; another drunkenly regaling the wife of one of the Bhundu Boys with his considered post-feminist thesis: 'At the end of the day, all women want is to be raped by bastards' – were enough to make me glad to be on the *outside*, under canvas with three actual members of the public.

The next year, the tickets had gone up to £38, but by then, innocence had fled the garden of Eden and I secured a pair for free. It also rained. However, we chose to camp among the people again, because, like refusing backstage accreditation, it felt like the karmic thing to do. That year, I was charged with reviewing the just-launched Comedy Tent for three days, quite a trudge in mud-caked boots from the Pyramid Stage, and thus I missed The Cure, Happy Mondays and Sinead O'Connor in favour of Rob Newman, Malcolm Hardee and deadpan accordionist Jon Moloney. It was a small sacrifice. I quite fancied myself as the paper's comedy correspondent. (Insert your own joke here.)

There was no Glastonbury in 1991. Something to do with the travellers. Everything was to do with the travellers in 1991. That was the year the Levellers sent me shit in a box.

In 1992 the festival was back, back, back, with weekend tickets now up to £49. I slept in the car. Worse, I slept in the car in the backstage paddock. I had crossed the line. My journey from punter to ligger was complete.

Was it a good Glastonbury? Well, it was dry. And for the *NME*, it was an experiment. One that went horribly wrong, and had far-reaching consequences.

This is how it worked: as the event had expanded over the years, more and more writers had to be dispatched to different stages and different tents on different days in order for the paper to boast full coverage. But with the festival finishing on the Sunday night it was impractical for the *NME* to get that coverage away in time for the following week's paper, which 'went to bed', to use print trade parlance, on the Monday. It hit the printers on the Tuesday and came back in those exciting bundles tied with string on a Wednesday.

So why not get the writers to file their copy on a Monday morning? Because it was considered too risky to rely on such a large ensemble of hacks to each come down off their festival cloud and deliver anything readable overnight. Either way, full-colour coverage was still technically impossible. In the inky world, your colour pages, cover included, must leave the building on a Friday. Monday can only accommodate last-minute black-and-white changes, in other words any news stories Terry and Steve might have rustled up after a conversation with Jeff Barratt or Alan McGee at the Bull & Gate on Saturday.

By the time our Glasto coverage appeared, a week and a half after the festival, it was the very definition of old news. End of story.

Enter Danny Kelly, in his scorched-earth ideas juggernaut. After Alan was promoted 'upstairs' at the end of 1990, he had quickly established himself as a bold, fearless, noisy leader. In 1992, he made a bold, fearless, noisy decision. He would dispatch just *two* writers to cover the entire 1992 Glastonbury festival. Let's run through those figures again: *two* writers. These trusted captains would spend three days onsite, soaking up the sights and sounds, return to civilisation on Sunday and write the report up *overnight*, delivering their joint Conradian epic on Monday morning. For the first time in its forty-year history, the *NME* would have its Glastonbury coverage on the newsstands by Wednesday, albeit in black and white. It was revolutionary.

Those captains were myself and David Quantick. Can-do features editor and veteran freelancer. The dream ticket. What could possibly go wrong?

We planned it like a military operation using maps, charts, highlighter pens and tiny models of ourselves: for three days, Quantick would be wherever I wasn't, and vice versa, all the while on the move, like sharks, taking copious notes and snatching interviews with the stars. We arranged to *rendezvous* at the backstage beer tent on Sunday afternoon, from whence I would drive us back to London in my Vauxhall Nova. We would hammer away at a hot keyboard all night and I, the responsible staffer, would hand-deliver our dynamic, vivid, evocative, Hunter S. Thompson-style copy on floppy disk to the offices of the typesetters in Farringdon the next morning. I would then oversee the layout with Danny and Brendan at the coalface. The operation would be as vital and real as if we worked on a daily newspaper, albeit without anyone actually 'phoning it in', as gentlemen of the press are mythically believed to do.

The *NME* would provide a unique service. We would confound expectation by turning round yesterday's news today. We would *deliver*. More importantly, we would beat *Melody Maker*, our arch-rivals-owned-by-the-same-company-whose-office-was-one-floor-away-and-who-ate-in-the-same-canteen-as-us. That would show 'em.

By the end of the festival, I realised that Quantick had certainly been everywhere I wasn't. In fact, he'd spent a good deal of the festival in a place where nobody else was. A special place, where motes of Toni Halliday's make-up danced in the air before his very eyes when she cornered him for calling Curve 'the Goth Eurythmics'. His notes resembled the hiero-glyphics of a serial killer in the last stages of mania before being caught. The only audible thing on his tape was an exclusive interview he'd conducted with our old editor Alan Lewis: 'WHY? WHY? WHY, ALAN? *WHY?*'

Unfortunately, he'd found himself with the House of Love in a marquee that served complimentary Pimm's. The height of perceived sophistication this sticky, reddish, gin-based drink might be, but by the bucket it will set you, like Quantick, on the road to ruin. To his eternal credit, he had thrown himself, self-marinated, into the spirit of the festival and soaked up every aspect of the atmosphere for three days. If only there had been a way of extracting any of this fine essence for use in the *NME*'s four-page extravaganza.

I'm not claiming to have been a choirboy myself, but driv-ing offsite in a Vauxhall Nova had at least guaranteed sobriety all day Sunday, and some of my notes were in English. We were the *NME*'s crack squad and between us, we reasoned, we had enough to fill four pages. That turned out to be true. We certainly filled those pages, just as the Levellers had filled that box.

In a comic parody of the co-writing arrangement reached by myself and Stuart, I typed and Quantick mostly slept. Without recourse to stay-awake drugs, we finished the piece before breakfast and I took it to Farringdon by hand, still acclimatising to the fumes and hassle of urban life after the three-day pastoral idyll of a cow field in Shepton Mallet. Quantick went home to get some more sleep. The great thing about a tight deadline is that there's no time for quibbling over the small matter of quality. The mere act of punctual delivery brings praise and gratitude. This may, indeed, be the secret of a lasting career in journalism.

So we'd done it. Mission accomplished. We'd met the deadline, fulfilled our brief, produced four pages of impressionistic rubbish, and revolutionised festival coverage for music weeklies for ever. Never mind the quality; feel the width.

The sound of backs being slapped and corks being popped resonated around King's Reach Tower.

This joyous sound continued for some time. Actually, it continued for a very specific amount of time: until the new issue of *Select* came out ten days later. With sixteen pages of Glastonbury coverage in full colour. Written by people who hadn't seen motes of Toni Halliday's make-up dancing in the air.

I had to write and congratulate everyone involved with the Glastonbury review. It was amazing! All of the other 'weakly' papers totally bollocksed their reviews up, well, if you could call them reviews. Exactly what you expect for your money!
Leo Miles, Didsbury, Manchester

Select letters page, August 1992

Select was a problem for the *NME*. It shouldn't have been. It was, after all, a monthly, not a direct competitor. United had launched it in the summer of 1990 as a shameless me-too challenge to *Q* and our very own *Vox*, whose launch it admirably beat by four months. Its first issue had a Prince lookalike called Guner Behich on the cover. Panicked IPC executives did not leap from the twenty-eighth floor. Instead, while *Q* ploughed its new furrow with ambition and confidence, *Vox* and *Select* competed to be as average as each other every month, and we got on with being the *NME*.

That was until 1991 when United sold its music titles to Emap, who promptly shut down *Sounds* (a black day for Mission fans and freelance rock journalists). They also decided to take the radical step of making *Select* good. They kept all the decent people, jettisoned the dead wood and drafted in Mark Ellen, one of the launch editors of *Q* and former *Whistle Test* and Live Aid presenter. Emap's fortunes had been built on the back of *Smash Hits*, whose commercial nose and wry use of unnecessary "double" "quote" "marks" now characterised everything they published, from *Kerrang!* to *Big* to *Sky*.

Emap did quite a number on *Select*. It began, brightly and irreverently, to surf the post-shoegazing, pre-grunge wave with writers as various and adept as Miranda Sawyer from *Smash Hits*, Dave Cavanagh from *Sounds* and Graham Linehan of the Irish *Hot Press*. All this plus a Fleet Street sense of story: 'CRACK. HEROIN. *GANGRENE*? THE ALBUM THAT ALMOST KILLED HAPPY MONDAYS.' They even groomed up their own whizzkid new editor from within: a drug-free raver called Andrew Harrison, whose name, if not height, struck fresh fear into the heart of his competitors.

What else was *Select*'s Glastonbury 1992 coverage going to be if not witty, evocative, vivid, literate, arch, colourful and sixteen pages long? The very day this pull-out extravaganza appeared, it set a new industry standard. Of course, they'd had more time to work on it than us, but the clincher was planning. Questions were asked at IPC, one of which was: 'How come the *NME*'s coverage was so shit?'

Danny, bold and fearless but suddenly a little less noisy, was carpeted by Alan for coming second in a race he didn't even know he'd entered. He came away feeling humiliated, bruised, unloved and back-stabbed by his old running mate and mentor. But hey, that's showbiz. As Danny used to say: 'Move on! Tomorrow's chip paper!'

However, what might otherwise have been water off a bold and fearless editor's back was poor timing indeed by IPC management, for Danny was already nursing a managerial wound. *Vox* had recently undergone a fairly swift change of editor and he hadn't even been considered for the job. He didn't even want it, but it's nice to be asked. QED: he felt taken for granted by his employers. He'd given the *NME* the best years of his life and this was how they repaid him? And, unknown to IPC, he was at that very moment being courted by the enemy.

Emap had made overtures. They were headhunting. Danny had politely turned them down, but the door remained open. Then came the Glastonbury incident, and Danny crossed the floor.

Six senior staffers applied for Danny's job, me included. Of course, the more melodramatic among us felt betrayed when Danny announced he was leaving, but it's possible to lose your head up there in the eyrie. Like Kurtz, operating without any sense of perspective, there is a temptation to believe every album review you write makes a difference and that you are all fighting a private war. When in fact you're just doing a job and taking a salary and delivering consumers to advertisers for accounts departments with targets to hit and books to balance and acquisitions and mergers to finance based on projections for the next fiscal year. Danny had betrayed us a bit, though.

I didn't even want to be the editor of the *NME*. I was fairly sure Stuart didn't want to be, living in Birmingham and everything, and Gavin would surely rather languish behind the media desk until they prised the telephone from his cold, dead hands. But we all felt that it was our duty to throw our hats into the ring. That's how it is with in-house job opportunities. Posts become available; you automatically apply for them. It's expected, and it looks bad if you don't.

Beyond the servicing of the photocopier and the occasional fire alarm, these games of musical chairs are the closest office life comes to intrigue and suspense. It's little wonder we set so much store by them.

Alan interviewed all six of us in a genial, bearded manner. Not one of us even got a second interview. Management had other ideas.

The snowball started to roll. The official announcement of *NME*'s new editor came so swiftly the rumours still had wet ink on them.

'I heard it's Steve Sutherland.'

'Steve Sutherland? Bollocks!'

'He *hates* us!'

'That's what *I* heard.'

'He definitely went for it.'

'Sutherland? Dogshit and diamonds?'

Steve, cueball-headed assistant editor of *Melody Maker*, had penned a live review for his paper that had become semi-legendary. A forced and witless comparison between Suede and Kingmaker, he'd fashioned it into a manifesto, drawing a line in the sand between the two IPC-owned weeklies in a post-*Sounds* world. It broke the unwritten rule: never mention the other paper. *Melody Maker*, Steve disambiguated, was embodied by Suede: glamorous, vibrant, ambitious, *diamonds*. Kingmaker, meanwhile, summed up the *NME*: workmanlike, dull, average, *dogshit*.

As prose it was marginally more effective than when he'd called Vic Reeves 'Prick Reeves' over the length of an album review, but as a gauntlet clanging to the ground between adjacent floors of a high-rise building in Waterloo, it hit its mark.

No matter that neither paper actually had a clear-cut musical agenda, nor that both papers regularly featured enthusiastic coverage of Suede and Kingmaker, it ruffled the intended feathers. Turns out it was a cry for help. Steve actually dreamed of working for the *NME*, and Danny's defection was his chance to make it come true.

'Sutho? Bollocks.'

Before our wounded and slack-jawed indignation at the official announcement had time to ferment into internecine outrage and actual territorial pissings, Sutho was being wheeled by Alan into a conference room like the accused at a murder trial – rather than a mild-mannered, enthusiastic, personable new boss with his heart in the West Coast of America and his accent on the South Coast of England.

If there was a villain in the room it was not the blameless Sutho, but our own collective closed mind, brand loyalty that had soured into xenophobia. Alan understood our grievances but a decision had been made and he'd appreciate it if we gave the guy a chance and were professional enough to try to work with him. Sutho assured us he was a lifelong fan of the *NME* and one of the reasons he wanted to work here was the prospect of doing so alongside such fantastic people. He hoped we'd give him a chance and be professional enough to try to work with him.

Steve Lamacq was the first to hand in his resignation. It was already typed up and sealed, and he gave it to Alan at the end of the meeting. Mary Anne was right behind him with hers. Alan accepted them like commiserations at a funeral.

I went back to my desk and typed up my own, taking it into Alan before I left work. My impotent rage at Sutho's appointment had found priapic shape in recklessness. I had resigned from a job I loved too much. I had cut off my face to spite my face. That would show me. Take *that*, me! If you love the *NME* so much, why don't you go and not work there?

*

I'm watching Lenny Kravitz on the Pyramid Stage. I despise him but I've never seen the coffee-table Hendrix before and he's starting to make profound sense. Maybe it's the time of day. Maybe it's the time of man. I don't know.

'We're one big happy family!' he shouts, between songs. He must really think this, as he says it again, three songs later.

We are one big something. Glastonbury can be a monumentally forgiving audience. Tom Jones went down a storm here last year, and Rolf Harris repeated the same trick with the students and Friday night comedown crowd yesterday lunchtime with 'ROLF RULES OK' written on the back of his leather jacket and a bit of mild swearing thrown into his chuckling repartee. If it's wet, people are even more determined to enjoy themselves. If it's dry, as it is this year, a state of test-match grace takes over. People will clap and wolf-whistle and form human pyramids to anything, even Lenny Kravitz, so long as he plays the hits.

I'm here because it's my job and yet, in the complimentary pink light of the magic hour, buoyed by enough paper cups of watery trade union lager to actually get a buzz on, I have an epiphany. *That's* what 'Mr Cab Driver' is about. A racist cab driver who won't pick Lenny up because he doesn't like the colour of his skin. Of course. How could I have been so dim?

I find myself nodding, eyes closed, to the too-clean, too-precise funk-rock of Lenny's band of sessioneers, basking in the early-evening sun, brimming with empathy for poor old Lenny, standing there by the side of the road, the cabs rushing past him. Won't Mr Cab Driver stop to let him in? Mr Cab Drah-vurrrr!

I get all this down in my notepad. I'm having a profound, abandoned and meaningful time, on my own, watching Lenny Kravitz point cloudward like John Travolta. Excuse me while he kisses the sky! I'm in my Glastonbury moment, dancing like a tit and reviewing the whole of the festival, by myself.

I'll be in the office, Monday morning, typing it all up. It's Saturday night and I've already seen it all. I've seen The Wishplants smash up their guitars when they surely can't afford second ones. I've seen the reformed Velvet Underground stand in a row and effect a synchronised bow, as if they'd just performed a school play about the Velvet Underground. I've seen Robert Plant and The Auteurs and The Black Crowes and Barenaked Ladies and Dodgy and Verve and Jamiroquai and a band called Chulm Factory who did a song called 'Motherfuckers' that just went 'Motherfuckers! Motherfuckers!' And Peter Garrett of Midnight Oil told us to support Greenpeace because 'it's the only planetary organisation dedicated to stopping the shit come down!' and Andy Kershaw introduced a Greenpeace rep onto the stage who told us all to boycott Norwegian products because of their whaling policy ('No way, Norway!') and I've yet to think of a Norwegian product I can actually stop buying, but I want to because it's *important*, and I'm getting it all down in my notepad, that is, when I'm not looking beatifically up at the sky and wondering where Stuart is.

Stuart has managed to blag a lift off site with a Wigan band he knows called The Tansads. He lasted two nights in his pressed shorts, sleeping in the *Select* hire car and washing his fringe in Evian, but the privations of Glastonbury are not for him.

The privations of Glastonbury are very much for me. This is my fourth festival. I feel like a veteran. Back at the car, which I now have to myself, I turn on Radio Avalon 87.7. On Thursday, as we crawled into the site, two DJs calling themselves Mr Yodel and Captain Hawkwind – possibly not the names on their supplementary benefit forms – read out a message from Wilf, saying, 'Please meet Geg up at the Green Futures Field.' At which point, we knew we'd arrived. Tonight, a different DJ puts out an APB: 'Remember – people are still stealing things!'

I think he's forgetting that we're one big happy family. I hope the sun holds out and the river of actual human piss doesn't burst its banks before Lenny Kravitz is helicoptered off the site.

My resignation from the *NME* was, in the event, less decisive than Steve's and Mary Anne's. After a charm offensive, Alan and Sutho talked me into staying. I allowed the priapic nature of my recklessness to subside in the name of compromise. *Music Week*, the boring, overpriced music-biz trade magazine written by The Man, rather flatteringly named me in 'Dooley's Diary' as the 'mystery third *NME* staffer' who'd resigned but withdrawn his resignation. There was no mystery. I'd simply lost my nerve in the face of unemployment. As a former gossip columnist, I can't blame Dooley for spinning it, whoever he is.

I dutifully served under Sutho for two months, getting to know him as a colleague and a man. Was he a monster, or an incompetent, or a charlatan, or a tool? None of the above. He was fine. He flamboyantly took on a couple of writers from *Smash Hits* who didn't seem willing to lay down their lives for The Wedding Present, and he wasn't very good at tortuous puns, but these were hardly war crimes.

Then, just before Christmas 1992, Mark Ellen called. He was looking for a *Select* features editor, having manoeuvred his own, Andrew Harrison, into the editor's chair.

He lured me to a clandestine meeting in what I quickly came to know as the *Select* pub, the Old Coffee House on the brilliantly named Beak Street, which forms a T with Carnaby Street. I liked Mark instantly; he was just as I'd hoped he would be after *Whistle Test* and Live Aid: voluble, generous and slightly too tall and long-limbed for his soft, counsellor's clothes. I already liked his magazine, which had farsightedly taken on Steve Lamacq, so it wouldn't be too much like start-ing a new school.

(I respected Steve, and had done since the moment I found out he could do shorthand. My respect for him doubled when

I found out that he arranged his holidays around the tour itineraries of indie bands: Kingmaker, Therapy?, Mega City Four. And it tripled when he broke his foot after kicking an office chair because Danny wouldn't let him have one of 'his' bands on the cover. We sent him a get-well-soon card with the words 'YOU TOOL' on the front, one of his own Essex catch-phrases.)

I took the job. The *NME* just wasn't quite the same without Danny and Steve and Mary Anne. James had gone, too. Having been denied the editorship twice in succession, he was placated by the offer of developing a brand-new IPC title, a project that appealed to his ego. The office joke was that it would be called *Lager and Shouting*. Without these key players it was like *Invasion of the Bodysnatchers* on the twenty-fifth floor. The same but different. The genetic sequence in its DNA had been altered. Leaving this *NME* would not be as unthinkable as leaving the old one.

The difference between working on a 'weakly' and a monthly is this: instead of marks out of ten, you award albums boxes out of five. This may not sound earth-shattering, but a lot of the subtlety and nuance are blunted by the five-box method. If I wanted to give a Levellers album three out of ten at *Select* I'd have to give it either one box or two boxes. Either way, I expect the Levellers would still have awarded me one box.

There are also fewer features to commission. That's the nub. When you've put out a newspaper every week for four years, with a week off for Christmas, the notion of putting a magazine out every four weeks seems the height of decadence. But it comes with added pressure: you can weather a couple of underperforming *NME*s over the course of a year (Psychedelic Furs, Cud, Chapterhouse), but every one of your twelve issues of *Select* counts. There is less opportunity for chair-kicking over cover decisions. The sell is harder. The nights towards the end of the cycle are longer.

The average *NME* is sixty-four pages. The average *Select* is twice that, at around 124. But you get four times as long to put it together. So, the difference between working on a 'weakly' and a monthly is that you can spend twice as much time on each page.

Galton and Simpson once articulated the difference between writing a sitcom for the BBC and for ITV. It was six minutes, the equivalent of the ad breaks. This they called Integrity Time.

That's more like it, a decent toilet. A row of decent toilets. Clean, bright, gender-specific, fully illuminated, the ablutive equal of King's Reach Tower. Now this is a gents I can really work with. I've stopped buying the *Big Issue*. There's only so far mortgage-guilt will carry you, and we've moved to a much wider thoroughfare – easier to avoid the vendors.

Just as *NME* was brought under the parental wing of IPC in 1988, *Select* has been reeled in and relocated at one of the offices of Emap, where the top brass can keep an eye on us. We've been in Mappin House since March. It's a bijou but well-appointed five-storey block whose entrance is tucked behind a jeans emporium and a Brazilian bar off London's busy Oxford Street.

Emap (whose name, incidentally, is an acronym for East Midlands Allied Press – we both come from the East Midlands!) has satellites across London and Peterborough. The one that puts out the music, entertainment and teen titles is called Emap Metro, housed at Mappin. The one that does the women's mags is called, rather pretentiously, Emap Élan, and so on. In board meetings you probably hear talk of the 'family of titles'. Perhaps even the 'portfolio'. Emap is much smaller than IPC but fancies itself rotten.

Never mind the corporate structure. The team at *Select* use their Integrity Time well. The finesse and love applied to each layout of the magazine give it the edge over all comers. While

Q is austere and functional, and *Smash Hits* bitty and improvised, *Select* is a thing of approachable, stylish beauty. Each of
the issues I've worked on has been worthy of framing. No chip
paper here.

I certainly made an impact when I arrived. The first piece I ever
wrote for the magazine almost got us sued. I'd never managed
that at the *NME*. Perhaps m'learned friends take glossy magazines more seriously? Well, they do look more important.

The offending article was called 'Comedy Babylon' – a headline cooked up by Mark and Andrew in search of a feature to
wrap round it, based on the notion that if comedy is *indeed* the
new rock'n'roll, then comedians must be living the rock'n'roll
lifestyle. It was my job to find out. There is a certain salacious-
ness at *Select* about sex and drugs. It's as if the magazine is run
from a vicarage.

For 'Comedy Babylon' I was to vault the security barriers of
the burgeoning comedy industry, one with which, happily, I
had a substantial 'in', due to my dalliances with stand-ups at the
NME and *Vox*.

It wasn't difficult to secure interviews with the likes of Sean
Hughes and Eddie Izzard, as I had their phone numbers, but
my overtures to Rob Newman and Dave Baddiel, fresh from a
sold-out rock-venue tour, including four Hammersmith
Odeons, were blocked by their manager, Jon Thoday, who runs
Avalon. The closest comedy has to its own major record label,
Avalon manages, books, promotes and has its own in-house PR.
I expect they offer a nice shoeshine service for their comedians,
too – for a small percentage.

'I'd like to speak to Rob and Dave,' I told Jon down the
phone.

'You can't,' he said, bluntly. This threw me a bit. I had a
good relationship with Jon as I'd been his point of contact at
the *NME*, and I imagined that this phonecall was a mere

formality. I could have just phoned Rob at home, after all, but wanted to do things by the book.

'Why not?'

'Because they haven't got any *product* out in February.'

Bingo! In *not* securing an interview with comedy's hippest new superstars, I had in fact stumbled on the mother lode. Here was the perfect crystallisation of comedy as rock'n'roll: *product.* Andrew was overjoyed. I arranged an interview with Jon himself, to talk about the way the business was run, which was conducted in a poky Soho café near Avalon's poky office. He told me many things, on the record, into my tape recorder. I've never used the phrase 'on the record' before, but legal action puts a new perspective on the otherwise bumbling job you do. One of the things Jon – who is after all their manager – told me was how much Rob and Dave had earned through touring in 1992, which was £300,000 *each.* This went straight in the piece.

It was splashed across six pages, and flagged on the cover with the single headline, 'DEPRAVITY!' Sean admitted to some casual sex, Eddie gave a lurid insight into the world of comedy clubs, rising star Stewart Lee told of drawing obscene pictures on the backs of cat paintings in a B&B, and I was able to retell the story of Rob being banned from four comedy venues for calling an audience member a cunt.

My maiden voyage on the glossy seas of monthly magazine publishing had gone rather well. This was almost investigative journalism. And then we had a letter from Avalon's lawyers.

The problem, it turned out, was something Eddie Izzard had said, which I now know enough about libel not to repeat here. Unfortunately I didn't know enough about libel when I put it in the piece to *not put it in the piece.* A piece that was going in a magazine of which I was features editor.

Years spent under the publish-and-be-damned regime of Alan Lewis had not exactly sown the seeds of caution, but I was still pretty dim to think a 'relationship' with somebody meant they wouldn't take legal umbrage at a damaging slur. The whole sorry tale at least taught me to choose my words carefully, and other people's. I was lucky Emap didn't dock my first month's wages.

Still, better than launching my monthly career by writing a negative review of the new Belly album.

Andrew Harrison, who generates energy like a Van Der Graaf generator with glasses, affects only to like two guitar bands, The Smiths and New Order, preferring fax-machine techno in his butcher's son's bones. To his credit, he knows that the best way to sell a mass-market music title is to put bankable rock stars on the cover – Kurt Cobain, Bono, Kurt Cobain – and conceal your inordinate amount of hardcore club culture within.

Andrew is like James Brown after charm school: equally plugged in and tightly wound, just a little less likely to go off in your face and more likely to be in the country when you need to ask him something. Hands on the magazine, hands off the coat-tails of rock stars, he's an ideas-interrogator, something handed down to him from Mark, and it makes for a brisk and stimulating office culture.

'We should do a piece on Radiohead,' I might pipe up.

'Why?'

'Because they're really good.'

'Are they, though?'

'Yes.'

'They sound like just another indie rock band to me.'

At this point, accustomed after four years to just putting a band in the *NME* for no greater reason than they've got a record out and there's a dog-leg to fill, you'll start to find Andrew's squinting face irksome rather than endearing.

'Have you *heard* "Creep"?'

He shrugs. 'More self-loathing for middle-class students.'

'Their album went to number twenty-five.'

'So?'

'So, people *like* them.'

'Not that many people if they can only get to twenty-five.' (Is he playing devil's advocate now, or does he mean it?)

'I really think we should do them. Steve likes them, don't you?'

Steve joins the brainstorm. 'I think their singer could be a real star.'

'Yeah. Thom Yorke.'

Andrew absorbs this new information. He detects an angle. At a monthly, you always need an *angle*.

'So, this guy's a potential star? Indie doesn't exactly *do* stars.'

'Well, that's how we sell it. Thom Yorke: saving indie rock from no-personality doom. We could do a sidebar about the other potential stars of indie – Loz from Kingmaker, Carl Puttnam ...' (Always worth throwing in the name of the Cud singer – Andrew went to Leeds University and has a soft spot for anybody else who did.)

'Right. It's three pages.'

'Is that all? Their album went to twenty-five!'

And so it goes. I like Andrew, despite his tendency towards cultural snobbery. Under his leadership, *Select* is so bracing.

I'll repair to the toilets – knowing that I've found my next spiritual home – to get some thinking done.

8

Letting Down Steve Wright

Wow, it's like a great big car park. A great big car park full of screaming girls. Excuse me while I try something.

'Bad Boys Inc!'

'Yeeeeeeeeeeeeeeaaaaaaaaaaaaaaaaaaaaaaaaaaaaahhhhh!'

All you have to do is shout out the name of teen sensations Bad Boys Inc and they go wild. Let's try it again.

'Bad Boys Inc!'

'Yeeeeeeeeeeeeeeaaaaaaaaaaaaaaaaaaaaaaaaaaaaahhhhh!'

They're putty in our hands; deafening, prepubescent, partisan putty. Is this what absolute power feels like? If so, it may yet corrupt me absolutely – if I didn't feel such a ruddy idiot.

A warmish Tuesday morning in July 1994, beginning of the school holidays, Centenary Square, Birmingham city centre. Wet Wet Wet have been at number one with 'Love Is All Around' for five weeks, the World Cup's into its final throes in America and a pall of national mourning hangs over North Korea after the death of President Kim Il Sung, the twentieth century's longest serving dictator. Against which background, welcome to our first Radio 1 Roadshow. I suspect, if Stuart Maconie's face is anything to go by, it will also be our last.

I'm stage left; Stuart is stage right. I'm wearing shorts, he's not, but that's to be expected. We both grip the same props: an oversized, 'One FM'-branded roving mic in one hand and a page of hastily convened script in the other, still warm from the printer. We attempt to prowl the stage and make eye contact with the audience, like an early-morning Run-DMC, but it's tricky to read and prowl, so we resort instead to skulking and making eye contact with our scripts.

Behind us, breakfast DJ Mark Goodier mans the desk, something he's done countless times in the past, a grandmaster at this type of thing; in front of us, hundreds of screaming girls, who wish we would get the hell off and usher the much-advertised Bad Boys Inc the hell on. The screaming will then reach ear-popping pitch as the band pump their loins, hope to hell nobody at *Smash Hits* ever finds out how old they really are, and mime their hit single 'Take Me Away (I'll Follow You)', a thought Stuart and I have both harboured once or twice during this most unusual of breakfasts.

The normal run of things is this: Mark plays the records and introduces the traffic news and, at regular half-hourly intervals, announces that it's time to go over to 'our chums Collins and Maconie in the kitchen'. Here, backed by an 'FX' loop of pots and pans – our own little piece of radio magic – we practise that time-honoured shuffle: making funny gags about stories from the morning newspapers, enlivened at an unearthly hour by machine coffee and the crystallised sugar on the glaze of Danish pastries.

Mark is temporary host of the breakfast show, the most important show on Radio 1, listened to by millions, while management decide who's taking it over permanently. Our slot has been working out just fine in the comfort and safety of the studio, a knockabout read and a matey bit of banter with our chum Mark, who is always kind enough to laugh out loud at our punchlines and allow us to poke gentle fun at him. We are the Don MacLean and Peter Glaze to his Ed Stewart. And this morning we're standing in front of screaming girls, on stage, in a square, in Birmingham.

Minutes ago we were in a Portakabin, wishing that the dot-matrix printer was a bit livelier and that the runner would hurry up with the Styrofoam cups of instant coffee from a nearby café. Now we're out here.

'Collins and Maconie, how are you?' asks Mark, ever chipper.

'As well as can be expected under the circumstances,' replies Stuart, his fixed grin failing to disguise the existential dread coiled like a boa constrictor around his very soul.

Mark chuckles. 'I think I know what you're saying.'

Stuart soldiers on with what's printed on his sheet of A4, while the crowd wait patiently for the next Bad Boys Inc announcement: 'Big news of the morning is that Fraser Hines is set to quit *Emmerdale* after twenty years.'

'Tragic news,' says Mark, gamely.

'He *is Emmerdale*,' I ad-lib. '*Emmerdale* is his unwieldy middle name.'

In fact, 'unwieldy middle name' is our unwieldy middle name – one of those quirky phrases that we have, in our short career in radio japery, come to look upon as a standby. 'Unwieldy middle name', 'in a very real sense', and '*crème de menthe* and eggnog'.

'He's consistently thrilled critics with his sensitive portrayal of Joe Sugden, the tortured intellectual farmhand, down the years, and sadly that's going to be no more.'

It's patently obvious that this erudite schtick is not designed for a live teenage audience, but it's either see it through or walk out of a promising career at Britain's biggest radio station.

I pick up the story, as per what we've written in the Portakabin: 'Given sensational developments in the plot of *Emmerdale* recently, what with the air disaster, burning fuselage raining down on people, how is he gonna die? That's what we wanna know. Will he be shot down in a hail of bullets by helicopters on the top of the Empire State Building?'

Think of the millions listening at home, not the hundreds of PJ & Duncan fans crushed up against the barrier. They might be enjoying it.

'Will he be torn apart by demented polar bears in a bizarre supermarket siege?'

Mark giggles. You have to love him for that. I wonder how this actually sounds through a big PA across the other side of Centenary Square? Can the good burghers of Birmingham on their way to do an honest day's work actually hear our dignity draining away?

'Anything's possible. His first acting job after the show will be to appear on the end of Bournemouth pier with Linda Lusardi in *Not Now, Darling.*'

'Look out for his Lear at Stratford later this year.'

Cultural snobbery, the last resort of the scoundrel. The wall of teen silence is no more than we deserve with material like this.

'On the same sort of tack, Nigel Le Vaillant from *Casualty*, who left so he wouldn't be typecast as a doctor, is going to play … a police doctor in a new BBC series.'

'Is there no end to Nigel's capabilities? What next? *Doctor Finlay's Casebook*? *Doctor Kildare*? *The Young Doctors*? Actually, I'm only joking; he's a hell of a nice guy.'

'Just before the writ comes in …' Mark interjects, already starting up 'I Swear' by All-4-One underneath our desperate voices. 'Collins and Maconie!'

We put down our mics and exit, pursued by no one. But hey, chin up; for the next half an hour we've got some knock-'em-dead stuff about Jimmy Knapp and the comet that astrologists predict will crash into Jupiter.

It is a short walk from a late-night Radio 5 magazine show to the Radio 1 breakfast show; from contributors to comedy sidekicks. In helpful illustrative tandem, it is a short walk from Broadcasting House to the more humble Egton House, home of Radio 1.

It's fitting that Radio 1 is housed in a separate annexe from the rest of the BBC. After all, wacky things go on there and all that thumping acid-house-style rave music would have the *Today* programme banging on the ceiling with a broom.

Just turn right at Ariel, poised above the heavy wooden doors of Broadcasting House, cross the narrow road with the parking meters and the bike rack, and walk down the steps of what looks like a government building from the outside. Of course, both are, lest we forget, government buildings. There's no statue above the door of Egton House, but if there were it would be of Kylie.

Here, past the garish neon sign announcing 'One FM', you will be greeted by the same, ever-smiling security guard, whose main job is to prevent not nutters or terrorists but record-pluggers from getting into the bowels of the building. This is why Egton reception is always wall-to-wall with record-pluggers, the mercurial human link between the music industry and the broadcast medium. There are probably nutters and terrorists in here, too – all they'd need is a box of CD singles and one of the new mobile phones to blend in.

I believe the collective noun is a *bottleneck* of pluggers: chatty, bag-lugging, caffeinated, *Music Week*-reading enthusiasts, not all of them as young as their trainers would have you think, some of them old enough to have known the last days of Emperor Rosko, and one or two with apocryphal tales of a time when jiffy bags contained more than just promo singles. They feign nonchalance as they loiter around the playlist that's drawing-pinned to the noticeboard once a week, but can pounce in the blink of an eye, their very existence tied into the possibility of thrusting a Del Amitri single, third-off-the-album-out-on-the-twenty-fourth-it's-the-rocky-one, into the hands of Simon Mayo as he breezes through to the lift. Because even Simon Mayo has to wait for the lift.

What pluggers don't need to feign is camaraderie. That's genuine. Even though they all work for different companies, locked in permanent competition, they are all in this together.

It's popular music's great game, a caper, a scam, a line-dance, and, deep down, they all know it. But such is the power of Radio 1, the biggest radio station in Britain, if not Europe, a disproportionate amount of effort, energy and expense are invested in the airplay quadrille.

Think of half an hour of national daytime radio as seven three-minute gaps. These gaps must be plugged. The pluggers must plug them. Radio abhors a vacuum. Silence is known as 'dead air'. Counter to which, pop music is live air.

Stuart and I spend a lot of time down here with the pluggers, for although we are on Radio 1, comedy sidekicks are one evolutionary step down from the members of Steve Wright's posse. Although our appearance on Mark's programmes is prefixed by some kind of modest look-who-it-is fanfare, nobody's putting our faces on postcards just yet, and we still have to wait to be collected from reception. It's an otherworldly existence, caught in limbo between legitimacy and the visitor's-pass carousel. Because, as journalists, we are 'serviced' by record company press officers (their terminology, not mine) and thus get all the free records we can sell, we are of little practical use to the pluggers, other than for company.

'Have you got the new Del Amitri? Third-off-the-album-out-on-the-twenty-fourth-it's-the-rocky-one?'

'Yes thanks.' It's-already-in-my-selling-pile.

'Beautiful South?'

'Got it.'

'Sleeper?'

In addition to our day jobs, we've been providing humorous items for Mark Goodier for over eighteen months now, moving with him around the schedules like a couple of loyal gundogs. We were initially approached by producer Jeff Smith, an owlish, far-sighted chap with a roving ear, keen to bring a comedic aspect to the *Evening Session*, an otherwise po-faced indie stockade that, at the time, marked the end of daytime by playing the

Senseless Things and Gigolo Aunts. Our first slot was called *Eyewitness Reports*. Pre-recorded once a week and 'dropped in' as an on-the-spot insert, a typical report went something like this:

> 'And now it's time to go over to our roving reporters Collins and Maconie.' [Just up from reception.]
>
> [FX: traffic noise]
>
> 'Well, Mark, I hope you can hear us over the sleek purring of expensive traffic. Andrew and I are right outside the Swedish Embassy in Belgravia, London. We're hoping to get an official statement from the Swedish Ambassador.'
>
> 'Yes, but oddly enough, they haven't been all that keen to speak to us. Don't know why. This is a matter of national import!'
>
> 'It certainly is. And we demand answers! On behalf of the *Evening Session*'s one thousand listeners—'
>
> 'It's more than that, you fool!'
>
> 'Sorry. On behalf of the *Evening Session*'s one thousand-plus listeners, we ask the question: Ace of Base; is it a spelling mistake or what?'
>
> 'Ace of Base, spelled B.A.S.E., which means support, foundation, headquarters, or vulgar. Can any of these words really be what the talented Swedish quartet meant? Ace of Headquarters? Surely not! Ace of Vulgar? I don't think so! Ace of Support—'
>
> 'All right, all right, don't labour the point.'

At which, we would labour the point for another minute and a half, signing off with, 'This is Collins and Maconie, *Eyewitness Reports*, One FM.'

It was, let's not be shy, an enormous amount of fun, not least for being able to type the letters 'FX' and know that Jeff would be able to rustle up purring traffic or idling traffic or heavy traffic or whatever kind of traffic we required. In the early days we faxed the script over in advance, but as the arrangement solidified into routine, more often than not we would turn up with it in our hands and read it without anyone seeing it first. Sometimes, if we were in a rush, *we'd* barely even seen it first.

When Mark ceded control of the *Evening Session* and moved to the higher-profile afternoon show, we went with him, broadening our net beyond pop music to cover, well, anything at all, with the more combative slot we called *On the Case*. For instance:

'Right, today we're on the case of …'

'Yasser Arafat.'

'The leader of the PLO, who has ended twenty-seven years in exile and returned to Israeli soil, sworn in as head of the new Gaza-Jericho self-rule authority. What a guy!'

'World peace? He invented it. Forging historic links between the Arabs and the Israelis? Yasser's your man. Setting up a Palestinian state with Jerusalem as its capital and undoing the effects of the 1967 Six-Day War is his middle name!'

'But there's a problem with Yasser Arafat, isn't there? And we think you know what it is …'

'That tea-towel.'

'That tea-towel. Now don't be coy! We're not undermining the culture from which the wearing of a head-dress derives. You know we're not! Funny hats are what makes this crazy old world such a rich, varied and rewarding place to live in. *Vive la difference! A la recherche du temps perdu!*'

'But Yasser Arafat has been wearing the same tea-towel for twenty-nine years! And we don't mean the same kind of head-dress, but *exactly the same one!*'

'Black and white, tassles, the sort of dogtooth check design you get on tablecloths in tea shops in Scotland.'

'We can only assume that Mr Arafat's been advised to wear the same tea-towel for twenty-nine years so as to imprint his public persona on the world stage.'

'It's worked.'

'It certainly has. You're watching the news, it's the state funeral of some obscure political leader in Syria. Hmmm, I wonder who that bloke is in the olive-green military-style jacket and the black and white tea-towel from a Scottish tea shop?'

'Is it Boutros Boutros Ghali, the UN Secretary-General? No, because I've no idea what he looks like.'

'Is it Vietnamese Prime Minister Vo Van Kiet? Nah, he'd never been seen out in a black and white tea-towel from a Scottish … Why, it's Yasser Arafat, the distinctive PLO leader!'

'Get a new one, Yasser. Because we're on your case!'

Pretty edgy for the afternoon on Radio 1, I think you'll agree. Knockabout repartee about Middle Eastern politics with a Marcel Proust reference, sandwiched between Whigfield and Pato Banton? Our name's Ben Elton, goodnight!

We knocked out five *On the Cases* a week. Some days it was like stretching a piece of satirical chewing gum until it snapped, but the discipline of writing these slots was rigorous and the demanding routine improved our licks. Coming up with a couple of humorous items for *NME*'s 'Thrills' page was one thing; supplying radio comedy by the yard is another. And who would have guessed, before we made this audacious diagonal career move, that the evil Svengali behind our new job description would be Mark Goodier?

Mark *Good*-ier, Mark Goodi-*err*, as his singsong Radio 1 ident insists.

My earliest memory of Mark must have been his debut appearance on *Top of the Pops* alongside Peter Powell in 1988, when I thought his surname was Goodyear. Hey, who didn't? Can he really have had a moustache? It certainly felt like it. His subsequent rise through the ranks at Radio 1 has been by stealth, now identified as a 'safe pair of hands', which in music radio is less of a backhanded compliment than it sounds. He's a can-do sort of bloke. For some reason, I identify with that. By the time Stuart and I were sort-of-poached from Radio 5, Mark had achieved an osmotic level of credibility at the *Evening Session*, while still able chirpily to read out the Top 40 rundown every Sunday like a radio Janus.

When he did lower the flag and hand over post-teatime power it was to the next generation, as the *Evening Session* sought a hip, younger gunslinger to host it. Four hopefuls tried out – it was like the indie *Search for a Star*. After a live on-air audition each, involving rock chick Claire Sturgess and Steve Wright posse leader Richard Easter (rumoured power behind Wrighty's comedic throne), the job went to … Steve Lamacq and a former *Word* researcher called Jo Whiley. I'm sure she'd done more than that, but her last job was *Word* researcher and it meant she had a hand in booking Nirvana, so what more needed to be asked.

Yes, *our* Steve Lamacq, who'd edged into radio at London's new alternative commercial station Xfm and found a voice, or at least found a version of John Peel's voice, as all male DJs of a certain vintage are predestined to do. Radio 1 was unable to choose between Steve and Jo, presumably because each sounded as nervous as the other, but both had the correct credentials – Doc Martens – and the decision was made to launch them as a Reading Festival version of Bruno and Liz. Steve's promotion from *NME* desk jockey to national disc jockey gave the likes of Stuart and I succour.

I can't imagine a more exciting time to have arrived at Radio 1. If there had been a skip at the back of Egton House, it must have been brimful of dead wood, such was the clearout under ruddy-cheeked, cheroot-sucking new controller Matthew Bannister. New faces abounded: Mark Tonderai, Lisa I'Anson, Wendy Lloyd, John Cavanagh, Kevin Greening, Clive Warren, Emma Freud, Danny Baker, Richard Herring, Stewart Lee …

I wonder if the pluggers tried to press copies of the new Sleeper single on Simon Bates, Dave Lee Travis, Bruno Brookes, Gary Davies and the rest as they passed through reception for the last time? I'm sure every one of them was a hell of a nice guy.

It wasn't quite a handover, but we did land an impromptu audience with Batesy once, quite by accident. It was meaningful in its own way.

Having paid our dues in reception one afternoon, we were allowed up, and strode into a studio to pre-record a couple of *On the Cases*. We pulled open the outer heavy door and shouldered open the heavy inner one. Somebody was in there.

'Oops. Sorry,' we said, not recognising him at first.

'Are you in here?' Batesy said, turning to greet us.

'Y-yes, we're pre-recording some items for Mark Goodier's programme?'

'Ah. I thought this studio had been booked out.'

'I don't know. It must have been Fergus who booked it.'

'Don't worry, loves. Crossed wires. I'll sort it out.' Meaning: I'll soon have you out of here.

A double-booking with one of the immortals of Radio 1 – this was surely a clash we could not win. Batesy picked up the phone, tapped in an internal four-digit number with his sausage fingers and spoke, one assumes, to his producer or other minion.

'Listen, love … ' He didn't even say who he was, confident that the baritone of his voice would be enough – *it was*. 'I think the studio's been double-booked. These guys are wanting to record something for Mark's show. OK. Well, we'd better look for somewhere else.'

He put the phone down. There had been enough urgency in

his voice to let the person on the other end know he was pissed off, and yet he used the patronising 'we' to soften the blow of what was an order: *you'd* better look for somewhere else.

'I'll get out of your way,' he said.

And to Batesy's eternal credit, he made his excuses and squeezed his not inconsiderable bulk past us. We thanked him kindly. I rather liked him. And he called us 'loves'.

Mark Goodier also uses the theatrical affectation 'love'. It's strange to hear someone who's so blokey and straight on the airwaves use Julian and Sandy-style Polari in real life. This is Mark:

'Will you be requiring a beer, love?'

Or:

'Showbiz showbiz, loves!'

Hey, he's a media mogul. He could smoke huge cigars if he wanted to and not a court in the land would convict him of pretence. Mark is head of his own media empire. Admittedly, it is housed in a store room behind a filing cabinet in the offices of a kindly radio promotions company, but this is just the start. Wise Buddah, its misspelled name a forced pun on popular American beer Budweiser, is a production and management company. Mark's been in the biz for long enough to know that your star can wane without warning, and he's nesting for the future. He has a wife and kids to support, and should his voice suddenly 'not fit' at Radio 1, he'll have a business to fall back on. Hence the zeal for bringing on new talent.

It's rather embarrassing to be called 'talent', but that is the way of things in radio and TV. If you are in front of the micro-phone or the camera, regardless of what you do, you're either the 'turn' or the 'talent'. It is a term used exclusively by those whose job requires their presence on the other side of the glass, and is applied with a withering irony. It has atrophied into shorthand because everyone knows that most 'talent' aren't that talented, and that most 'turns' couldn't do one.

It was Mark who suggested that Stuart and I go after our own programme on Radio 1. Lo, under his guidance, and with his experience as our collateral, we got it. A Wise Buddah production, our name was even above the title: *Collins & Maconie's Hit Parade*, a weekly, hour-long singles review – basically *Round Table* spruced up, stripped of insincerity and record-industry politics, and given a comedic slant for the nineties. It went out every Monday at 9 p.m., although we recorded it in the afternoon, when I should, by rights, have been at work. But then, presenting the *Hit Parade* was work. As mental as it may seem, finding new ways of using the phrase '*crème de menthe* and eggnog' was work:

> Welcome to *Collins and Maconie's Hit Parade* on Radio 1, a weekly forage in the forest of rock for the nuts and berries of opinion. He's Andrew Collins, I'm Stuart Maconie, you're my best mate you are, and our first record of the evening is 'The Osmond' by Crazy Horse. No, that's 'Crazy Horses' by the Osmonds, remixed for the modern age by our old pals the Utah Saints, U-U-U-Utah Saints ...

It seems that by default, Stuart and I are now 'talent'. But beyond that all-encompassing and slightly bitter umbrella, what do we actually do?

Are we comedians? We are definitely a double act, but we don't perform comedy; we don't stand up and tell jokes. Stewart Lee and Richard Herring, whose 9 p.m. to 10 p.m. slot we took over with the *Hit Parade*, are comedians.

When I interviewed Stewart Lee for 'Comedy Babylon', we sold him to *Select* readers unaware of his work as a Ben Watt lookalike. Our roles in that deal were clearly defined: I was the journalist; he was the comedian. I was the interviewer; he was the interviewee. What was I now doing taking over his slot on

Radio 1? Was I still a journalist, or had some shift occurred? Time bends. Space is boundless.

Lee and Herring, a proper double act, stand up and tell jokes for a living, write gags for *Week Ending*, and perform at Edinburgh. They are not journalists who do a bit of funny banter on the radio when they should be at work.

We're not DJs. We have no idea how to 'drive a desk', which means press the buttons and push the faders to make records come on and go off. Mark does all that for us. We just talk when the green light winks. Are we, then, broadcasters? We certainly broadcast, but the name conjures up bow-ties and dinner jackets.

We are writers, but we don't write for other people, just ourselves, selfishly. Sometimes I write for Stuart and he writes for me, but that's because we have developed a style that either of us can switch on, and because we've allowed certain aspects of our character to define us: he's the sophisticated one, not because he's sophisticated but because he's more sophisticated than me. He knows that Vaughan Williams is not a composer called Vaughan, but the surname of a composer called Ralph. I am the bit of rough, not because I am a bit of rough – after all, I hold down a very responsible job and read Kurt Vonnegut and have a lovely wife and drink a number of interesting, buttery New World chardonnays – but because I am just that bit less of a ponce than Stuart. It works, because all good double acts have characteristics that distinguish them. Sometimes Stuart plays the bluff northerner who has little time for the fripperies of London, and I play the metropolitan slicker. Sometimes, if we've rushed the script, we both play the ingénue and both play the cynic. I expect Mike and Bernie Winters had similarly vexed meetings about the blurring of their personas.

'Which one are you again?'

'The big fat one.'

'Oh, yeah.'

For a clue as to who we are, we consult the *Daily Star*,

Britain's 'No. 1 Paper For News', or so it claims, next to a colour pic of Eva Herzigova showing off her 'ample charms' in a Wonder Bra, whose sales she has boosted by £100,000 a week. ('Today the *Daily Star* launches a hunt for her successor! Can your wife or girlfriend measure up – Turn to Page 3.')

Let us, in fact, turn past Page 3, where readers are basically asked to send in pictures of their wives and girlfriends in a bra, and tear our eyes away from the story on Page 15 about a German holidaymaker who built a 'Colditz-style' castle on the beach and nearly died when it caved in and buried him ('DONNER SAND BLITZEN!'). Let us alight instead upon an oasis of culture, namely, 'Rave', the pull-out pop section that promises, 'A Party On Every Page'. This is still quite difficult to take in, and Stuart remains in a state of denial over the whole sorry business, but Page 19 – the 'cover' of 'Rave' – bears a full-page, full-colour photo of me and him.

Taken by in-house snapper Nick Tansley, whose glossy colour posters of East 17, Mark Owen and, yes, Bad Boys Inc, are available to buy with tokens inside, the offending photograph was taken on the roof of Broadcasting House. I'm in the foreground in red denim jacket and faded Blur 'baby' T-shirt, adopting a kind of hip-hop pose and grimacing, with all my crooked teeth exposed. Festival hair tumbles over my shoulders and a layer of designer stubble completes the look. Behind me Stuart looks icily detached in sunglasses and pressed pale-blue Ben Sherman. I squint gamely to camera, while he gazes tellingly into the middle distance. 'SMASHIE AND NICEY TURN GRIZZLY AND NASTY!' bawls the headline. 'RADIO 1 SWAPS "SUPER" IMAGE FOR DJS WHO SNAP 'N' SNARL.'

I know, I know. Inside, 'Rave' has devoted a two-page spread to Radio 1's 'two demonic DJs', even though we are not DJs. There are further pics, one of which sees me leaning in as if to stick my tongue in Stuart's recalcitrant ear. It is fair to say that he looks unamused by my antics. But then, he is Nasty.

And I am Grizzly.

What measure of madness is this? In what parallel universe does a national tabloid devote three of its precious pages to *us*? Were Let Loose unavailable for comment? Had not a single supermodel's top fallen off in the previous twenty-four hours?

The story is spurious in the extreme. Reading it, you would assume we had actually taken over the breakfast show and were now presenting it on a permanent basis: 'The nation's top pop station has changed its tune at last … putting its faith in crazy cult comics Collins & Maconie. They've even got the loony duo putting bite into breakfast time.' It goes on to say that we've been 'signed up for breakfast', as if perhaps we've been, I don't know, *signed up for breakfast.*

Loony is right. While it's flattering that Britain's shabbiest daily newspaper would devote so much space to us, it's also unnerving, as if perhaps there's been a major administrative blunder and the whole thing will be retracted in tomorrow's edition. When press guru Judy set up the interview with 'Rave' reporter Julia in a café near Broadcasting House, Stuart mysteriously found himself too busy to attend, so I spoke for both of us. Although the stakes are low, it's tedious to discover how abstract the correlation is between what was actually said in the café and what appears to come out of my mouth on the page.

'We just seem to make each other, and other people, laugh,' I apparently say. I am also 'often said to be a double of Marti Pellow of Wet Wet Wet', even though I'm not. We just both have long, dark hair. But *Star* readers will have heard of Marti Pellow; he's been at number one for eight weeks.

For Judy and the Radio 1 press office, it's the sort of publicity money can't buy at a time when Bannister-bashing is a tabloid sport. For me, it's a reminder how crooked my teeth are. For Stuart, it's all the motivation he needs to get onto Radio 4. Still, at least we know what we are now: crazy cult comics.

*

Steve Wright's on next, one of the last of the old school Radio 1 'jocks' to survive the Stalinist purge. He loiters behind the stage, already expectant with the smell of the crowd in his nostrils. You can tell he's dying to go on. What must he make of us? Two crazy-cult-comic stowaways soaking up the Roadshow vibes? Have we paid our dues on local radio? Did we start out making the tea or answering the mail like the posse? No. What are our qualifications for being onstage in front of all these screaming kids? None. Actually, Wrighty's here to help. Perhaps he knows we're dying.

He beckons me to the back of the stage conspiratorially, as if he's about to tell me a trade secret.

'Throw these out into the crowd,' he hisses, proffering a pair of Radio 1 boxer shorts.

I hesitate. This is a loaded moment. Steve Wright is handing me a baton in an underwear-based transfer of power. This is a confirmation; these pants are holy Radio 1 communion. Without thinking, I snatch the boxers off him, gratefully. I can't be sure, but I think he winks at me, as if to say: *Go on, my son. It's your time now.*

I rejoin Stuart out on the lip of the stage, the shorts screwed up in my hand, held behind my back for maximum pantomime effect. One well-aimed lob and I can make some young bobbysoxer's day.

Except I can't do it. I just can't summon up whatever it takes to throw a branded undergarment into a squealing crowd. Instead, I read out the last bit of topical satire, shout out, 'Bad Boys Inc!' one last, desperate time, and return to the wings, the freebie pants still in my hot hand. I casually drop them behind the DJ booth without anyone seeing. I'm sure Wrighty will find a home for them when he's out here brilliantly whipping the punters into an even higher pitch of frenzy later on. The keys to the kingdom were dangled in front of me, and I didn't have the right stuff, or the Wright stuff, to take them.

*

Stuart and I are downbeat after the show. I feel as if I have let the side down; worse, I have let Steve Wright down. Stuart just feels as if he's let Birmingham down. No amount of geeing-up from Mark will convince us that we have found our spiritual home on the Roadshow boards. Hosting a lighthearted, pre-recorded, hour-long singles-review show every week is one thing; pandering to prepubescent schoolgirls is another. Part of me thinks I could adapt, but no part of Stuart does, and since we only exist as a pair, going down the Smiley Miley route remains off-limits.

It's fantastic to be on Radio 1 in a kind of peripheral capacity, as grouting in the schedule, a sideshow, but we're too journalistic, too serious, too self-conscious, too aloof to sell our souls and accept the boxers, no matter what the *Daily Star* says. Whilst loitering backstage, decompressing, sipping our polystyrene cups of catering Nescafé and waiting for Judy, a pasty-faced young man catches my eye from the other side of the security barrier, whose job it is to protect the equipment and the boy bands, rather than separate us from the public.

'Can you sign this?' he asks, mechanically and without enthusiasm, holding out an autograph book.

He wants us to sign it because we have been on stage. Not because he knows who we are and loves our work, nor because he cares, just because *we're there.*

I sign with gusto. It is my first autograph and it feels … sad. Is this the way they say the future's supposed to feel?

9

Keeping the Door Open
for Johnny Vaughan

'Good luck, Jarvis!' I shout over to the passing Pulp frontman, whom I know well enough to shout over to, adding: 'Don't ruin it for us!'

Not just 'Don't ruin it' but 'Don't ruin it for *us*'?

Jarvis narrows his eyes, casts me a withering look, and walks on by in his brown pin-striped suit. Glastonbury 1995. At the eleventh hour Pulp have been gifted the headline slot on the Pyramid Stage, after the Stone Roses pulled out because of a broken arm. Another momentous generational and cultural handover. They keep happening. It's Britpop's big moment. The irony is *I've* ruined it. Assorted looks of disdain come from the rest of the social circle, camped around Robert Sandall's traditional picnic hamper in the backstage paddock.

It's easy to go too far when familiarity replaces professional detachment. I have no doubt that Pulp will pull one out of the hat and provide a fitting climax to this Saturday night. I call after Jarvis, shouting, 'I was only joking!' but to deaf ears. It came out all wrong, and my good luck wishes have turned to ash in my idiot mouth. I won't flatter myself that these ill-chosen words will now have dented Jarvis's confidence as the afternoon turns to evening via the magic hour and his band's graduation draws nearer, but they certainly won't have helped.

As I'm fond of saying, I've been in the music journalism caper for seven years now, and I should know better. They're the important ones, not us. They make the music, they take the risks, they tour the world; we just write about them doing it, give them marks out of ten, or boxes out of five, or stars out of five, and occasionally ride pillion. We don't make them. They make us.

Hard-and-fast rule: never make the mistake of thinking you are the band's friend. Never cross that line. It will only end in tears, or a stupid remark made in the over-confident heat of the moment. This is not the best behaviour of a *Q* features editor, which I now am.

At what point in life does being drunk stop being a legitimate excuse?

Six months earlier, 16 December 1994. An historic date for Blur, for *Q* magazine and for me.

Blur were playing to a half-full hall. Alex muffed the intro to 'Girls & Boys' and the band had to start again. He looked sheepish under his generous canopy of a fringe, but still supercool, fag perched where it is always perched. The half-an-audience didn't seem to mind. In fact, they loved it. Their own personal Blur fuck-up!

I was standing where all rock journalists ultimately desire to stand: side of stage, an impartial international observer with a unique smell-the-dry-ice vantage point. You know you've made it when you watch bands sideways on. Even though I lacked any kind of laminated backstage accreditation, confidence in my close relationship with the band is a preference for the habitual voyeur of what-is-known-as …

Q was actually getting an exclusive. Yes, after six long, thankless years in journalism, I was reporting on something worth reporting on; witnessing something secret and more newsworthy than My Bloody Valentine eating a pizza in their manager's house or Mark E. Smith taking the piss out of his keyboard player in the cafeteria of the National Film Theatre.

The half-full hall was in Colchester, Blur's spiritual birthplace, at the town's Sixth Form College, and half-full by almost petulant design. Damon – or Albarn, as formal Q orthodoxy demands that I call him, and I live by that orthodoxy – organised this secret, students-only show with his old music teacher to raise money for an expedition to India to help with an orphanage project. Usually when a band does something secret or to raise money for an orphanage project, they do so by telling everybody about it, holding a press conference and inviting the world's media. But Blur only invited Q. By which I mean me and jolly photographer Hugo. The national press was firmly refused entry, as was the local press, despite fulsome coverage in that day's *Colchester Evening Gazette*.

It was thrilling, clandestine stuff, all the better for not being a rock circus. I've attended plenty of those in my time. (Sorry, did I just say, 'in my time'? I'm starting to sound like some weatherbeaten old lag sucking on a roll-up.)

Mind you, I couldn't help but feel as if I had gone legit. After all, I was working for Q magazine, the adult rock monthly whose appearance on the coffee table signals a hardening of the musical arteries for the music fan no longer satisfied by the inconsistencies and three-out-of-ten prejudices of the inky rock weekly. *Select*, it turned out, was just a halfway house, somewhere for me to reacclimatise to the monthly way of life and bolster my alcohol threshold at lunchtimes with Dave Cavanagh.

I moved down the corridor at Emap at the end of 1993, and graduated from sitting on the pavement outside the Camden Falcon to ligging backstage at Earl's Court. Blur – and *all* this – represented a momentous handover of power, and one that, unlike Steve Wright's boxers, I found myself ready to accept. The cover story I had been parachuted into Colchester to write signified not just Blur's arrival in the wide-open seas of legitimacy, but my own.

What a long and decisive year 1994 had been. In January, just three issues of *Q* into the new job, I sat in my flat and tapped out on my little Mac Classic what I suspect now will be my last ever diary entries. Then life took over.

Saturday, 1 January 1994

First song heard after twelve: 'Today' by Smashing Pumpkins. A popular choice amongst those in my house at midnight. Greatest day. Ever known. All that. It was followed (on the tape) by Aimee Mann's 'I Should've Known'. Uplifting selections. All my favourite things can be good or bad. Long hair. Kissing. Living alone. Being the partner of Stuart Maconie. Honesty. Even Raymond Carver. It's such a bright, beautiful, clean-looking Saturday. Not a Saturday at all. Rotten telly. My phone has not yet rung. In 1993 I made a habit of *not* picking up the phone; let them speak to the machine until I know if I want to speak to *them* or not. Generally not. Timing's important. I have the ability to reject anyone at any turn; no harm intended; no offence. But I feel that 1994 deserves better of me.

Resolution number one. Become friends with Stuart Maconie. We are professionally joined now. Sole Agent: Vivienne Clore for the Richard Stone Partnership. Collins & Maconie, wry satirists, scatological humorists and 'rising cult comedy stars' (*Radio Times*, November 1993). Neither will admit to being the fat one. Yet we are strangers to one another. I tell him everything; he tells me nothing. One-way traffic. Let's get to know each other.

Resolution number two. Look people in the eye. This can be symbolic if you like. Take more notice of others. Stare them out. I have a bad habit of looking away, and it's not because I'm not interested. I am interested.

Resolution number three. Lose half a stone. Not much to ask. Turn that clothes-horse back into an exercise bike. Dave Cavanagh has lost three stone since he packed in the booze four months ago. I am not packing in the booze, but then, I don't wish to lose three stone.

This morning, my exercise bike read 000406 kilometres. It now reads 000412. My legs haven't felt this much like jelly since the Phonogram Christmas party. I am listening to the new Therapy? album, *Troublegum*, on tape. Haven't had a proper headache all day. I thought headaches might kill me in 1993. They did not, in fact; they receded noticeably in December. Blame the computer, or toothache, or drink, or rock'n'roll. I have done all the things I do when I'm alone: mimed the guitar in the mirror and shaken my long hair (to 'Pinch' by Acetone); eaten Start; washed up; typed; drunk tea; found out that all the little candles I left burning for most of last night have either melted or scorched that which they were stood upon (cupboard tops, cassette box). Coulda been a fire in here. How bad would it have been? All fires are bad.

I loathe, hate and detest Mr Nutz, the Nintendo squirrel. I can't bear the pathetic squeal he makes when he dies, and the *frequency* with which he dies. I hate his piss-poor jumping technique. I hate the way he moves, unattended, bobbing about like a moron. And I hate the fact that I can't get him through the first four stages of his so-called 'Woody' woodland world.

Accidentally recorded *nothing* over the top of half of 'Today' by Smashing Pumpkins.

Sunday, 2 January 1994

The bells are ringing. It must be Sunday. It could be any day. Last night in bed, triumphantly, I speed-read

Thunderball, the first book in *The Essential James Bond* (a doorstop I have agreed to review). I reckon if I speed-read two more (out of five) I will be able to pass comment with confidence and aplomb in *Q*.

Bought two Sunday papers. Still can't decide which way to swing. *Independent* or *The Times*? Both have things to offer. I ought to plump one way.

Cleaned out my U-bend as my sink had started to stink. Seven years of tea-stain.

Tuesday, 4 January 1994

Back to school. Therapy?'s album – which I am honoured to be reviewing; first result of the New Year at *Q* – had me in its iron grip all evening. I have given it four stars, because five says *any Q* reader could walk out and buy it and not be in any way disappointed. I'm too clever to believe that. But it's the rest of the world's loss: this album has the ability to frighten and reassure at the same time. *Troublegum*, released in February, fourteen tracks, is 1994's first truly magnificent record. I am its slave. It has me.

Work? Oh, boring, really. Lots of computer stare and Danny writing things on the board. We have ten working days to finish *Q*90 (February's issue). Can't be done. It will be done. Phoned three out of four women in the Phonogram press office: Dawn (she's arranging a Cocteau Twins interview for us); Sophie (her first day in a new job, welcome aboard, first day at big school); and Julie (because it would seem foolish not to when I'm thinking about her all day).

Wednesday, 5 January 1994

It was worth it. Apropos of nothing, Adrian and I got pissed this evening after work. It was almost a deliberate act. He drank Red Rock with intent, myself Kronenberg. Many pints. In the George, our second favourite pub in the area. Excellent conversation (girls, resolutions, Rome), which re-bonded us after the Christmas and New Year break. Adrian was in an attention-seeking bad mood all morning at work, his first day back, caused by a 'work' thing (Danny and I commissioning Stuart to do Eric Clapton, when Adrian claims we'd promised it to him – this situation has been reversed now). We're big mates again. Steve Lamacq unexpectedly joined us in the pub after his Radio 1 programme had finished (he was seeing Tony Smith in there, his manager, for a business meeting – a wide boy, but managers have to be). Steve and Adrian got on fine. Steve's now reviewing for *Q*, and you can tell he's proud of the fact. Quite right.

Thursday, 6 January 1994

Began my Friendship Programme with Stuart tonight over some vodka. Getting there.

Friday, 7 January 1994

Collins & Maconie are back in front of the mic. At 3.15 p.m., up to Radio 1 to record our first five *On the Case* inserts for Goodier's afternoon show. Producer Fergus recorded them, which infused us with confidence – a) He's never worked with us before, and he seemed to dig them, and b) He's the boss of the programme, and our previous segments were always recorded on auto-pilot, in a piss-poor studio called 'The Pit' with no feedback from the producer. Steve Wright's backroom comic genius Richard Easter introduced himself to us in the corridor and said he was a 'fan'. Fantastic, then.

Tuesday, 11 January 1994

Unable to write last night. Iestyn, news editor of the *NME*, and possibly one of the sanest figures at that beleaguered journal, turned twenty-eight yesterday. Joined him and selected friends at 7.30 p.m. at what used to be Shuttleworth's, now Downstairs at the Phoenix … the Theatre Bar anyhow. Cast: Bill, Iestyn's girlfriend The Lovely Pandora, her sister, Gavin Martin, Mrs Miles Hunt (Mary Anne), the Lamacqs, Johnny Dee and Cathy – a happy, easy crowd, all of whom know me, thus immediate comfort. Let's get on with the drinking and nonsense. One problem: I overdid the alcohol. Tennant's Extra (three pints) in Shuttleworth's, then more white wine than I ought to have done in Amalfi, a cute Italian in Soho. Waiter! Another bottle, please! It was like that. I was as drunk as if I hadn't eaten, except I *was* eating – hearty whitebait, rigatoni, and a yard of beautiful bread with olive oil. Didn't embarrass myself *per se*, merely talked quickly and clumsily and over-frankly to nearly everybody there, in turn. I could *hear* myself stumbling over my words. By midnight, home time, I was slaughtered. Slept all the way home in the cab, then bang. Out.

My only bad memory of the evening was Marc, fiery French art editor of the *NME*, having a pop at me in Shuttleworth's. I attempted to laugh it off, since I have endured his humourless venom plenty of times before. He actually can't help it – it's just his poor grip on bawdy office-style sarcasm. It's not personally malicious. Plus, the girlfriend he nicked off John was there for him to impress. He had a pop at my Carter T-shirt, if you must know, then muttered that I had put on weight. Luckily, we were leaving, and he wasn't coming on to eat, so the matter dropped, but I fear I would've been less patient later on.

This morning I lost the ability to function. More than a beer/wine hangover. I am not well. My stomach hasn't been right since Sunday, and a night of liquid carousing was not what the imaginary doctor ordered, was it? Felt civilisation-shatteringly rough when I woke up. Suffered all day. Hot, unhappy, unsettled, mixed up, tired. I ate a jacket potato in The Downstairs Café, but turned to bananas on Julie's advice. Go down easily. Body gets used to them. No acid. I ate one on the way to the pub with Adrian and John Naughton then drank three pints of Kronenberg. Is that good? Home by 10.00 p.m. Adrian was superb company, I had to stick around. He's a diamond this year already. Where is Stuart Maconie?

I keep bemoaning the hangover caused by beer and wine. I keep drinking beer and wine.

Wednesday, 12 January 1994

Afghan Whigs at the Astoria. Not tonight. Give me a rest. Still unsettled, digestively. Bananas for breakfast, followed by, of course, a curry for lunch. Hanway Street, a *Q* haunt, thali for £3.50 at lunchtime, plus the requisite ice-cold bottle of Cobra. I wouldn't have, but Bill did. It was quite the most wonderful single drink to pass my lips in 1994. However, a quick one in the Clachan with Bill and Lisa after work at 6.50 p.m. turned out to be almost equally magnificent: an ice-cold bottle of Elephant beer, which, unbeknown to me thus far, is 7.2 per cent proof. I drank two in the space of one, and we all happily left at 7.30 p.m.

Attempted some comedy writing back here tonight. Finally spoke to Stuart, who has promised to stay down tomorrow night. This alleviated the pressure, and I packed it in. He's done three features in three days for *Q* and *Select*. Too much for any writer; the quality threshold will, I predict, be low.

Thursday, 13 January 1994

Ha ha. We are funny. All done. One cheeky pint in the George with Mr Adrian, who was off to see Sting, and Stuart and I were home, producing words. That's three *On the Cases*, which I hope are funny, plus an entire *Hipster's Guide* to Martin Scorsese, which I believe is halfway to inspired. It was, really and truly, a spirit-lifting treat to see Stuart in the office today, and, as ever, the rest of them were happy to have him around for a brief period, too. People like Stuart; he should capitalise on it.

Friday, 14 January 1994

I have been unprofessional. No way out of this one. I was reviewing The Cranberries tonight at the Astoria 2, which, in *Q* style, involved three simple acts:

1) A short interview. OK, did that, pre-gig, 6.35 p.m., after an hour and a half's wait, the entire shifty, uncomfortable thing filmed for the band's own forthcoming video. They are quiet people. I'd never met them until a minute before someone shouted 'Action!' and I didn't want to show off. Fifteen minutes of muttering. At least I accomplished that bit, and the band warmed to me. Dolores complimented me on my hair.

2) Procuring a set list. Failed there. Asked Nick White from Island to get one, but I bet he forgot. This one is niggling me. Such a meagre task. But I was too drunk.

3) Review the gig. Well, I was *there*. Twice, I moved from the bar to see what Dolores was wearing, and make sure I wasn't missing anything *visual*. I wasn't. But now I feel like a cliché, a rock cliché. Reviewing a gig from the bar. Without the set list. What a fucker. Serves me right.

I am deeply cross with myself for tonight's unprofessionalism. It was, in truth, the least I could do; in fact, a bit less than that.

Saturday, 15 January 1994

I keep waking up with a hangover and attributing it to having eaten no food the night before. I have *always* eaten the night before. On Monday night it was a whole Italian meal; last night it was virtually a whole pizza, cooked back here at midnight. Ah well. Still half a stone down on New Year's Day! I'm either doing something right, or else I've stopped doing something wrong.

Adrian and I met in Shuttleworth's at 8.00 p.m. to have an indie night out in Central London. His Basingstoke mate 'Disgraceful' Kev the actor came, too. He and Kev are more like one another than Adrian and I since I went legitimate, but the three of us found plenty in common: *Carry On* films, instant mash potato, Tennants Extra on tap. Marquee to see Thrum. Old-fashioned Glaswegian folk-rockers, not so bad. Up to the Astoria 2 for *NME*'s 'On' night, just in time to see – or hear, since it was rammed – Elastica. It was Guest List Heaven.

Bumped into and conversed with, for varying lengths of time, Matt Hall (Channel X) and Tamsin (TV21); Damon; Louise; Mary Anne; Simon Williams (he sorted me out with after-shows, for which I am eternally grateful); Mark Lamarr; Swells; Steve Lamacq; Debbie from Curve; Dele; John Best and Miki; Sonya from Echobelly; Andrew Harrison; Polly and Jim Reid (who now seems to have accepted me after some initial resentment); Mark Ellen; Elastica themselves. Friendly kisses from Justine and Donna; they haven't forgotten me! Really enjoyed myself all night. I love the music industry when it can supply me with this much sociable interaction. And beer. When my taxi home passed Lambeth Town Hall I was amazed to see the clock say 12.45 a.m. What a lot of people I must've packed into my night! Thank you. I have Justine's phone number to do my *Q* interview tomorrow (it's Damon's as well, obviously).

Sunday, 16 January 1994

'No poker? What? Is there a war on?' Line from *Bilko*, just one of the TV programmes I watched between writing bursts today. *Doctor Who. Antiques Roadshow* from Exeter. *Moviewatch.* Lazy day, fundamentally. Didn't even get dressed, since I managed to get my Sunday *Independent* from a stall on Charing Cross Rd last night. Luxury! Half-wrote The Cranberries, Elastica, computer game reviews. Drank a gallon of tea. Ate salmon fish cakes for tea. Did it by the book, really. Spoke to Mum, Julie, Justine.

A key question, I think: what better way of spending the evening is there than sitting in front of *Manhattan* on video, drinking a chilled bottle of Chardonnay by yourself, with no lights on in the house but fairy lights? This was my way of a) treating myself after a hard week, and b) getting 'in the mood' for the reasonable *South Bank Show* Woody Allen interview at 11.00 p.m. I laughed out loud, freely, about three times. Answer: There is no better way.

Tuesday, 18 January 1994

Happy birthday, Sophie, twenty-three today. Met her and Phill and their mates Jo, Russell and Neil Perry in another George in Charing Cross. Last two days of this issue of *Q,* I was in the 'colour house' (Colour Systems, Islington) until 9.30 p.m., so it was a late starter all round. Minor alcoholic consumption; *Vox* secrets from Neil (he's subbing there currently).

Wednesday, 19 January 1994

My third ever *Q* was finished at 8.30 p.m. this evening, Islington. Cue: a celebratory pizza in the Hut for Danny, Bill and myself. No ice, and no telephone. This is not America.

Monday, 31 January 1994

Brussels: grey and uninspiring. Cocteau Twins live at the Lunatheater: beautiful, no other word describes it better. Interview for *Q*: Robin and Simon only. Fantastic, truthful; they treated me as a confidant. Trip: easy, full of daytime drink on plane and in bar, hungover by the evening.

It has seemed a very long January.

I landed the life-shaping job of *Q* features editor not long after the magazine started to go a bit we-are-weird in August 1992 – issue *Q*71, to be precise. Up to that point, it had been plain sailing. *Q* had struck magazine gold and found a gap in the market. Its reputation had curved exponentially. If it had a mission statement it was to treat the music it loved with equal parts holy reverence and bawdy irreverence; perfectly encapsulated by its choice of cover star and attendant arch cover lines. For instance:

'AW-*RAHT*!'

'UH-OH! IT'S THE HEAVY MOB!'

'OOPS! WRONG PLANET!'

'A MILDLY PRETENTIOUS INTERVIEW!'

And so on.

This was *Smash Hits* with a mortgage.

Next to box-office 'bankers' like Pink Floyd, Paul McCartney, Dire Straits, U2 and R.E.M., the idea of a risky *Q* cover star was the Pet Shop Boys or Tanita Tikaram. If anyone moderately youth-orientated such as the Stone Roses or Nirvana made their own little corner of a patchwork cover, the token oiks would find the likes of Prince or Annie Lennox acting as commercial guarantor. Sales soared and *Q* continued to act like cavity-wall insulation foam, filling that vacuum in the market that its founding fathers, Mark Ellen and his former *Whistle Test* and Live Aid co-host David 'Dave' 'Heppy'

Hepworth, had so astutely identified at the end of the eighties during the first summer of the Compact Disc.

The fact that *Q* became an illicit pleasure at the *NME*, literally read under desks like porn, tells you everything you need to know about its reach. Danny would sometimes catch us at it and huffily declare, 'If you like it so much why don't you all go and work there?' – at which we would put it away and start talking in earnest tones about Truman's Water, DC Basehead and The Family Cat.

And then came *Q*71.

At this juncture, the bitty, bet-hedging *Q* cover had begun to give ground to a bolder, more confident single image: Hendrix, Bono, Madonna, Guns N' Roses – basically anyone worthy of a realistic moving waxwork in Rock Circus. It was within this rubric in August 1992 that an exclusive one-on-one with Bruce Springsteen dominated the entire cover of *Q*71. Full-bleed, as they say in magazines. Nobody else had it. The magazine had even dispatched David Hepworth to conduct the interview – a man who had long since abandoned hands-on magazine-making and retired to an office marked Editorial Director, the avuncular national hero who'd made Bob Geldof swear at Live Aid ('Fuck the addresses') and Britain's most dogged Springsteen fan. And Bruce had two albums out. In the same week. Doubles all round.

Or not. The Springsteen issue was nailed to the shelves, despite *Human Touch* and *Lucky Town*, the horribly named twin albums, topping the chart. While everybody was too busy having a picnic to notice, the tide had turned. And, as if to prove it, the next issue, *Q*72, its cover dominated by Morrissey, sold like hot cakes. Emap flipcharts were furiously flipped and coloured markers squeaked frantic trails over whiteboards.

The conclusion astutely drawn was that a new generation of reader had begun to block vote in John Menzies. Yes, they still liked U2 and R.E.M., and certainly had a more circumspect and open-eared take on rock history than the average, indie-boned *NME* reader, but they were in their late twenties and early thirties as opposed to their late thirties and early forties. A crucial difference. To tap directly into this new constituency, *Q* wined and dined Danny Kelly of the *NME*, and the rest is recent history.

Danny was given the post of *Q* editor – or Mohicanned Tartar of Rock Publishing, as he preferred to call it – on the solemn understanding that he wouldn't just repopulate the staff of the magazine with ex-*NME* colleagues. He stood by this solemn promise … for about six months, then started repopulating the staff of the magazine with ex-*NME* colleagues. First Bill, the redoubtable, candy-floss-haired, Dylan-loving *NME* sub-editor. Then Stuart, who was ceremonially inducted as a star feature writer, much to the chagrin of long-standing star feature writer, Adrian Deevoy, who'd been with *Q* since birth. Then me.

At the job interview, more formal than I was used to and conducted by no less than the avuncular but stern Heppy himself, I was asked what I would 'bring to the magazine'. They always ask you that. 'My own pen' doesn't cut it as an answer.

'So what would you, Andrew Collins, bring to the magazine?' asked 'Dave', making his fingers into a steeple and swinging around in his swivel chair like a chat-show host.

'I'd bring The Wonder Stuff.'

As with all the best interview soundbites, I hadn't prepared this one, it just sort of tumbled from my mouth. I imagine this is what it's like to buzz in *University Challenge* in the split-second before your brain's had chance to access the answer.

'Go on.'

Too late. You've buzzed.

'Well, I think The Wonder Stuff are as important as Van Morrison. Whenever Van puts another album out, *Q* automatically runs a feature on him. Why? Is there really anything new to find out from another Van Morrison interview? Meanwhile, The Wonder Stuff have built up a huge following over three albums, and I think *Q* should give them as much credence as someone who's put out twenty. I'm not saying you shouldn't do Van Morrison, but there should be room for both at the table.'

I sort of half-believed it, and it turned out to be the kind of soundbite upon which interviews are won. So I brought The Wonder Stuff to *Q*. They really are a splendid and affable band. I've had my moments of feeling like the sixth member of The Wonder Stuff, having travelled across Europe with them in their xenophobic tour bus, so it felt good to offer them a seat at the *Q* table – and indeed to commission *myself* to fly to San Francisco to write about them. James Brown had taught me well.

What I also brought to the magazine was a now-formidable valance of grunge hair, a range of Pop Will Eat Itself tops and a pair of promotional L7 shorts, worn over battle-hardened oxblood Doctor Martens for that still-at-Glastonbury look. I appeared, for all the world, to be on some kind of exchange programme from the *NME*. I appeared, to the eyes of the more conservative gentlemen journalists of *Q*, many of whom had bylines in broadsheet newspapers and took their own hampers to festivals, like a student. It earned me the odious nickname of Andrew College. Ha ha. Very funny. College: it's a bit like Collins. I wish I had a better nickname.

I lobbied tirelessly for that Blur cover. It may not seem that risky to nail your colours to a band whose third album, *Parklife*, has gone briskly double-platinum. But this was *Q*, and there were only twelve covers in a year, soon allocated to R.E.M. or U2 or the Stones, depending on who had an album out, then to Eric Clapton, Paul McCartney, Prince, Madonna, Sinead O'Connor, Kate Bush (albeit every five years), Sting, Rod, Morrissey and Mick Hucknall, which only left one spare.

Come in, Blur!

I suppose the biggest irony is that when I invented Britpop at *Select* in 1993, Blur weren't even mentioned.

I didn't really invent Britpop, of course, but I will happily lay claim to the idea of putting Suede on the cover with a big Union Jack, in parody of the *Sun*'s 'Support Our Boys' poster during the Gulf. It was time to repel the grunge invasion with some symbolic *Dad's Army*-style triangles, and, thanks to the wit and wisdom of Andrew Harrison and Mark Ellen, with whom I cooked up the themed cover story in a poky café on Beak Street, the napkin became reality. We gathered together Suede, St Etienne, The Auteurs, Pulp and Denim, entrusted a grunge-resistant Stuart to write it, added a stirring piece by Andrew reclaiming the British flag from fascists and finished it with a patriotic playlist compiled by Carl from Cud, because he went to Leeds University. Even though Brett from Suede bridled somewhat at being photo-shopped onto the flag – which is why we hadn't asked him beforehand, obviously – *Select*'s Britpop issue was a treat, a real talking point, the sort of thing you can do on a glossy monthly, as you have the time to get it right. Well, almost right.

If only we'd had the foresight to involve Blur, who at that point had yet to unleash *Modern Life Is Rubbish* on the populace and actually define Britpop. History will need to be rewritten by the victors.

'Now, get into pairs and face each other.'

We comply. I pair up with a woman from *Just Seventeen*. We face each other. She's older than seventeen.

'What I want you to do is decide which one of you is going to lead.'

The woman from *Just Seventeen* and I nod meaningfully at each other. I'm going to lead.

'Then I want you to imagine that you're standing in front of a full-length mirror. The other person is your reflection.'

Oh God.

'I want you to start to move, *veeeeery* slowly, and I want the other person to copy your movements. OK?'

Smirking and giggling breaks out around the conference room, and not for the first time today. Resistance, however, is futile. As it was before lunch when we were each instructed to leave and re-enter the room, then try and get the rest of the trainees to guess which adjective we'd been given on a piece of paper, by the way we addressed them.

Angry.

Excited.

Depressed.

Nervous.

Humiliated.

'Off you go.'

The man from the training company, possibly a resting actor, *let's-call-him* Rufus – but hey, it's not about *him*, it's about *us* – clasps his hands together and steps back, perching his bottom on the edge of a desk. After a few seconds' contemplation about the fruitlessness of existence, we begin the exercise. I raise my right hand in front of me, fingers outstretched, like the alien greeting in *Close Encounters*. It's quite a profound moment. The woman from *Just Seventeen* does the same with her left, mirroring my every move as I gently raise my hand above my face and then out to the side, like Kate Bush. I think to myself: shouldn't I be helping oversee the layout of the cover of *Q* with Danny and Cowlesey? We gaze into each other's eyes, both trying desperately not to read the other's expression. Around us, other senior editorial hopefuls do likewise.

'Don't look at other people, concentrate on what you're doing,' says Rufus, in that gently reassuring voice he dips into when he senses we're feeling like mental patients.

What are we doing? What are we *actually* doing, besides very slow synchronised aerobics in a hired conference room? Well, we're trying to get on. We're showing willing. We're thanking Emap kindly, with bodily submission, for considering us worthy of Senior Editorial Training, a series of one-day initiatives designed by Americans to instil in us the values, skills and sensitivities required to 'head up' a team. Something all twelve of us, plucked from the day-to-day grind of titles as various as *More*, *Select* and *Smash Hits*, may someday have to do. One of which is the ability to pretend to be somebody's mirror image – a technique that could come in pretty handy if, say, your reviews editor had broken their mirror and you wanted to create the illusion that it wasn't broken, which might come up. After all, anything can happen in magazine publishing.

It's not about that.

'This exercise,' explains Rufus, 'is about responding to the needs of others – it helps us tune in to what other members of our team are doing and thinking and react in a sympathetic manner; in effect, to allow *them* to lead.'

Yes, it's bollocks. And we're going along with it because we're all sort of flattered that the company would single us out for entire awaydays of workshopping, group-thinking and role-playing. We're all lowly features editors and section editors and news editors and deputy editors, and that makes us … the next wave of potential editors when the current lot become managing editors.

Fuck me, I'm being groomed! I'm not sure I even want to *be* the bloody editor. Mind you, if a job comes up in the Broom Cupboard, I'll be primed and ready. The big joke is I have to leave this training day early, potentially curtailing my ability to be editorial in a senior fashion.

'Do you mind if we leave the door open?' asks Johnny Vaughan, already togged up in his ironic dinner jacket. Is he joking? He sounds like he's joking even when he's being sincere, and yet he sounds sincere even when he's joking. That's his schtick. The very schtick that saw him promoted from 'roving reporter' on the first series of *Naked City* to dinner-jacketed co-host on this one.

I've escaped the editorial training day and Johnny's in our dressing room. Savour that for a moment: *our* dressing room. A dressing room with the names 'Collins' and 'Maconie' on the door, albeit printed out on a piece of paper. It smells of dogs, for some reason, but it's still our dressing room, and we're not really at the tantrum level of our careers yet.

We could be in Johnny's dressing room, but he's in ours.

'I don't like being in a small enclosed space with two other men,' he explains – again, halfway between serious and not-serious. 'I get flashbacks.'

He's referring, with candour, to his time in prison. Our dressing room reminds him of his cell. Johnny's cool about it. We're certainly cool about it. Impressed, deep down, though. He's certainly the first ex-con I've ever known socially. And Johnny is very social. Although he's our age, he deliberately comes across as much older, like a relic from a more innocent light entertainment age. He calls us 'chaps', and regales us with Jimmy Tarbuck anecdotes.

It's cool being showbiz pals with Johnny Vaughan. But then, we do share a showbiz agent: Vivienne, a vivacious, no-nonsense woman who looks after Rory Bremner, Jo Brand and Mark Thomas, and once went out with the footballer Pat Nevin. She took us on at the end of last year after a recommendation from Katie Lander at Channel X. I still can't quite get my head round the fact that I've got an agent. Well, *we* have. Stuart and I are now officially an item. We appear in the little brochure as Collins & Maconie, just as Phil Hammond and Tony Gardner appear as Struck Off and Die, and Jim Sweeney and Steve Steen appear as Sweeney & Steen. It's like being actual comedians, even though we're not. Are we?

So, *Naked City*: how did we get this plum job? Our career thus far has been like a bar of chocolate: one chunk leads to another chunk. Signing up with an agent puts you in the marketplace and sets out your stall. Actually, you appear *not* to sign up with agents. It's all very Factory Records: done with a handshake and an understanding. After all – and this isn't something I ever thought about before entering this arcane world – if an agent doesn't procure for his or her client any paying work, they don't get paid either. It's all in the percentage. QED: it's incumbent upon the agent to scare up some work for the entertainer.

I'm slightly scared of Vivienne. The first thing she did was almost double our money on the Mark Goodier show and *Fabulous!* with one phonecall each. Ker-ching! Of course, my first paranoid thought was: I hope they don't get rid of us now we're twice as expensive to hire. But that's the game of showbiz brinkmanship. The second thing was to broker a meeting with the big cheeses at Rapido, makers of, well, *Rapido* and *Eurotrash*, where a TV version of our *Hipster's Guides* was conceived.

It wasn't rocket science. We simply adapted one of our existing radio scripts for the visual medium – that is, changed the 'Fx' to 'Inserts' – and they filmed an offline pilot, whatever that is, in a small room at their production office. We selected *The Hipster's Guide To The New Wave Of New Wave.*

Stuart looks calm, authoritative, Andrew seems agitated and fidgety. He is wearing a S*M*A*S*H T-shirt. 'Welcome to the *Hipster's Guide*, a weekly look at what's cool and happening in the world of rock'n'roll. I'm Stuart, and this is Andrew. [to Andrew] Sit still. [back to camera] Ahem. This week we'll be looking at – The New Wave Of New Wave! Punk Rock!'

'Sorry?'

'God Save The Queen! No Future! Get pissed, destroy! Cash From Chaos! Who Killed Bambi! One Two Three Four! Because there's gonna be a borstal breakout!'

'Crikey!'

Cue: 'Anarchy in the UK'.

'I am an ant Christ, I am an anarchist!'

'It's not ant Christ. It's *anti* Christ, and you're C of E … *and* you vote Liberal Democrat.'

'That's all in the past, Mr Thatcher … because now I'm New Wave of New Wave.'

'Oh dear, can you see what's happened here, viewers? Andrew, like many other impressionable young people of low IQ, has fallen hook, line and, indeed, sinker for something he has read about in *i-D* and the *NME*: the New Wave of New Wave.'

'The most exciting thing to happen to British music/culture since Madchester …'

'Ambient House …'

'… or Acid Jazz.'

'But what *is* New Wave of New Wave, I hear you ask? To answer that question we need to take a journey back in time … a journey back in time … a journey back in time … '

'The seventies! Anthea Redfern! The Wombles! Martin Chivers! Labour governments! Clackers!'

'But it wasn't all *Abigail's Party* and Cresta. The kids on the street, in the graffiti-daubed underpasses of Britain's high-rise monstrosities, had no future! … until Punk Rock!'

'Kids who had previously made model aeroplanes and frugged to Greenslade and 10CC became deranged punk rock monsters, hell bent on overthrowing the monarchy and instituting the People's Republic Of New Wave.'

'Of new wave … Of new wave … Of new wave …'

'But what has this to do with us in the present? I'll tell you! The new wave is back! Skinny ties, drainpipe trousers, V-neck jumpers, short, unattractive haircuts that are a bit too long at the sides: it's the New Wave Of New Wave.'

'The New Wave of New Wave – so christened by the *NME* because it's, like, a new wave of bands who are New Wave – is here to give the tired old music industry an amphetamine-fuelled kick up the backside, and to kill off boring hippy has-beens like Pink Floyd, The Milltown Brothers, Clannad and Technotronik Featuring Ya Kid K.'

'Like every youth movement before it, NWONW ...'

'What?'

'N.W.O.N.W. – New Wave Of New Wave. Keep up. NWONW has its own drug: speed! Whizz! Sulphate! Beak! Kedgeree! Indonesian Wensleydale! Swarf! Impetigo! Call it what you will, it's speed!'

'Like the music, it provides an immediate rush of adrenalin. Like the music, it's fast, it's cheap, it's NOW. Like the music, it's white. Although the really good stuff's more sort of browny yellowy.'

'And, just to prove how great speed is, Andrew and I are now going to take some, on air. Andrew, the speed!'

At this point, I bring out a tray with decanter and two small sherry glasses. We sip the sherry.

'So, while Andrew and I enjoy this noggin of speed, we'll hand you back to Johnny and Caitlin.'

'Cheers!'

It went well enough for Rapido to sign us up to provide one satirical item a week for ten weeks. Which is why we find ourselves in our own dressing room that smells of dogs in a studio in Wandsworth on a Thursday afternoon when I should, by rights, still be at Senior Editorial Training in a conference room in Central London.

On the telly, *The Hipster's Guide* is presented from an old sofa on a gantry, heralded by the same theme tune we use on *Fabulous!*, 'Take Five' by the Dave Brubeck Five. It's hard to think of a gantry and not think of *Nozin' Around*, the mock-yoof

TV programme on *The Young Ones* – especially when *Naked City* is a yoof TV programme, replete with wacky rooftop set with wire fencing and chimneys, live bands, filmed items about how to be acid jazz, and a 'relaxed' attitude to drugs, illustrated by a controversial, in-studio joint-building competition between Mr C of The Shamen, Fish out of Marillion and Tony Banks MP. But this is a show that fancies itself a cut above the usual patronising yoof hi-jinks, with a veil of we-know-what-we're-doing postmodernism, embodied by Johnny Vaughan's dinner suit. And if nothing else they book some really top-quality bands: Blur, Pulp, the Manics, S*M*A*S*H, These Animal Men, Senser, Arrested Development, Shara Nelson, Sounds of Blackness, Honky, Urban Species and Fun-Da-Mental. They get dressing rooms, too.

Johnny is called away for a run-through.

'See you later, chaps!'

As he heads for the studio floor, he shouts out, 'Any sign of that air freshener? The boys can't work in these conditions!'

Earlier, he asked one of the runners to go out and fetch an air freshener for our dog-smelling dressing room. It was just a bit of fun, but you never can tell with Johnny Vaughan. It certainly wouldn't cross our mind to ask a runner to fetch anything for us.

Stuart and I close the door and rehearse the opening lines of this week's *Hipster's Guide to Comedy*, which has been turned into a proper shooting script by whoever does that. There is something perilously postmodern and knowing about two rock journalists posing as comedians doing a comedic routine about comedy being the new rock'n'roll, but what the hell. There's a good bit about Paul McCartney moving into stand-up, which Stuart delivers in the voice of Les Dawson: 'I'm not saying my wife's a prominent vegetarian cook, an accomplished photographer and an animal rights activist but ...'

We're pretty sure that's funny. But does it make us comedians? I expect Michael Smiley, a seasoned stand-up who, this series, acts as *Naked City*'s roving reporter, would have us down as interloping fly-by-nights. Which we are. There's something about being on telly that legitimises what we do in a way that radio doesn't. Look, there we are! On late-night Channel 4! Johnny Vaughan has just introduced us as 'our chums, Collins and Maconie'. Me on the left with my long hair and him on the right with his fringe, playing up to our self-anointed stereotypes of fool and sophisticate. Anything can happen, as long as it's within the fairly rigid framework of two men bursting with archness and reading out lists where the fourth or fifth item is deliberately wrong or uncool.

'Comedians like … '

'Rob Newman.'

'Sean Hughes.'

'Vic Reeves.'

'Freddie "Parrot Face" Davies.'

'And Howard Stableford.'

Do you see what we did there? I hope so, as we do it every week, from our gantry. The item itself is pre-recorded earlier in the afternoon, then the audience of surly youths is bussed in, and we top and tail it, as live, in front of them, so that the camera can pan across their heads up to our scaffolding eyrie, and pan away again. This is more nerve-racking than the pre-record, because of the knowledge that if we fluff it, the audience will have to stand around disconsolately while the shot is re-set and then applaud, again, on cue. It would be nice to think the kids enjoy our satirical humour, but it's much easier to become convinced that they hate us and wish that the Boo Radleys would hurry up and come on.

It's weird when a band we know is booked to play – and booking policy means they do tend to be the kind of band one or other of us has been to Utrecht with. They will inevitably ask, 'What are *you* doing here?' when they run into us backstage, expecting us to say that we're here to interview one of the other bands. 'We do a *sort of* comedy item on the show,' we'll say, the degree of awkwardness flagged up by the 'sort of'. That's what we are, then: *sort of* comedians. Still, there's nothing *sort of* about this dressing room. It's a dressing room.

'Right, let's do it one more time.'

'Welcome to the *Hipster's Guide*, a weekly look at what's hot and sticky in the world of rock'n'roll ...'

A knock on the door. Perhaps it's genial producer Kenton, who also likes to hang out at our dressing room, despite the canine odour.

'Come in!' we shout, simultaneously, like a pair of Norma Desmonds.

Ah, it's the runner, *let's-call-him* Dom. He's carrying the familiar blue-and-white-striped plastic bag of a mini-mart.

'Here's your air freshener,' Dom announces, with a smile playing around his lips. True to his word, he's been out to buy us an aerosol can of Glade. He hands us the bag, and leaves. We remove the can, only to discover he's also purchased us twenty Rothmans and a copy of *Razzle*, presumably on Johnny's orders. It's a satire, we imagine, on the sort of thing prima donna show-biz types might send a runner out for. We've really arrived.

Q has been a maturing influence. Since taking up my desk there, I have, unprompted, grown to like two debut albums that would have been unthinkable at the *NME* or *Select*. One is *Tuesday Night Music Club* by Sheryl Crow; the other is *Whatever* by Aimee Mann.

Believe me, in my former life, these records would have found themselves automatically filed in my sell-pile without a cursory listen, had A&M or Warners sent them to me in the first place. These are Adult-Orientated Rock records – a description that strikes fear into the heart of a young man with the weekly music press still in his veins – a world apart from Kingmaker's *Eat Yourself Whole*, with its cover image of a cartoon sperm, or

Suede by Suede, with its two androgynes kissing away with every hope of frightening the horses.

Nary a neigh would be heard from the stables if you were to place either Crow or Mann in the CD drawer. Existing outside the vagaries of fashion, immune to any flimsy notions of credibility, these are singer-songwriters with grown-up concerns and rootsy leanings about which they are unabashed. *One of them wears a denim shirt.* They are signed to major labels and not to self-conscious imprints designed to look as if they are independents when they are in fact major labels. Sheryl Crow is thirty-two. Aimee Mann is thirty-four. I like them. I like them both, and I don't mind who knows it. I am proud to like these records. I am not yet thirty, but the big day is approaching, I can smell the creosote.

It was all very different at Glastonbury 1994, my first as an ambassador of *Q*, when I found myself being interviewed, live on national television, in the middle of the night, by Mark Radcliffe, who was hosting Channel 4's inaugural coverage of the festival from a double-decker bus parked backstage. I was, it is fair to say, somewhat refreshed at that late hour, as any reveller might be. Dazed, yes, but not confused enough to have failed to arrive at the bus at the allotted time of 11.30 p.m. and saved myself the humiliation.

I reported for punditry duty to genial Geordie producer Malcolm Gerrie. Lit by the dancing flames of a bonfire made from Workers Beer Company cups, Malcolm and I had, as I remember it, a perfectly cogent conversation while I waited my turn.

I have never seen the footage, nor do I wish to, but people have relayed back the general content with a certain amount of cruel glee. I only recall it through a glass darkly, but I'm reliably informed that, at one stage, I asked Mark to stroke my grunge-length hair. The joke I made about the band Galliano is lost in the mists of time, but it had something to do with hats and I had been rehearsing it all evening.

In fact, the clearest mental image I have of that night is of Danny Kelly, my boss, watching the coverage on television at home in East London that night, with, by his own account, a glass of red wine balanced on his stomach. When *Q*'s features editor appeared in his red Cure top, gazing dreamily into the middle-distance, Danny almost dropped his bottle. He sat bolt upright, willing the live feed to cut out. Imagine his relief when the caption came up beneath my grinning face: Andrew Collins, Radio 1.

But that was then. They can call me College as much as they like, but inside I'm growing up. If anything, I'm a mature student.

Pulp don't ruin Glastonbury 1995 for us. Far from it. They pull one out of the hat. We watch their triumphant headliner not from the side of the stage, but at the top of the hill. Like normal people. Like common people. It is magnificent beyond belief.

10

On a Yacht with Will Smith

We are on a jetty at Cannes, about to board a speedboat. Stylish publisher Jerry looks my brand-new beige suit up and down and says with a note of withering disdain: 'What is that? Hessian?'

I'm not sure what it's made of. It's from Marks & Spencer, and I rather fancied it as redolent of Mickey Rourke in *Angel Heart*. I have another one at home, same make, same cut, same Hessian-like material, also from M&S but slightly darker – one might even call it butterscotch. When you're the editor, you really should wear a suit.

So, suit inventory, May 1995: if you add the two Hessians to the grey Top Man with the eighties electric-blue lining, and the bottle-green Top Man, and the grey Hugo Boss three-piece I bought for my wedding, that's five suits. Though a newlywed, I remain, at heart, a boy, but a boy with five suits to his name. Get me. In another echo of Mickey Rourke in *Angel Heart*, I have sold my thirty-year-old Northampton soul to the devil. In return I get to board a speedboat, which will take us to the yacht, which is my yacht. Well, *our* yacht.

Jerry is not the devil. His skin is too smooth, his eyes too blue and his hair too wispy for that. He's not strictly my publisher – he publishes Emap's music titles – but as commercial director he holds jurisdiction over the ad sales teams, including the ad sales team at *Empire*, the magazine of which, somewhat improbably, I am now the editor. Jerry's 'a suit', which is ironic, as so am I, and yet I'm not.

I get on well with Jerry; our relationship is cordial and candid, and, despite having a wife and baby, he retains an air of mischief. We are men of the world. And he's within his rights to take the piss out of my suit – just preferably not *here*, exposed, out on a jetty in front of people I've never met, clients, media buyers, heads of ad agencies, the people who keep magazines like ours afloat.

Perhaps Jerry would show me a little more respect if he knew that I have been invited out for lunch with Patrick Bergin, star of *Lawnmower Man II: Beyond Cyberspace*.

I flew into Nice this morning, in my Hessian suit, travelling light brown. Minibus into Cannes from the airport. With barely time to unpack my toiletries at the *Empire* apartment, the phone rang in a peculiarly French way. Mark, my features editor and something of a Cannes veteran, picked up.

'It's for you,' he said, handing over the receiver with a mixture of disbelief and jealousy. He's the features editor. He wanted to be the editor when the job vacancy came up, and he applied for it with an insider's confidence. Magazines do tend to recruit from within. But for whatever reason, it is not yet Mark's *time*. Instead, it appears to be mine, recruited from next door; I am the editor and, again improbably, I am Mark's boss. However, he's been at *Empire* for years and knows the ropes, and I've been at *Empire* for a month and need showing the ropes. It's a very delicate power balance. A handover of rope knowledge.

The voice on the other end of the phone, upbeat and over-familiar, says, 'Hi, Andrew?'

'Yes.'

'This is *let's-call-her* Jocasta from New Line. How's it going?'

'It's going fine.' I have barely unpacked my toiletries.

'I'd like to invite you to lunch with Patrick Bergin.'

'Who?' I realise this is rude, but his name does not ring any bells and she's saying it as if I should know who he is.

'Patrick Bergin. He's here promoting *Lawnmower Man II*, and he'd very much like to have lunch with you.'

'With me?'

'You are the editor of *Empire*?'

Now she's thrown me. I am the editor of *Empire*, Britain's biggest-selling movie magazine – and I have the Hessian daywear to prove it – but I didn't realise it was my passport to lunch with actors I have never heard of, who are starring in sequels that sound shit.

'Yes.'

'Well, Patrick would *really* like to have lunch with you.'

'I'm afraid I can't.' In other words: I'm afraid I don't want to. 'I'm only here for two days and I've got … *stuff* I have to do.'

'That's a shame. Well, we're here at the Majestic. Drop by and say hi.'

'OK. Thanks. Bye.'

I explained who it was to Mark and watched the envy evaporate from his puppyish face.

Welcome, I thought to myself, to the Cannes Film Festival. I hope Patrick Bergin found someone else equally important to dine with. I'll be on my yacht.

Geographically, *Empire* sits between *Select* and *Q*. We're next-door neighbours. This corridor of Mappin House is actually starting to resemble an architectural manifestation of my CV since leaving *NME*. It would be nice to try another corridor someday. For now, though, this is my own equivalent of Magazine Avenue from the Lloyd Cole song 'Pretty Gone', from his underrated *Easy Pieces* album, not that I'm interested in music any more. I'm interested in films. We're always in and out of each other's offices, borrowing Sellotape, looking for mugs, poaching staff.

I was happy enough at *Q*, Danny's number two. But even those without a masterplan soon find themselves sucked into the hierarchy at a magazine. Freelance writer covets the job of reviews editor, reviews editor covets the job of features editor, features editor covets the job of assistant editor, assistant editor covets the job of editor, editor covets the job of managing editor … then, once over the parapet of those jobs actually connected with putting magazines together, you're into the coveting of publisher, then executive publishing director, then editorial director, then managing director, then group managing editor, then chief executive, and suddenly the erstwhile freelance writer has either forgotten how to write a pithy review of a Bobby Fuller Four reissue, or there simply isn't the time any more.

I was happy being features editor at *Q*, commissioning the features, writing the occasional feature, doing some reviews for John, the odd round trip to Utrecht. Without the buffer of an assistant editor, if I was to covet any position, it had to be Danny's. But Danny wasn't going anywhere. He was General Franco or Fidel Castro. Just as he had solidified into the leader's role at the *NME* after Alan, he'd shaped *Q*, and the office culture of *Q*, in his own lager-than-life image. Everything was just kind of bigger, more overstated and pub-based. The thought of Danny leaving *Q* seemed as likely as the Queen Mother dying. He treated the magazine market as a battlefield, with rousing speeches made from an imaginary balcony in which he spoke of driving other titles into the sea. When another publisher launched a direct broadside against *Q* – a shameless *Rolling Stone* rip-off called *Encore* – Danny didn't blink before undermining it in the 'spine message' that runs up the side of the magazine. On our latest Morrissey cover, in homage to Moz's *Kill Uncle* album, it read 'Kill *Encore*'. How we laughed when *Encore* belied its own hopeful name and folded before the second issue.

The big man had left me in charge for a few issues when he'd become embroiled with *Total Sport*, a potential new Emap magazine launch being concocted behind a shroud of secrecy upstairs. But once the dummy issue had been made and given away free with the ghastly *FHM* so that they could 'research' it, Danny returned to his desk. And I returned to mine. To be honest, I enjoyed my brief taste of executive power, but it was power without responsibility. Danny and his military epigrams were only a flight of stairs away, and he was thus consulted at every stage.

Some people in publishing – indeed, any other office-based job – are driven by ambition. They are the air-kissers at parties who constantly glance over your shoulder, in case someone more advantageous has entered the room. Today, reviews editor; tomorrow, the world. For these people, a job is a means rather than an end. You always get the feeling that these people are passing through.

Being a can-do sort of bloke, I feel I can turn my hand to almost anything, so long as it doesn't involve physical danger, deep water or whistling. This is not because I am particularly clever, but because most things in the media are easy. Let me qualify that: most things in the media are easy *to do*, but not necessarily easy *to do well*. You can get by with very little in the way of acumen or experience or talent, providing you are prepared to busk furiously, and do a lot of huffing and puffing for the benefit of others, so that what you're doing looks more difficult.

When *Empire*'s editor, the terribly nice Phil – a man whose niceness actually extends to wearing a turtleneck sweater under a checked shirt – moved upstairs, as all editors careful not to rock the boat are wont to do, his job was advertised in the normal way. For some reason, it piqued my dormant ambition glands. I consulted the people on the fifth floor and asked, candidly, if there was any chance of Danny being moved off *Q* permanently. The people on the fifth floor said absolutely no chance.

So I applied for the top job at *Empire*.

I was interviewed for the top job at *Empire*.

And I got the top job at *Empire*.

'What's the greatest film of all time?'

'*The Poseidon Adventure.*'

'Welcome to Hollywood!'

I think I got the job because I had wisely shed my shoulder-length hair and sported a much less threatening bob to the interview. They didn't ask me if I would be prepared to go the whole hog and wear *long trousers* to the office should they offer me the position, but it was hinted at. I hinted back that yes I would. Unlike Malcolm X, I was prepared to sell out.

I was sad to leave my friends at *Q*. I really liked John and John and John and Adrian and Bill and Kim and Claire and Tim and Isabel and Lisa and Ken and Chris and Hugo and all the writers with the broadsheet bylines, and of course I really liked Danny, who had taught me all he knew, such as to put on the Helmet of Destiny when making difficult phonecalls to important record company people. (This existed; it was actually an orange hard hat he'd been given at a KLF stunt, with 'Helmet of Destiny' written on it, and he really did put it on when, say, he had to ring up Kenneth Pitt, David Bowie's manager between 1967 and 1970, and tell him that we'd lost a priceless photo of Bowie he'd lent us.)

When I left *Q*, in May, it was a bit like the moment in *The Jerk* where Steve Martin is seen off by his family, walks to the end of the drive and waits for the bus. I popped next door to my destiny, with a short detour across Oxford Street to Marks & Spencer's men's department.

'I'm looking for something in butterscotch … '

The Jerk is a film. I'm interested in films now.

*

So, here we are, at my inaugural Cannes, the *48e festival international du film*. As I take my first, awed steps along the world-famous Croisette in the mid-afternoon heat haze, I wonder how many more of these glamorous beanfeasts I will attend, and whether perhaps in future years the laminated pass slung round my neck will actually get me *into* anything, such as a film. Due to my very recent arrival in the film industry, my accreditation was applied for belatedly. As a result, it is yellow. Oh, it's official – it bears my name, my mugshot, the words 'Grande Bretagne', the Cannes laurel, the worrying serial number '0000', and it comes on a lanyard – but it actually gets me into less things than a member of the public. It barely got me into France. However, it hangs from my neck and that's all that matters. And I have Mark to look after me every step of the way.

'One thing you'll notice,' he informs me with a conspiratorial wink as we glide down the promenade, 'is that there are some very beautiful women at Cannes.'

I'm glad he told me this. I might not have spotted it otherwise.

Mark, a compact fellow with blue eyes and the sort of hair that would earn him the ironic nickname Curly in prison, acts as if he *owns* Cannes. This is clearly the sensible way to approach what is a carnival of vacuity, bullshit and pomp in a seaside town whose restaurants all put up their prices for a week every May. It's all about attitude. Behave like a tourist and you'll be treated like one by burly men in headsets and puffa jackets. I'm starting to think I have actually made a very astute suit choice. It may be cheap and made of sack but it behaves like an expensive suit from a distance and that's all that matters. I'm starting to look upon it as my Cannes suit. My Hollywood uniform.

We stroll into one of the big hotels to make contact with one of the big PR firms, DDA, and we do so with such confidence that nobody stops us or even affords us a questioning glance. And yet, outside the hotel on the pavement, members of the public gawp from behind barriers, forgetting that *anyone* can walk into a hotel. It's just a hotel. So even with a laminate that actually makes me the laughing stock of the international press corps and may as well actually be an albatross on a lanyard, I have learned to swan.

Mark and I catch up with the *Empire* top brass, Phil, Jerry and garrulous executive publishing director Barry, at Le Petit Majestic, favoured watering hole of British hacks, where we order traditional French pizza, feeling very much as if we are on holiday. Next, Mark escorts me to the British Pavilion, to which my joke laminate actually grants entrance and where I do my best not to look as if I am scanning the room for stars from behind my cheap Top Man shades. I don't see any stars, as there aren't any. If there were, my pass wouldn't have got me in here, would it?

Far more than in the rock world I know so well, the film business is a case of us and them.

'Quick, lads! It's Marisa Tomei on a jetty!'

Ah, that must be the international press corps.

Two months and two issues in, and although this is not something I'd bandy around, I can now say with some confidence that being the editor of a magazine is not as taxing as you might imagine, merely time-consuming and mind-consuming. It's just a series of decisions. You're not an eye surgeon; these decisions are not life or death.

Who goes on the cover?

What else is flagged up on the cover?

What colour do you make the 'flash' that runs across the bottom of the cover? Answer: yellow; it's been scientifically proven to be the best colour for a flash, so this particular decision doesn't take long.

How much are you willing to pay for a photograph of Bruce Willis to accompany the cover feature?

Are you prepared to pay for a writer to fly to LA to attend a press junket for a film on the vague promise of a 'one on one'?

Who wants to go to the pub?

Make a bad choice of cover and you could fail to reach projected sales figures for that issue, but nobody dies. Unless the amount of unsold copies are so vast that a man in WHSmith gives himself a heart attack trying to lift them back into the warehouse. Trade secret: projected sales figures are calculated by looking at last year's and adding a bit on. They're made-up figures. Nevertheless if you don't hit them, there will be an inquisition, at which your lighthearted response, 'But they're *made-up figures,*' can be used once and once only.

As the editor of a magazine, part of your job is to manage the staff. You are, in employment terms, a manager. The staff of *Empire* is small and manageable. There are six of us in total. Under my jurisdiction are an art editor (the smooth-talking, silk-shirted Boomer, so named because when he speaks you can hear him in reception), a features editor (the aforementioned ambitious godsend Mark), a reviews editor (the young, thrusting Ian), a news editor (Caroline, a superkeen émigré from *Smash Hits,* and another team-member with a faulty volume knob), and an editorial assistant (the life-saving Susie, who is actually my secretary, among other tasks, except we don't use that word any more). There's a further tier of freelance staff: a production editor (Bon Jovi fan Neil, who is actually on a short contract), a picture editor (the slumming-it Debs, also officially freelance), and a US editor (Jeff, who's on the other end of a transatlantic phone-line in LA, should we ever need to save on travel fares). I am their boss. They look up to *me,* and I look up to Phil, who is my managing editor.

I have never really been anyone's boss before. It feels a bit daft. Bosses are figures of fun – I've seen the sitcoms. Fortunately, *Empire* operates an open-plan office, so I am anything but a remote, ogre-like figure. I'm just sat over there.

Hello.

Who wants to go to the pub?

Here's the best thing about running a film magazine: you don't always need a cover story! Unlike a music magazine, where readers have been conditioned to expect a big star like Bono or Michael Stipe or Damon Albarn on the cover with a full and frank, in-depth interview inside, at *Empire*, you can just put a *film* on the cover.

My first issue, dated July 1995, had as its cover story a preview of films that are due out in the remainder of the year, which included *Batman Forever*. This meant we could just put a picture of Val Kilmer dressed as Batman on the cover. No interview with him inside or anything, just some information about the film and a quote from the director about Val's 'tremendous amount of depth, sensitivity and mystery'. What a piece of piss. Imagine if *Q* could just put a photo of Michael Stipe on the cover because R.E.M. have an album out later in the year. No need to take the photo – Warner Bros have already taken one for publicity purposes and it's free to use! Slap it on. Yellow flash. Ker-ching!

Free film-studio pictures are called 'specials'. They're not that special, but for a magazine like *Empire,* they are bread and butter – gratis high-quality transparencies of film stars, ready to use. However, because they are stage-managed and provided by the studio, their usage subtracts from the magazine's editorial independence and risks drawing accusations that *Empire* is merely a PR wing of the film industry, which it is.

So, here's my first *Empire* cover: 'KER-POW! *Batman Forever* Heads Up Our ULTIMATE SUMMER PREVIEW!' Ten pages of films that the readers can't see yet. In some cases, not until Christmas! And this passes for a cover story – not a bad-selling one either.

No takers for the pub, then?

I think the staff were scared of me when I arrived, or at least by my over-the-fence reputation, because rock'n'roll animals they are not. There is no pub culture at *Empire*. I had to drag them all round the corner to the Champion in my first week, individually, under the pretext of getting to know them. Their image of me was of some wild rebel boozehound – an image I systemically failed to dispel at the Emap Awards, an annual event that just happened to coincide with my arrival, proving at least that a haircut and a new suit had not sapped my superpowers. I believe I informed my new staff, with overbearing emphasis, that they were my best mates. I certainly put my arm around young Ian with the assurance, 'I've got big plans for you.'

The very act of putting my arm around a younger member of staff, albeit informed by strong drink, proved my first fatherly act. No matter that I am only a couple of years older than most of the staff – and possibly younger than Boomer – I am their editor, their protector, their dad, their cheerleader and their champion. I'd like to buy them all a drink, but they won't let me.

When *Select* moved over to Mappin House in 1993, the Champion instantaneously became the *Select* pub. It continues to serve Emap well – a nice, dingy, wooden cornerhouse set far enough back to avoid the tourist trade, with stained-glass windows depicting moustachioed champions of the past. It's a Samuel Smith pub, which means a constant parade of newcomers confidently ordering a Budweiser at the bar and being told, 'We only sell Sam Smith's beer.'

It's a rather quaint set-up, lacking only sawdust and dray horses. When you know your way around the Yorkshire-brewed Sam Smith range of beers, it's like being a member of a private club. Of the bottled beers, there's the Organic Lager, the Pure Brewed and the Imperial stout. On draught, it's a pint of either Old Brewery bitter; Cooking Lager, as it's known round Emap, the weakest at 4.5 per cent, and actually called Prinz; or Ayingerbrau, which is stronger (5.0 per cent) and colloquially referred to as 'a pint of Little Man' because of its distinctive pump featuring a small, alpine gentleman in a glass box. Then there's the Ayingerbrau D Pils, which is 5.9 per cent proof – you know when you've had two and a half pints of *that* at lunchtime.

This is not the kind of pub you expect to find in the South of England, never mind Central London, and yet there are three Sam Smith's pubs within easy walking distance of Mappin House. It's that little piece of W1 that will be forever Tadcaster.

Anyway, we drank an awful lot of beer there. And ate a lot of McCoys and nuts. Andrew Harrison once declared that the next *Select* staff meeting would be held at the Champ. I have tried to follow his example, but *Empire* are not *Q*, or *Select*, and it's unfair to try and mould them into that shape.

They're film people. Oh yes, and so am I.

Wow, there are a lot of bloody jellyfish in the sea. It's pulsating with live, translucent, toxic jelly. The sharks are all up here though, on the sun-sautéed terrace of the Hotel Du Cap, posh-est hotel in the world and perched on the sheer cliffs of the Cap D'Antibes peninsula. This is how exclusive and scum-resistant it is – they don't accept credit cards. Even suites, which we have to assume are the other side of pricey, must be paid for with cash. The surreal vision of Elizabeth Taylor or Bruce Willis or Princess Caroline of Monaco turning up with a wheelbarrow full of crisp francs appeals to me.

Mark's inside, interviewing Nicole Kidman for her new film, which is called *To Die For*. Nicole Kidman! The ginger one out of *Malice* and *Dead Calm*. She's famous and sexy! It's a round-table interview, a movie promo convention by which the star is interviewed by up to a dozen foreign journalists at once, round a table, who each then go back to their constituencies and write the interview up as if it was a one-on-one, which by definition, it wasn't. I'm sitting out here, one-on-nobody, a cold beer in hand, gazing at the primordial waves crashing on the rocks beneath and wondering how long it will be before I am ejected from the premises because of the cut of my suit, even though I have cash, and I understand cash is accepted here.

I know. The hierarchy's a bit wonky. It's as though I'm Mark's assistant, his bagman, his sidekick, twiddling my thumbs while he secures gold-dust copy for the magazine and gets to flirt with a film star into the bargain. The only film stars I ever interviewed as a music journalist were Josh Charles, Jim Belushi and Frances Barber. Josh Charles? He was one of the pupils in *Dead Poets Society*.

'*Excusez-moi, Monsieur …*'

Oh, here we go. I turn around to see a crisp waiter hovering at my table. I've been found out. Now, how best to deal with this? I crane my neck past the waiter, looking for Mark. He'll vouch for me. He knows the PR company. Maybe I should say I'm waiting for Patrick Bergin.

'Can I get you another drink?'

This blindsides me.

'Yes. P-please,' I stutter, forgetting my O-level French oral. 'Another beer?'

'Certainly, Monsieur.'

I swear he does a little bow before turning on his heels. Does this mean I've made it? Me? At the Hotel Du Cap? On the terrace? In my Cannes suit? Flashing the exact same currency as Sharon Stone or Johnny Depp or Greta Scacchi? Is that all it takes to join the international jet set on the French Riviera? A Hessian jacket and trousers from Marks & Spencer and some cheap plastic shades from Top Man?

Maybe it's the beer, but I suddenly feel invincible, like a Master of the Universe, like someone who's entitled to order a beer in a seaside hotel bar and pay for it. And look who's just standing there, three tables away, holding a colourless drink with lime and a sprig of mint in it – Christopher Penn! *Reservoir Dogs*! He's also wearing a light-coloured suit and sunglasses. It's the uniform. In this head-rush of confidence, I feel like waving over to him.

'Hey, Chris! Loved you as Nice Guy Eddie!'

'Thanks, man.'

I'd stand up and extend my hand. He'd come over. 'Andrew. Editor of *Empire*. Britain's biggest-selling movie magazine.'

'Good to meet you.' He'd pump my hand. 'I love London. Had some major times there.'

'Well, next time you're in town …'

Chris would look around and peer back at me over his sunglasses. 'Hey, I hate all this movie star wheelbarrow bullshit – let's hop in a cab and hit the bars.'

'I can't. I have to wait for Mark.'

'Hey, fuck Mark!' There's a hint of menace in his voice now. He downs his drink.

'Yeah, fuck Mark,' I reply. 'I'm *his* boss, he's not *my* boss.'

'Right on.'

I'd toss a coupla notes down on the table and follow Chris Penn out of that terrace, through the lobby and into a waiting car. Me and Chris.

'What is that?' he'd ask. 'Hessian?'

The speedboat – which I believe is actually called a 'launch' in seafaring parlance – pulls alongside the jetty, outboard motor still running. Its job is to ferry Jerry, the men from the agency and I out to the *Empire* yacht, which is just a hired yacht, but we hired it. Its name is the *Rosenkavalier*.

I'm not a great one for boats. Last time I reluctantly found myself on open water was a pleasure cruise to the Isle of Mull in 1990 and I was sick over the side. But the purpose of this trip is not pleasure, it's in the line of duty. The *Empire* yacht awaits, with a buffet lunch, drinks and some very special guests promised, and even though I've turned down Patrick Bergin and walked into two hotels without being stopped and seen Christopher Penn in the flesh, I can't yet walk on water.

The cost of the yacht and the speedboat and the buffet and the booze will be absorbed by *Empire*'s marketing budget. This will be pretty steep – Jerry tells me that the *Rosenkavalier* costs £80K to hire for two days alone, and there's no such thing as a free launch – but it's difficult to put a price on 'presence' at an international film festival. Ask the makers of *Barb Wire*, who have hoardings up the length of the Croisette for Pamela Anderson's first theatrical post-*Baywatch* excursion, and it's not even out until next year. They've only got a poster. And Pamela Anderson's tits.

Mark may be nominally out here to cover the festival, to secure interviews and see some preview screenings, but our number one job is ambassadorial. We're here to represent the magazine, to help with its brand extension, to be seen where the beautiful people are seen, to move and shake, to press flesh, to grip and grin, to bow and scrape if appropriate, and to let the Riviera know that *Empire* is in town. For the advertisers being entertained by Jerry, it's one big jolly. For us, it's abject misery, obviously.

I can safely say this is the first yacht I have ever boarded. In many ways, it's a stupid parody of the high life – I mean, what's so great about having a drink in the sea? I only hope I'm not sick over the side. The other Emap bigwigs – Barry, Phil, business manager Delyth – are already aboard, along with Matt, benign and lanky editor of *Premiere*, and Mark, doing his bit, probably longing for all the 'beautiful women' back on the Croisette, or his new girlfriend Nicole Kidman.

Barry spots me as I collect my flute of champagne from a proffered tray. 'College!' he exclaims, garrulously.

Thanks, Barry – just what I need in front of account managers to cement my authority. Perhaps I should tell everybody that you got Delyth to iron your trousers back at the *Empire* apartment this morning. (Mine don't need ironing; they're supposed to look crumpled.)

The Emap suits and their freeloading clients all appear very confident and entitled out here on the deck, eating canapés and sipping champagne and swapping small talk. I mingle, hoping that the bubbly will quickly buoy my confidence in case I have to put on some kind of show as the editor. I no longer feel like a Master of the Universe. I feel like a boy on a boat. I feel like College.

'Will Smith's here,' Mark whispers to me, bursting with excitement. 'And Jerry Bruckheimer.'

Fuck. Will Smith *and* Jerry Bruckheimer. On the *Empire* yacht. How the hell did we lure them out here? It's not as if it's that easy to get away once you're aboard. More to the point: *who* are Will Smith and Jerry Bruckheimer?

I'm the editor of Britain's biggest film magazine and I can't place either Will Smith or Jerry Bruckheimer. Where are they? Perhaps I'll recognise them if I see them. Maybe they'll have cigars, to help differentiate them from the other guests.

'Where are they?' I ask Mark.

'Inside somewhere.'

'Have you seen them?'

'I interviewed Bruckheimer, but I haven't seen Will Smith.'

I scan the deck of the *Good Ship Brand Extension*. Everybody looks famous and nobody does. That's Cannes. That's sunglasses, actually. It's clear that I should be pretty impressed by the presence of Will Smith and Jerry Bruckheimer, and I am – in theory. I hope that's exactly how I look – impressed – but I really don't have a clue who they are. They must be famous, or else why the *sotto voce*? And why would Mark be interviewing one of them? But I can hardly ask my own features editor who they are. It's bad enough that I am already reliant on Mark for, well, *everything*, without showing my music journalist's ignorance.

We're joined by Belinda, who works for one of Emap's women's magazines, I think.

'Will Smith's here,' Mark whispers to her.

'Wow!' she says.

'And Jerry Bruckheimer,' I add, in what I consider a pretty slick move.

'Who?' she says, clearly unselfconscious about the knowledge hierarchy.

Good question. Mark leaps to my defence.

'Simpson and Bruckheimer,' he says, as if this explains everything. She's none the wiser. 'They produced *Bad Boys*.'

Brilliant. He's a producer. In other words, who gives a toss? Who cares about producers? I mean, I'm glad he's here, on our yacht, if he produced this *Bad Boys* film, and I'm happy that Mark managed to secure an interview with him, but really, he's no Chris Penn, is he?

It becomes apparent from the conversation that Will Smith is in *Bad Boys*, which is why he's with this Bruckheimer fella. Mustn't grumble: I'm on a yacht with Will Smith, the actor, whoever he is, and his producer. I'm still a star magnet.

'More champagne?'

'Yes, please!'

After half an hour, it transpires that Will Smith and Jerry Bruckheimer have left the yacht. They probably took the very launch that ferried us out here back to dry land. I don't think anybody actually *saw* Will Smith. Perhaps nobody else knows what he looks like either. Perhaps he was never here and I never was on a yacht with him. Perhaps I'm not such a twat.

No, thinking about it, I am.

'Hi. I'm Andrew, editor of *Empire*!'

'All right, mate!' There follows an enthusiastic shake of hands. We're both shouting to be heard above the din.

'You were great!'

'Thanks! Decent party!'

'Thanks!'

At last, I am talking to a star at the Cannes Film Festival.

Admittedly, it's the baldy bloke out of Freak Power, who've just played a set at the *Empire* party, but it's someone to tick off, and at least he's friendly. The irony is crushing: I'm the editor of a film magazine, and I'm talking to a pop star.

The party is just one of many being held in Cannes tonight, but it's still a big deal for the magazine, being the first time we've dipped a toe in this particular body of promotional water. Also, it's on the beach, which means Barry and Jerry and their clients can glamorously arrive on a launch from the *Rosenkavalier* and step off the boat and straight into the do. Apparently, after I'd left the yacht to go back to the apartment, it was boarded by pirates – the Hawaiian Tropic girls: a dozen tall, tanned blondes promoting sun-tan lotion, who stayed for two hours, flirted outrageously and left with bottles of champagne.

We're actually piggybacking the beach party with MTV. It's officially the MTV/*Empire* Party, although everybody calls it the MTV Party except for Emap employees. I spent much of the afternoon *literally* extending our brand with Phil and Mark, putting up large *Empire* posters all around the venue with gaffer tape. I felt noble for getting my hands dirty in the name of the magazine. It reminded me of when Alan Lewis got behind the counter of the *NME* stall at Glastonbury all those years ago. This is the *Empire* stall, except we're not selling boxer shorts and cassettes, we're selling … *Empire*. The idea of *Empire*. The notion of *Empire*. Essence of *Empire*. I know, it's bollocks.

Apart from Freak Power, who are here to do a job of work, the party – thronging with revellers grooving ironically to disco tunes – appears to be devoid of stars. Everybody at Cannes seems to be somewhere else. On another yacht, at another party, in another hotel. We're here to convince the industry that *Empire* is a player. But *Empire* is a magazine.

Eventually, I decide to trudge home. At about 10.30 p.m., word went round the party that Tina Turner had turned up. I strained my neck trying to catch a glimpse of her – the top of her thatched hair would have done it. I know she's also ostensibly a pop star, but she was in *Mad Max III: Beyond Thunderdome* and *Tommy*, which makes her a film star, too, and you have to take what you can get in this carnival of vacuity, bullshit and pomp. I wanted another tick. But the second she arrived, she was whisked away from the main party to a private VIP enclosure – an enclosure to which I, as editor of the magazine who are half-throwing the party, had no access. This rather summed up my frustration with the whole experience.

Without making any fond farewells, I push my way out, back onto the Croisette. I am warned by the bouncers that I won't be let back in once I've left, and I say that this is fine, as I'm not coming back.

Enjoying the cool breeze through the pores in my Hessian suit, I trot confidently back towards the apartment, using my natural compass for finding my way back to places in foreign cities, honed during my years as a rock journalist in Chicago and Utrecht. Cannes is one of the highlights of the film calendar, but if you ask me, it's also a bit rubbish.

I'm first back at the apartment, so I tuck myself up in my camp bed in the living room and drift off to sleep, pondering that evergreen philosophical conundrum: If an ageing soul singer arrives at a party and no one sees her, was she really there at all?

I'm not sure I've found my next spiritual home.

11

Having My Hair Mocked by Noel Gallagher

It's been another long year, 1996, and this is my reward. This simple wooden box, which is designed to give me the extra physical stature to match my perceived stature. Plenty of that round the waist, of course, pushing against the buttons of my Hugo Boss, but I need about six inches underfoot, otherwise the statuesque Mark Ellen will tower over me.

Yes, the man who interviewed me for the *Select* job four Christmases and four jobs ago, and with whom I plotted the invention of Britpop in a poky Beak Street café, is my co-host. He and I will co-present the 1996 *Q* Awards from this very stage at one o'clock today, and, thanks to the timely intervention of this box, we will address the assembled music-biz luminaries at roughly the same height.

Ad revenue, ad spend, marketing spend, ad yield, flat plans, promotions, projections, paginations, cover mounts, house ads, subscription offers, year-on-year increases, period-on-period increases, budget meetings, production weeks, awaydays, Frontline, Colour Systems, Cooper Clegg, St Ives, account numbers, assessments – welcome to my world.

There is nowhere to park around Mappin House, no Emap underground car park or anything. It's all sky-high NCPs and coin-gobbling parking meters. Hence, I don't actually drive my company car into work at the company that has bestowed the car upon me. Nor does anyone else. It's literally for private use only. A token. A metallic-green status symbol. How did that happen?

The world looks very different today. At least, the world looks very different from my office. Which used to be Danny's office. The Helmet of Destiny is still here, on the bookshelf next to the back issues, but I choose not to wear it. That was Danny's gag.

I'm not Danny, although I have put on a cummerbund of weight since I got the top-dog job. I now weigh in at about thirteen and a half stone. I was twelve when I started. I was too embarrassed to take my shirt off when we were on holiday. That's the weight of responsibility. One and a half stone of responsibility.

So, big fat boss man, what happened to being a music journalist? Wasn't that once the amazing Technicolour dream job? I rarely interview bands any more. In August I asked John, who's now features editor, to commission me to interview Billy Bragg, and it was entirely pleasant, blowing the dust off my old Dictaphone and doing a bit of transcription. At least it put my byline on a feature across four pages. Hello! I'm still here! The work I now do is almost entirely unseen. Being the editor of the World's Greatest Music Monthly is an invisible labour. Unlike presenting a late-night ITV film review programme. But enough of such frippery. Don't give up the day job.

I have been the editor of *Q* for a year and a bit. That's proper. That's tantamount to a tenure. The beginnings of a reign. That's about sixteen planning meetings; thirty-two late nights at Colour Systems (two per issue); one round of staff assessments and pay rises; one *Q* Awards; one Senior Editorial Conference at a hotel in Sussex; six sets of ABC circulation figures; and a lot of Pils. Taking over *Q* in the summer of 1995 was like being winched in a breeches buoy from the deck of a destroyer onto the deck of an aircraft carrier. You are, in that wind-buffeted instance, a speck, dangling. Your passage from one vessel to the next makes no difference to the trajectory of either. They both keep steaming along on the same, fixed course. You just end up on the bridge of a new ship, where the crew already have matters in hand. A new editor's impact on a large-circulation, mass-market glossy magazine is minimal. It's a rearrangement of deckchairs at best.

After my brief baptism-by-bullshit on *Empire* (and we'll talk about *how* brief in a moment), I felt I was versed enough in the ways of man-management to move on to a fresh challenge. Actually, that's toss. Fate intervened. What actually happened was this: I attended the three-day Senior Editorial Conference at a country house hotel in deepest Sussex, and it emerged, in a stage-managed kind of way, that the company had signed off on the launch of a brand-new title.

This was a big deal for Metro, as launches – which notoriously cost around £1 million – are few and far between. Andrew Harrison, my old boss from *Select*, had, it seemed, been toiling away on failed launches in a broom cupboard for years. (We like to think of them all as variations on a fictional title called *Techno for the Smaller Man*, but then we are cruel.) Anyway, to suitable fanfare, with the whole of Metro's senior editorial, marketing and advertising staff seated, hungover, around a large doughnut of tables in a conference room at a country house hotel in deepest Sussex, with blotters and crystal decanters of lime and blackcurrant cordial present, and unfounded dread about team-building assault courses being sprung upon us hanging in the air, the launch was made official.

It was … *Total Sport.*

And its launch editor was to be … Danny Kelly.

Wait a minute. Had I not been assured by the people on the fifth floor that Danny Kelly would *never* leave his post at *Q*? And was that not the only reason I had disloyally jumped ship and gone all films? I felt shafted, albeit shafted in that very specific way when you are offered a really good job, with share options and pension scheme and bonuses. I can never hope to really understand what goes on in Danny's mind, but you have to ask yourself: had he been planning to leave *Q* all along and go all sport? When you are established as a specialist in one field, it raises eyebrows when you move sideways into another. Anyone who knows Danny even on a very shallow, down-the-pub level, which is, let's face it, most of us, knows that he is obsessed by music and sport. With a bit of military history thrown in. But is sport his true calling? Has music been a twelve-year distraction? Facing his forties now, does he feel it's time to settle down and ease into a new role as car-coated sports pundit in the dugout? Could I reverse my defection and ease back into my original role as rock pundit?

At the next tea break, I approached Barry, now managing director.

'College!' he probably exclaimed, as he always did. It was bad enough when he did it as executive publishing director.

'Barry, can I have a quiet word?'

'Let me guess,' he twinkled.

We moved outside onto the terrace, balancing our teacups in our saucers. Barry's not as wide as Danny, but he's taller, so I'm just as physically dwarfed by the man's presence, even in his casuals.

'If Danny's launching *Total Sport* …'

Barry knew what was coming next.

'… who's going to run *Q*?'

'We'll advertise the job and see who comes forward.'

'But isn't it a bit shortsighted, taking Danny off the magazine that pays for all the other magazines and leaving it without an editor?'

Emap is a great company. You can accuse the managing director of being shortsighted, over coffee. He's also just Barry, who started out as a music journalist like the rest of us. He used to write pithy reviews of Bobby Fuller Four reissues and fly to

Utrecht with A Flock of Seagulls. Now he's the top man. He is the garrulous, Northern Irish embodiment of the Emap Dream.

'I hear what you're saying, College. Let's talk further back at Mappin.'

He could sense my panic. I loved *Q*. I loved it like I used to love the *NME*. I only left because I'd reached a career bottleneck, and Danny was *never* going to leave, even though nobody *never* leaves. We're all just specks, dangling. I had found myself the editor of *Empire*. I'd bought Mickey Rourke suits and been on a yacht with Jerry Bruckheimer and denounced rock'n'roll. I was a Hollywood player now. And Danny was about to leave *Q* with the door wide open. Fuck! Somebody else might get the job that was rightfully mine!

This was an entirely new sense of panic. I was thirty years old. I had been in gainful, deskbound employment for an unbroken period of five years. The ink was not yet dry on my job description at *Empire*. I had entered a new world. When Hugh Grant was caught with his penis in the mouth of a prostitute on Sunset Boulevard in June, I was sought out for comment by the *Sun*. I didn't even have anything profound to say ('stars have withstood these kinds of scandals in the past'), but I was quoted anyway, as the editor of *Empire*. I had arrived. I was part of the warp and weft of the movie world. I had even managed to do what all editors do: fast-track a couple of my old mates onto the freelance writing staff of the magazine.

Stuart Maconie was dispatched to interview Gillian Anderson, which went off without a hitch, while Dave Cavanagh was sent off on two set visits, *Fierce Creatures* and *Stealing Beauty*, where he proved himself something of an acquired taste among the film PRs there to nursemaid him. A man of few words, except on the page, he didn't say much, which is the Cav's style, honed over years of insinuating himself into the inner circles of world-famous rock bands – there's nothing like *not* getting on R.E.M. or Nirvana's nerves in the dressing room or tour bus if you want them to treat you as one of their own, and laconic, nonchalant indifference actually pays dividends in this *milieu*. It doesn't play so well when you're levered into the well-oiled mechanical workings of the movie biz, where gushing is required etiquette, 'hanging out' a luxury open only to *Vanity Fair* and *Esquire*, and actually getting up in the middle of a 'roundtable' interview because it's not very interesting is a crime punishable by excommunication. The Cav did this during one of the roundtables for *Stealing Beauty*. Just got up, wordlessly, from the table of foreign hacks and went back to his room, probably inwardly disgusted by the whole sterile set-up and wishing he was on the road with Urge Overkill. I'm quite proud, looking back, to have put a small pole into the film industry's spokes. They have it too easy.

I'd done *all that*, and yet here I was, in a country house hotel in Sussex, aquiver. This is what happens inside the feudal system of publishing. I had become one of those people who look over shoulders. I was literally looking over the shoulder of *Empire* in case *Q* should walk in. Not content with being the editor of one best-selling magazine, I wanted to be the editor of another. Greedy, greedy bastard. This was the panic of avarice.

Q does pay for all the other magazines, by the way. I've seen the spreadsheets. I've attended Delyth's lectures. Without the revenue of Metro's top earners, which includes *Empire*, and, coming up on the inside leg, the ghastly *FHM*, the other magazines would have to play the mouth organ in Oxford Street for their picture budgets.

Back at Mappin, after the conference, I had my audience with Barry, and it turned out to be the shortest job interview I'd sat since Sainsbury's in 1981, albeit for much higher stakes.

'So, you want to be the editor of *Q*, do you?'

'Yes, please.'

'OK then.'

I know my truncated tenure at *Empire* has gone down in Emap folklore as one issue, but it was actually three issues: the Ultimate Summer Preview, the 100 Sexiest Movie Stars of All Time and *Die Hard With a Vengeance* – suitably arch coverline: 'Is it hot in here or is it Bruce Willis?' – at least one of which heralded a proper, one-on-one interview with an actual film star in the old-school style, albeit one we had to buy in from an American stringer. It's none the less a triptych. A trilogy. A triathlon.

Chief benefactor of my exit from *Empire* was, naturally, Mark, my loyal, Sancho Panza-like features editor whose *time* had arrived sooner than expected. He filled the editor's shoes with minimum fuss, Ian got Mark's job ('I've got big plans for you'), and the assorted Jocastas of film PR probably breathed a sigh of relief. No more taciturn, maverick rock journalists on set visits. The staff must have been happy, too: no more meetings in the pub.

The game of musical chairs continued. Danny became managing editor of *Q,* a job he was to combine with being editor of *Total Sport* (or *Partial Sport* as we all call it, since it appears mainly to be about football, and we are cruel). Before he went, he kindly poached me John Harris from the *NME* to be *Q*'s new features editor – a mustard-keen young pamphleteer and Oxbridge grad from Wilmslow's Labour ghetto who'd started out filing reviews of Thousand Yard Stare from Manchester, where he was on a postgraduate politics course. We were lucky to have him.

And the migration from *NME* to *Q* goes on to this day. Now, thanks to the steady, low-octane progress of *Mojo* – or *Nojokes* as we call it, because we are cruel – there's even somewhere for old *Q* writers to retire. Fred Dellar ended up there, and quite right, too. Not every music journalist is a film correspondent or a sports writer trying to get out. Some stick to what they know best, and God bless them. God bless me, in fact, as finally I think I have found my spiritual home.

*

'Are you going to the IPD Awards?' February 1996. Delyth was clearly in something of a flap.

'Never heard of them.'

'International Press Directory?'

'Nope.'

'You've won one.'

'I have?'

'*Q* has. Best International Something …'

'Quite an honour.'

'Somebody should go and accept it.'

'Absolutely. When is it?'

'Tonight. Dorchester Hotel. Six-thirty for seven. I've got a spare invite up here. Can you make it?'

At which point I sighed and tutted like a teenager who's just been told to tidy his room. 'Do I *have* to?'

'It's Best International Something!'

She talked me into it. This was the editor's burden. Still sighing, I went round the corner to Moss Bros, hired a dinner suit, white shirt and dicky bow, cancelled all plans, which probably involved going to see the Boo Radleys, and started work on a speech, without actually knowing what the award was for, who was giving it to me, or why. It snowed that night. The do itself was very formal, no fun at all, populated by balding, middle-aged middle managers from across the European publishing spectrum called things like Xavier and Fabio and François, who talked all the way through the dogged warm-up routine by Kryten from *Red Dwarf*. When I was finally called up onstage to collect the award for Best International Something, which was fashioned after a giant roll-on deodorant, I was determined to lighten the mood with some jokes of my own, to amuse Delyth and the advertising types on our table if nothing else. I began with this misjudged drugs innuendo:

'Well, I'm more used to attending music business award ceremonies, so it's quite a change to have the snow on the *outside* of the building.'

Response: nothing.

I considering explaining that 'snow' was slang for 'cocaine', which certain people in the music biz are rumoured to ingest, but instead soldiered on with some pre-prepared family material about those magazines that never win awards: *Men's Ill-Health*, *Impractical Boat Owner* and *Macramé Monthly* incorporating *What Knot?* Tried and tested zingers that have generated howls of laughter around pub tables, these raised barely a titter. Lost in translation, I'm saying. In fact, *Men's Ill-Health* elicited some booing from the publishers of … *Men's Health*, who thought I was taking the piss out of their secretly gay publication.

I exited, pursued by a deafening silence, and handed gladly back to Kryten – who wasn't even dressed as Kryten for instant robot-faced laughs, but as the chap who plays him, not that I think any of these ageing Iberian lotharios had heard of *Red Dwarf* anyway.

If I learned anything that soulless night it was to get myself to Burton's, buy myself a serviceable black suit for similar future emergencies, and a bow-tie, which I would keep inside the Helmet of Destiny on the bookshelf. On the plus side, I got my face in *Hello!* magazine. They printed a line-up shot of the winners in the following week's edition because their proprietor Eduardo Sánchez Junco had won something. There we all were, clutching our deodorants, and only one of us making a stupid, ungrateful, sneery face for the camera. Very grown-up.

Editor's daily routine: rise at 7 a.m. regardless of what time I went to bed the night before. Choose regulation Ben Sherman to wear with black suit, my seventh, purchased from Burton's to save time and money hiring evening wear for awards ceremonies.

Leave the flat with no breakfast inside me – no time or appetite for that. Catch my usual two buses to Brixton, take the Tube to Oxford Circus, my mind already spinning with *Q*-related matters. You can never switch off. Pick up an orange juice and a McDonald's Big Breakfast, i.e. a polystyrene plate with a polystyrene lid containing, with military precision, two hash browns, some bacon, a kind of burger which is actually a sausage and some wet scrambled egg that's suspiciously white and not the traditional yellow. Arrive at the office at 8.30 a.m., an hour before anyone else gets in, and two hours before the phones start ringing, and creep into my office to consume my takeaway fuel without pleasure or sensation. Make attempt to reduce size of in-tray. Take two Anadin Extra with orange juice. Draw up a list of things to do, based on things carried over from previous day's list of things to do. Wander over to design department out-tray to check chromalins. Go and sit in sanctuary-like toilet cubicle with head in hands. Wait for the day to start.

Lunchtime, convince staffer or visiting freelance writer to accompany me to the Champ, there to consume the requisite two and a half pints of Pils. Feel enjoyably woozy and cauterised. Line stomach on the way back to the office by dropping into McDonald's for either Big Mac or Double Cheeseburger, depending on enormity of afternoon ahead, accompanied by extra-large Coke, or Snapple from newsagent, again, depending on enormity. Retreat to my office again to consume this parody of lunch, designed only to reduce effects of alcohol in preparation for whatever meetings the rest of the day holds. My PA Julie knows to hold all my calls while I'm getting special sauce all over my face.

Work through until around 6 p.m., beating the mid-afternoon lull into submission with cakes for the office from Marks & Spencer. If it's a production week, in which case evenings are built-in for senior staff, further refreshments will be provided. Some days I'm more of a caterer than an editor.

The last two nights of an issue's production cycle are spent at Colour Systems in Islington, where our layouts are turned into four-colour films, and passed on-site by a quorum of myself, Bill, John, art editor Shem and Danny Eccleston, the beaming, Communist-raised production editor we poached from the *NME*. Our reward for this unpaid overtime is a curry on Chapel Market. As editor, I'm the last man out of the building, which can be as late as one or two o'clock in the morning. When I was features editor, Danny Kelly would magnanimously send the rest of us home at midnight in account cabs, so that's what I do, although Danny Eccleston or Shem might feel duty-bound to stick it out until the last set of films is taped up inside a huge cardboard folder and handed over personally to the Welsh cab driver who ferries this precious cargo back to Caerphilly, where, improbably, *Q* is printed.

After this final late night, even I will stay in bed the next morning. But by midday, we're all back in the office, filling out expenses, and the whole damn thing starts all over again.

What a difference a year and a bit in the saddle makes. If I'm actually *not* the editor of *Q* and in fact it's all been an elaborate practical joke, then what have I been doing for the last sixteen months? Shouldn't a giggling Noel Edmonds jump out at some point and cast off his disguise?

I attended my second Senior Editorial Conference in the summer, this time something of a practised old-timer. It was held at the same country house hotel in deepest Sussex, but this time I was there alongside John Harris, who'd left *Q* to become editor of *Select*, a lightning ascent up the greasy pole. We were peers now, decision-makers, top dogs, and we celebrated that fact by, frankly, mucking about like schoolboys after the blotters and decanters had been put aside for the evening. At one particularly abandoned juncture, we led an athletic but nihilistic game of repeatedly diving off the terrace into some bushes, joined by some of the younger ad execs. This was dismissed by our superiors as a healthy release of steam after another day of workshopping and overhead-projector presentations. It's something of a blur, but I believe I may have climbed a sturdy vine up the side of the hotel and entered the building via a first-floor window. A memorable team-building exercise.

Unfortunately, Emap was informed after the conference that certain rare, irreplaceable shrubs in the hotel grounds were irreparably damaged during our stay and that we would not be welcome back there on future occasions. Rock and roll!

What kind of editor have I turned out to be? Not exactly legendary, notorious or earth-moving. I doubt I strike the fear of God into anybody, and I certainly never do much more than raise a few smiles at meetings on the fifth floor. But I'll settle for a crowd-pleaser. Danny was nothing if not an entertaining Mohicanned Tartar of Rock Publishing, and I'd like to think that I have at least carried on the fine tradition: a happy office is a hard-working office. Don't ask your team to do anything you wouldn't be prepared to do. Lead from the front: first at the bar, last in the taxi. Although I have always had my bedrock PA Julie, a blonde surfer-against-sewage who's mates with The Jesus and Mary Chain and dreams of being in Fuerteventura whenever she's not, I have made it my business to fill the industrial-sized teapot with boiling water at regular intervals. If that's my legacy, I can live with it: he sometimes made the tea.

And when it's someone's birthday, or someone's leaving, or the quarterly ABC figures are up, or it's Friday, I'll nip round the corner to Oddbins for beers of the world and champagne. If John Harris wants to have a screen-grab of Eric Manchester professionally blown up to poster size for the office wall, I will sign it off as a legitimate expense – Eric Manchester being the thinly veiled parody of Beatles press officer Derek Taylor in *The Rutles*. If the office stereo is looking a bit sad, I'll arrange for systems editor Rob to rustle up a brand-new set of separates from Richer Sounds in exchange for a three-page feature. If Pizza Hut introduces something called a Stuffed Crust Pizza, which appears to conceal an inner tube of stringy melted cheese about its doughy rim, I'll suggest a team-building lunch at that very eaterie. I may not be a legend, but I do a good lunchtime.

Yes, we have lived high on the hog at *Q* for the past year, with a record ABC circulation in our tenth anniversary year of 215,000 to keep us in the manner to which we have all become dangerously accustomed.

And to cap it all: we have a guest list for the 1996 *Q* Awards that actually beggars belief. Having turned up for the last two years, our old pal Tony Blair is on tape ('Ten years in power with no opposition – sounds good to me'), as is Alanis Morissette ('I'm in Mexico right now'), and Burt Bacharach is represented by a telegram sent from the almost-famous zip code Beverly Hills 90212 congratulating Elvis Costello, but everybody else is here. And I mean *everybody else*.

Underworld's 'Born Slippy' accompanies a video montage of every *Q* front cover to date, *shouting, lager, lager, lager, lager,* eighteen of which I worked on as features editor or acting editor, fourteen of which I worked on as editor. *Lager, lager,* it's actually physically impossible not to let out a little yelp of excitement as each one of these flashes past, *lager, lager,* with a quiet moment of knowing reflection when Bruce Springsteen, *lager, lager* is followed by Morrissey and the trajectory of so many lives in this room was altered for ever, *lager, lager* … followed by a parade of birthday messages from the likes of Belinda Carlisle, Phil Collins, Ian Hislop, Mike Mills, Sheryl Crow, Peter Gabriel, Joe Cocker, Luther Vandross and Damon, a galaxy ruined only by Tom Petty, who tries to kill the party mood by saying, 'We're not down with doing gratuitous shit for English rock magazines. Maybe when we're really broke we'll do that kind of shit, we'll grovel to English rock magazines. For now, fuck you!'

No, fuck you, horse face! We're having the lunchtime of our lives here.

Next, a specially filmed item from the set of *Brookside*, organised by my new pal Mal Young, outgoing series producer and massive *Q* fan, in which Sinbad and Julia Brogan argue over a copy of the magazine outside Ron Dicko's Trading Post: 'I'm in the middle of reading about that Liam Galahad fella,' she shrieks. Meanwhile, that Liam Galahad fella sucks down another gratis Carlsberg while Patsy explains the joke to him on table fourteen.

I should have stayed off the booze, but I needed something to calm my nerves and had a snifter for elevenses, and now I'm standing here, waiting to mount the podium, my heart racing, perspiration gathering beneath my viciously waxed quiff. Mark's done this every year since the *Q* Awards began, in 1990 at Ronnie Scott's. This is my first time. It's important. We take the stage, I step up on my wooden box and the prizegiving can commence. Yes, the Hugo Boss is new. It's pure wool. That's eight suits, although the first three are now very much out of service so don't really count.

All 350 guests are seated before us. I can't see the whites of their eyes but I know Mick Jagger and Bono and Rod Stewart and Johnny Marr and George Martin and Elvis and Bob Geldof and Brian Eno and Neil Tennant and Shaun Ryder and the Galahad brothers and Peter Blake and Jarvis Cocker and the Manics and three of Take That and Apple press officer Derek Taylor (Eric Manchester!) and Everything But The Girl and Caroline Aherne and Baddiel and Skinner and Ian Broudie and Father Ted are out there. I also know that one of our most important guests is still somewhere out near Heston services on the M4, but the 'limo bike' that's delivering him here from Chelsea's training ground just outside Heathrow's Terminal 4 is going at 'a fair old lick', so fingers crossed he'll make it for the penultimate award.

The next forty-five minutes are something of a blur. It's all over far too quickly, despite one or two lengthy citations from the elder statesmen and a couple of long walks from the back of the ballroom. One is so seeped in significance it's worth describing in detail.

Oasis win Best Act in the World Today, an award minted in 1990 and literally handed back and forth between R.E.M. and U2 ever since, like the Ashes. However, it might have been named specifically for the Gallagher brothers, to whom it seems less an honour, more a birthright. They both lap up the full quota of glory as they wind their way to the stage from table fourteen accompanied by 'Acquiesce'. Liam theatrically lights a B&H before embarking on the walk-up and takes an elongated drag. En route, followed by the spotlight, he comes past Mick Jagger and, with the dictionary definition of 'attitude', flicks cigarette ash on the living legend's head. Jagger is apparently oblivious to what is an almost Oedipal gesture: the defilement of the father figure. This sort of thing stops you in your tracks and reminds you, once again, that you are a mere spectator.

All I know is that I don't muff any of the scripted links, the true disparity of presenter height is only revealed when Mark and I emerge, statesmanlike, from behind our podium to greet each award-giver and winner, and that I shake hands with every member of U2, Johnny Marr, Ruud Gullit (for it is he, piped onstage by the carefully chosen walk-up music, 'Blue is the Colour') and star of the show Rod Stewart, who bends down, flips up the back of his finely tailored jacket and shakes his rump at an appreciative crowd, before thanking his label Warner Brothers for twenty-five years of service with the well-chosen words, 'Fucking money you've earned!' One short burst of Riverdance from Father Ted and a slurred speech by Bono later, and it's all over. Mark and I kindly leave the stage, and naughty Liam Galahad himself is the first to line himself up for the group photo, public-spirited behaviour indeed from a man who will refuse to get on a plane for an American tour if he doesn't feel like it and thinks nothing of using Mick Jagger's hair as an ashtray.

This is my reward for working myself ragged and eating myself to death for the last year and a bit. A wooden box, Liam coaxing other rock stars back onto the stage like a bluecoat, and a warm hand on my exit.

Passing between tables during the aftermath with Stuart, his lengthy fringe a telegenic counterpoint to my own waxed pompadour, we stop to say hello to Noel Gallagher, elegantly slumped next to table fourteen in his pricey brown anorak, an item he has kept zipped up for the duration, sipping from a bottle of Carlsberg and still clutching his Best Act in the World Today award.

'You two,' he says, preparing perhaps to say something complimentary about our radio work or recalling our first meeting backstage at the Brits, 'have got the worst fucking haircuts I have ever seen.'

It is, of course, an honour.

'At least I change mine occasionally,' comes my witty retort. Regrettably, I say it to Stuart as we walk away.

The postscript to every *Q* Awards is the aftershow, which follows the aftermath. Fittingly, for the best *Q* Awards ever, this is the best aftershow ever. The drill in previous years, once the staff of the Park Lane get the hoovers out, has been to repair to a nearby private members' club with Danny Baker and a few major record company heads of press, therein to drink the afternoon away until it turns into the evening, then see what happens. Last year, we went all formal and booked a room at the Hard Rock Café, and one or two actual pop stars tagged along: Louise Wener, Danny Goffey out of Supergrass and his wife. This year, high on that hog, we tapped up Delyth and booked the St James's Club in Piccadilly, staggering distance from the hotel, a nice place for a late-afternoon disco, and a cut above.

The room itself is dark and functional and the music is loud, but what makes it special is the private apartment. Anyone wearing a *Q* staff laminate is granted access to a private lift and whisked up to the penthouse floor. The upper sanctum. Here, as a reward for working so hard all year, *Q* staff have been gifted their own West End pied-à-terre for one night only. A roaring fire warms the sitting room, a private bar supplies our every liquid need and the bathroom is marbled with gold-plated fittings and kitted out with folded white face flannels and luxurious foreign ointments, fragrances and creams. There's even a bedroom, with access to a roof terrace, but the bedroom door is closed, even to *Q* laminates. It has been officially requisitioned by a higher power, otherwise known as Warner Brothers. *Fucking money they've earned!* In other words, by Barbara Charone, legendary head of press and *numero uno* 'friend of *Q*' – hey, she looks after Madonna, R.E.M., Cher and Rod. She's more powerful than any editor.

As we speak, outside in the street, Liam Galahad is being accosted by a reporter and photographer from the *News of the World,* who are brandishing a snap of the junior Oasis sibling with 'a mystery raven-haired beauty' taken in the Drum & Monkey pub in Maida Vale while Patsy was away filming in Wales. Liam very much objects to these gentlemen of the press having lain in wait for him outside the St James, hoping to stir up some trouble, and he responds in a manner best described as physical.

Upstairs, unaware of the tabloid sensation unfolding in the street below, I manage to gain entry to the bedroom using a combination of the 'special knock' and 'being the editor'. Barbara's lit-up face appears at the crack in the door, sees me, shouts, 'Andrew!' in her croaky Chicago voice and disappears back inside. A word ensues. She opens the door again and I'm in.

It's a very nice bedroom. It has Rod Stewart in it. Barbara has effectively created a VIP area within a VIP area. This is why she is head of press. The *News of the World* won't be brandishing anything at her member of rock nobility.

Later that evening, way past the hour when actual rock and pop stars are still to be found hanging around at the *Q* Awards aftershow – even Ian Broudie's gone home – Rod is on fine, crowd-pleasing form, unruffled by one guest telling him that her mum *really* loves him. Out on the roof, unseasonably warm for November, he regales all and sundry, and their plus-ones. The *Q* staff are a bit tired and emotional after a very long day, but Rod, fifty-one, is in full flight. Earlier, back in the bedroom, although the memory is so colour-saturated and exaggerated by refreshment it already seems unreal, he and I disappeared into a wardrobe, to continue a discussion of vital import away from the hubbub of his already-filling private boudoir. His bouncer guarded the door. Of the wardrobe. I did actually think in that moment my career had finally peaked and I should probably retire now. After all, once you've been in a wardrobe with Rod Stewart where else is there left to go? Under a desk with Elton John? Behind a filing cabinet with Jon Bon Jovi?

Jerry, publisher, makes his excuses and, with some reluctance, goes to leave.

'Ah, come on, Jerry!' I shout. 'Have another beer! We're on the roof! We've got Rod Stewart!'

'Yeah, come on, Jerry!' Rod joins in, truly a giant among *Q* Merit Award winners.

'I promised my wife I'd be back by ten,' Jerry insists. It is past ten.

'You got a phone?' Rod asks, warming up.

'Yeah, why?' asks Jerry. Trust Jerry to be the sort of media high-flyer with a mobile phone.

'Call your wife up and give me the phone.'

To howls of encouragement, Jerry does as Rod instructs. Getting a dialing tone, he hands his phone over.

'Hello, darling. It's Rod Stewart.'

A brief pause as he allows this information to sink in and for Mrs Jerry to pick herself up off the floor.

'Yeah, look, I've got Jerry here, and we're at the *Q* Awards party, and it's my fault, but it's going on a bit longer than expected.'

Jerry looks halfway between mortified and elated. It is, after all, the ultimate Get-Out-Of-*Le-Maison-Du-Chien*-Free card.

'So if it's OK with you, darling, 'cos it's only once a year, he's going to stay for one more drink. Is that all right?'

It's a rhetorical question, like, 'Do ya think I'm sexy?' Of course it's all right. Everything's all right. I'm all right. He's all right. We're all all right. And I've got the worst fucking haircut Noel Gallagher has ever seen.

Just try to imagine Beethoven, standing there on that podium, holding his baton ... he pronounces it bat-*on*, in the American way ... gracefully through the air, and the orchestra in his mind is playing perfectly ... if there's an orchestra in my mind, they're underwater, that's how my head feels, *underwater* ... How long have I been here, prone, on this settee? How many days have I been down? Longer than a week? Without a job to go to, I don't know what day it is ... Concentrate on the film ... Try to stay awake for the film ... There is a story that in order to write his music Beethoven literally sawed the legs off his piano so that he could lay his body flat on the ground with his ear pressed to the floor ... I don't want to be on the floor, I like it on the settee, the settee is like a bed, like a daytime bed, with my head pressed to the arm ... Mr Holland's getting emotional, something about pounding the keys to hear the vibrations, and he's welling up, it must be to do with his son, his son's deaf ... I can feel the vibrations ... the camera pans up so that we're looking down on the vinyl record going round and round, an out-of-body experience, looking down, I wish I was out of this body, but I'm in it, stuck right in it, the spinning vinyl dissolves into footage of a helicopter ... the Seventh Symphony into rotor blades ... Vietnam! ... John Lennon ...

trouble breathing ... a pull on my inhaler ... pipes clogged ... anti-war placards, Martin Luther King, Bobby Kennedy, time passing too quickly, too obviously ... my life has slowed down to a grinding halt, limbo, and Mr Holland's world is speeding up ... Richard Dreyfuss has grown a moustache ... time bends, Woodstock, another hanky, too damp to find an unused patch, reach for the toilet roll, it hurts to stretch my arm out ... go to sleep, let it go, you can't sneeze or blow your nose in sleep ... there's his deaf kid ... and no religion too ... No religion either! It should be no religion *either*! ... the deaf kid's having a tantrum, I don't know what you want, I don't know what you want! ... I want to die ... I don't want to live like this ... Nixon, Ford, Carter, Reagan, now some redhead is singing Gershwin and Mr Holland really likes her ... have I missed a bit? ... I'm missing everything ... just try and imagine Mr Holland standing there on that podium, holding his bat-*on* ... just try to imagine me standing.

If this enforced, delirious leave has taught me anything, it's that I've been working too hard. I had the prescribed 'few days' off between Christmas and New Year, tried not to think about *Q* for that entire time, even though we were strictly mid-issue, then the germs attacked, as they always do when you slow down, as they always do at Christmas and New Year, and I put up with it, relaxed into the healing power of illness. Just a cold. Maybe even a touch of flu. Work through it. Danny would have. I don't remember Danny having a day off. He's built like an ox, though. He claims never to get jet-lag either. Says it's a myth invented by poofs. He also used to buy the *Guardian* every day and theatrically throw *G2* into the bin without reading it, knowing that the rest of us preferred *G2* to the main paper. It was an affectation, like the jet-lag denial, but a committed one, and that's what counts.

I'm not, it seems, built like an ox. On the first day back at the office after New Year, I got up at the usual hour, still stuffed up and wheezy from my touch of flu but looking to a hectic production schedule to unblock my pipes and help me forget. I threw on a crisp Ben Sherman and my black Burton's suit, ready to catch my two buses to Brixton, kissed my wife goodbye and left the flat as normal. Except by the time I reached the first bus stop I had almost lost the use of my legs. I felt about eighty years old. I realised something was wrong and staggered back home. I threw the suit and the Ben Sherman in a pile and took to my bed. For the first time in my working life, I called in sick, except I was the boss calling in sick. You're supposed to call your boss when you're sick, but I was it. So I called John, who's my deputy.

I had every right to be sick, but I felt guilty for leaving them without an editor on the first day back, what with the production cycle being a week behind due to the Christmas break. I put John in charge of the February issue. He'll love being in charge, I thought. I assured him I'd probably be back on track in a couple of days and that I'd call him the following day.

That was two weeks ago. I'm only now starting to feel human again. I've spent two weeks on my back. I don't know what I've had. We can all call it flu – 'I've been off work with flu', 'Andrew's got flu', 'How's your flu?' – but flu doesn't feel like that. Flu doesn't lay you out for a fortnight and pin you to the settee, suck the marrow out of your bones and remove even the slightest interest in the outside world. I reached a point where I couldn't care less if *Q* came out or not. Actually, I knew that Tom had already been out to do U2, so we had a cover story, and Danny Eccleston was in Cologne with Ben Folds Five as I lay there under my sodden duvet, and so I went back to sleep. Again.

My body cleansed by the poisonous sweat of a fortnight's down-time, I was there at the climax of *Q*126 at Colour Systems, and saw the latest U2 cover into the Welsh minicab. It was sure to be a big-seller. It was sure to be a bigger seller than *Q*125, with Kula Shaker on the cover ('BLIMEY! THE WORLD'S MOST EXCITING

BAND!'), and I couldn't even claim to have been ill when we put that one together. Move on!

And the week after that I handed in my notice. It was as much of a surprise to me as it was to Jerry and Barry, but I didn't want to be the editor of *Q* any more. It was killing me. I was underpaid and overweight and I had no interest in becoming an executive anything, which was the only rung on offer. After all, I had been in a wardrobe with Rod Stewart, and it had been all downhill since then.

12

Writing Comedy Gold
for Judith Hann

In 1679, the last dodo was killed in Mauritius by British sailors. A Navy spokesman said, 'It's regrettable, but these lads have got to let off steam when they go into town at the weekend, and believe me, some of these birds are no angels, you know.'

Is that funny?

In 1687, Sir Isaac Newton discovered gravity when an apple fell on his head. Before this happy accident, 'he didn't understand the gravity of the situation', said court humorists Lord Hale and Viscount Pace.

Groans rather than merry laughter. Move on!

In 1689, the Protestant William of Orange took over the English crown. This pleased everyone, except the Poet Laureate.

Do you get it? Orange! There are no words that rhyme with orange! Any joke you have to explain isn't going to play on ITV.

In Russia, Peter the Great came to power. Though some said he was overrated.

Boom! Boom!

Elsewhere in the building, unseen, a harem of blonde beauties go about their business like handmaidens in a James Bond villain's lair, while Stuart and I read out gags based on the last millennium to Clive James in his producer's office, hoping to raise a smile.

In 1924, an enormous queue snaked round Red Square for Lenin's funeral as ordinary Russians waited to pay their respects to the great leader. Seeing the queue, many joined in error, assuming that a packet of sausages had arrived from Finland.

'That's very good,' chuckles Clive. Does that mean all the others haven't been? Does he know how much Stuart and I worship the ground he laconically walks upon? Does he know how *weird* this is?

Clive – and we are allowed to call him Clive – has, perhaps predictably, been commissioned by ITV to produce a three-hour satirical review of the last one thousand years for New Year's Eve 1999, very much in the spirit of his previous showbiz almanacs: studio-based, audience-cheered, and special-guest-punctuated. It's a tall order, even for a wit and thinker of his planet-sized magnitude.

As a rule, he writes his own material. Always has done. Of course. Before he became a highbrow light entertainment star, Clive was a working journalist. He's never stopped being a journalist. A true polymath, who's currently learning Japanese so that he can fully appreciate Japanese poetry, and considers the tango a matter of life and death, Clive James has called in co-writers, possibly under sufferance from his business partner and producer Richard, and co-conspirator Elaine. They will have informed him that he can't possibly write a three-hour show on his own.

In truth, he probably could. But we're helping him anyway. Journalists who want to be on telly should stick together.

The first ever Winter Olympics were held in 1924 in Chamonix, with thrills and spills among the snowy slopes. The newly formed Winter Olympic committee were soon besieged by accusations of bribery and corruption when they announced that the second games had gone to Dubai.

Murmurs. Too subtle. Fuck me, this is enough to make any man sweat.

In 1925, the publishing sensation of the year in Germany was *Mein Kampf* by Adolf Hitler. This was just the first in a long list of best-sellers from the popular author, including the self-help book *Men Are From Munich, Women Are From Heidelberg*, and the Christmas stocking-filler *101 Uses for a Dead General*.

'There's some good stuff here, chaps,' says Clive, who may be a highbrow light entertainment legend who went to Cambridge with Germaine Greer and Eric Idle, redefined the role of the TV critic at the *Observer*, has three volumes of auto-biography behind him, and acts as occasional cultural consultant to Prince Charles, but he's also kind enough to laugh at the jokes of two ex-music journalists who fancy them-selves as comedy writers. When he laughs his eyes disappear even further back into his famous head.

You're so used to seeing Clive James on television, perhaps even on *Clive James On Television*, wearing a suit and tie, it's disarming to see him ambling around the office of his TV production company, smaller and craggier than TV portrays him, open-necked, usually in shirtsleeves, sometimes in what can only be described as a gardening jumper. It's hard for Stuart and I. We *love* Clive James. Absolutely *love* him. To *work* with him – that is, collaborate with him, breathe the same show-biz air as him – is like *Jim'll Fix It*.

When we first met the great man, in this very office, he leaned in and proffered his hand, turned on that Clive James twinkle, and said, in fluent showbiz, 'Thank you for *being you*.'

We first worked for Clive without ever meeting him. Watchmaker, his production company – formed when every-body else was forming theirs, albeit named, rather more loftily, after an Albert Einstein quote ('The release of atom power has changed everything except our way of thinking … the solution to this problem lies in the heart of mankind. If only I had known, I should have become a watchmaker') – made *Collins & Maconie's Movie Club* for ITV.

A cheap-and-cheerful, make-do-and-mend, low-concept weekly movie review show presented from Row D of a repertory cinema in Hammersmith, the *Movie Club* was originally commissioned for six months, but ITV let it run for eighteen, which was a glorious, unbroken run and a nice amount of time to be on terrestrial telly, usually at 12.40 a.m., sometimes at a less convenient time than that. Produced by Andy Rowe, our old mucker from *Fabulous!*, with a no-passengers crew of six (camera, sound, production secretary, makeup, researcher, runner), we had what can only be described as the time of our lives. The siege mentality again. A merry band of shoestring late-night television desperados, we'd arrive first thing every other Thursday and do two shows in a day while the cinema was closed to the public. Andy oversaw the locking-off of the identical camera shot with Sarah, AJ fiddled with his boom, Amber checked the script, Mike or Verity fetched the bacon rolls from a nearby café and Rich set up the fake movie projector at the back of the auditorium – a single spotlight shone through a dry-ice machine, whose output needed expertly wafting with a bit of cardboard. Meanwhile, Stuart and I would share a joke in makeup, albeit not in a makeup room, but a corridor leading to the fire exit, our suits and shirts waiting for us not in a dressing room but a musty old walk-in store cupboard. We couldn't afford autocue, so Stuart and I would learn each link by heart. We couldn't afford wardrobe, so we just brought in a couple of our own shirts and changed between recordings to create the illusion of a week having passed. The lie that TV tells.

Partway through the run, Andy managed to scare up sufficient petty cash to send one of Watchmaker's harem out to buy us two trendy shirts each, in camera-friendly red and purple. These were by John Rocha, whom we'd never heard of but who is apparently a top designer. They had inordinately long sleeves and buttonless cuffs, which at least allowed us to crack this joke every week, to great merriment: 'John Rocha: *pour le singe.*'

In-jokes become the lifeblood of a small TV crew working on a long-running series. Like a unit just back from a tour of duty in Vietnam, none of us will ever be able to fully explain to anyone from *outside* why a book called *Dressing for Television* by Robert Dougall, or the words 'smoky smoker!' are funny. But let me tell you, they are fucking funny.

The format was pretty rigid: four film reviews, two humorous items, one video round-up and a competition. Within this framework, we found plenty of opportunity for horseplay and hi-jinks, such as Stuart punching me really hard in the face with a *ker-pow* sound effect added in post-production, or Mike dressing up as a tramp and emerging from Row C while the end credits rolled, as if perhaps he'd been sleeping there for the whole show. Such things were there to entertain us, but they seemed to appeal to a reasonably loyal fistful of late-night ITV viewers, too – that is to say, students, bar staff and minicab drivers. This is an accurate cross-section. During and after the run Stuart and I found ourselves recognised exclusively by students, bar staff and minicab drivers.

I remember being in a black cab and catching the driver's eye in his rear-view mirror. I knew from his furrowed brow what was coming next.

'You do that film programme don't you?'

'Yep.'

'With that other fella.'

'That's right.'

'Are you Colin or Marconi?'

This is the first rule of fame: the people may love you, but they don't know your name.

'I'm Collins, he's Maconie.'

'Oh, right.' The cab pulls onto the roundabout at Hyde Park Corner. 'Yeah, I often catch your programme when I get in. It's on about – what? – one-thirty?'

'Can be as late as that, yeah.' Rub it in, why don't you?

'Yeah, it's very good. Do you know what I like about your programme?'

'Go on.'

'It's the sort of programme that doesn't use the word *genre*.'

Garry Bushell may affect the persona of a cab driver in his TV critiques but there's no beating a real one. In actual fact it *was* the sort of programme to use the word *genre* but you could see what he meant. It was definitely not for cineastes, the *Movie Club*. It was for, well … it was for students, bar staff and you get the idea. Do you know what I loved about that cab driver? He was the sort of cab driver that used the word *genre*.

So, those eighteen months were a blast. They bridged a momentous change in circumstance for me: I was the editor of a magazine when we started, and a freelance writer by the time we finished. Not that we ever thought it would finish, but a new Director of Programmes arrived at ITV, David Liddiment, who cancelled our little show for the main reason that he hadn't commissioned it – or at least that's the bitter conclusion we leaped to. New station controllers are just like new magazine editors: they must rearrange the furniture to mark their arrival, or else what's the point of them being winched aboard?

Students, bar staff and minicab drivers must have been bereft. I also know for a fact that Eddie Izzard watched it, as he told us so at the Brits. And Joe Strummer. For a little programme made for tuppence that went out after bedtime and was mainly two blokes in suits, one with a quiff, the other with a floppy fringe, can't remember which is which, saying what they thought of some films, it meant a lot to a few. I interviewed Strummer for *Q* up at the top of London's most unlikely architectural folly, the Ark, so called because it is shaped like an ark, albeit an empty one, as nobody wants to work there, except Seagram, the distiller, who happened to have just bought Joe's record company, PolyGram.

He screwed his eyes up at me. 'Have we met before?'

'I don't think so.'

'Yeah we have. I know you from somewhere.'

You don't want to disagree with Joe Strummer of The Clash, but we really had never met. I would have remembered it. He is, after all, Joe Strummer.

'You might have seen me on telly,' I mutter, always slightly embarrassed to suggest this option.

His eyes lit up. 'That movie show, man!' he exclaimed. 'With the other guy!'

'That'll be it.'

Why am I surprised that Joe Strummer, inveterate dope-smoker and resident of Bridgwater in Somerset, might be up at 1.40 a.m., watching the telly?

'When's that show coming back, man?'

'Never,' I tell him. 'It was cancelled by ITV.' I expect Benny Hill had conversations like this in Kwik Save after Thames dropped *The Benny Hill Show*.

'We should get down to ITV and tell them what's what! Get the *Movie Show* back on!'

It was a sweet thought: the leader of The Clash – at that point noisily campaigning for the release of John Mawdsley, a twenty-six-year-old human-rights activist imprisoned in Burma for distributing pro-democracy leaflets – taking on the cause of a cancelled late-night movie review programme and storming the barricades.

But even Joe Strummer couldn't bring back *Colin & Marconi's Movie Show*.

'OK, let's see what the next batch of archive throws up. I'm going to take a break. Boys, do you want to come to my office in an hour and we'll work on the latest version together?'

Clive is already on his way out. We both nod, eagerly. We are 'the boys'. I'm thirty-four, Stuart's thirty-nine. Only in light entertainment are we 'boys'. 'Thanks, everyone!'

And with that, he's gone, like a *Late Night Line-Up* version of Young Mr Grace.

'That went pretty well,' offers Andy.

'You know what he's like,' smiles Richard, who really does know what he's like. Richard is a light entertainment producer of the old school. As well as Clive's shows, he used to do *Aspel* and *An Audience With … Dame Edna, Kenneth Williams, Dudley Moore* etc. If he told you he used to work on *Variety Bandbox*, you wouldn't raise an objection. He's Clive's business partner and great friend, and the only person on earth in a position to criticise him.

Before starting work on our gags for *A Night of a Thousand Years*, as the three-hour ITV spectacular is now called, Stuart and I were sent the first-draft script Clive had done, based on years of doing what can only be described as 'this type of thing'. It was, of course, effortlessly witty, literate and urbane: 'It was during World War One that the question arose of why Franconia and Estonia had joined Korea and the Crimea to seize the sisal silos of Silesia and the hairier areas of the even scarier Bavaria.' Instantly recognisable as a Clive James script, the only problem was that it was instantly recognisable as a Clive James script written in 1987. Some might call the humour timeless. Some might call it a bit knackered – a heresy both of us felt guilty for even entertaining. There was a reference in it to Club Med. Isn't that a bit, I don't know, 1960s? Hasn't Clive heard of Club 18-30? Actually, even Club 18-30 is a bit 1980s. Perhaps this is why someone had the bright idea of bringing in boys. Just in case you've forgotten, Stuart and I are 'the boys'. I expect the Chuckle Brothers are also known as 'the boys', and they're old enough to look like each other's dads.

Representing the kids – with their disposable income a valuable target audience for ITV's advertisers – Stuart and I are here to jolly the programme up a bit, drag in a few references post-Gerald Ford. But it's a Sisyphean struggle. No, make that a Sisyphean honour.

To punctuate the show in time-honoured fashion, Clive plans to present awards to figures from the last millennium at the end of each segment. It's worked before on his end-of-year spectaculars, it'll work again. These will be presented by modern celebrities, and collected on behalf of historical figures who-can't-be-with-us-tonight-because-they're-dead by another tier of celebrities. The first is Villain of the Millennium. Who could we get to present it?

'How about Christopher Lee?' suggests Clive.

Murmurs of approval.

'Isn't he a bit old?' I ask, rather impertinently in the circumstances.

'He's still working,' says Richard.

'The Prince of Darkness! The audience'll *love* it!' Clive enthuses.

'Shouldn't we get someone a bit more … modern?' asks Stuart, boldly. We've been in enough of these meetings in Richard's office now to know that our opinions are at least theoretically welcome.

'What about Martin Kemp?' I throw in.

'Who's Martin Kemp?' Clive asks. He can speak eight languages, but he's never heard of Martin Kemp.

'He's the villain on *EastEnders*.'

'I've never heard of him,' says Richard, backing up Clive. They're of a similar vintage.

'No, but a lot of other people have. It's watched by fifteen million people!' Stuart has a point.

'Ah yes,' counters Richard. 'But that means there are thirty-five million people who *don't* watch it!'

He and Clive seem rather pleased with this argument. Stuart and I stop arguing and concentrate instead on getting in our Viking gag about Ikea the Affordable.

*

Judith Hann is dressed in seventeenth-century finery. She moves slowly and deliberately towards the camera, the classic TV presenter's 'walk and talk' she's been doing all her professional life. She is holding an apple.

'The ordinary apple,' she says. 'Found in any orchard. A crunchy treat that helps to keep the doctor away ... but not all doctors. Not Doctor of Physics, Sir Isaac Newton, a man dismissed by the scientific establishment as little more than a strange old fruit ... until now, that is.'

Comedy gold! It's hard to convey what a bizarre thrill this is. Judith Hann, the first female presenter on *Tomorrow's World* who notched up twenty years with the classic popular science programme, is gamely dressed in historical garb and saying amusing words Stuart and I have written for her, and which now scroll up on her autocue. She enunciates them in precisely the way she used to before leaving the show in 1994, her style imprinted on the national consciousness.

While Clive continues to concentrate on his own links, Stuart and I have been charged with rustling up some sketches, based on recognisable TV formats, that deal with key moments in history – hardly the most original approach, but one that seems appropriate. And three hours is a lot of primetime ITV to fill, even with ad breaks.

Judith continues: 'Newton has just published a controversial new study that has shocked the world of physics to its very *core*.'

These sketches will be played back to the live studio audience tomorrow evening on VT monitors, hopefully generating appreciative laughter. The 'core' gag will probably raise no more than an audible smile. It's not a zinger. It's a sugar lump for those who are really paying attention.

'For centuries, scientists have clung to the belief that apples fall upwards, but Newton has taken this theory in another direction. Downwards. Take this Cox's Pippin. Look what happens when I drop it.'

She drops the apple to the ground.

'Down it goes. Let's see that again.'

Later, in post, a slow-motion replay will be dropped in, with the caption, 'AppleCam'. To be honest, this material is only funny because Judith Hann is doing it, and because it's been shot on the floor here in Studio 1 at LWT with exacting verisimilitude. On the page, it's pretty weak, but production brings it to life. Budget brings it to life! And Clive James commands budget!

'Professor Newton has run extensive tests on apples, pears, greengages and certain plums, and it seems that in a controlled environment, what grows up must come down. Religious leaders have described Newton's Theory of Gravity as heresy, and wherever he goes, they drop rotten fruit on him from below.'

It's OK, there's a zinger to finish.

'Now over to Michael with the latest development in flameproof Catholics.'

We both breathe out. Andy and director Terry ask Judith for another take, as the apple didn't drop very well. There's a lot to shoot before tomorrow night: the *Top Gear* sketch with Quentin Wilson; the *That's Life* sketch with Esther Rantzen and Adrian Mills; the *Sky at Night* sketch with Sir Patrick Moore; the *Holiday* sketch with Judith Chalmers; and the football pundits sketch with Bob Wilson, Ron Atkinson and Barry Venison. There are venerable television personalities coming and going all day today, like an edition of the *All-Star Record Breakers*. It's all tremendously exciting and a long, long way from the old *Movie Club* days, when our names were above the title, as it were.

Stuart and I are fifth and sixth on the bill according to the monster 172-page yellow shooting script, after executive producer, senior producer, producer and director. There we are: writers. Apparently more important than assistant producer, archive consultant, production manager and production co-ordinator. I know it doesn't matter in the broader scheme of things – it's just names typed on a cover sheet – but it's good to know your place.

While Clive is camera-rehearsing his links, behind the familiar oversized light entertainment desk, he'll often ask for 'the boys' if a line doesn't feel right, and we'll be despatched from the gallery to the studio floor for some on-the-spot surgery. He doesn't really need us, but we're there so he might as well use us.

It's odd to be invisible again, after eighteen months of high visibility at 1.40 a.m. This one's all about Clive and his giant, ever-pulsating brain at the centre of the light entertainment world. We, like the blonde beauties around the Watchmaker office, are handmaidens. (There are some brunette beauties, by the way. Clive is an equal opportunities employer.) In comedy-gold downtime, Stuart and I have been fantasising about forming our own production company, Giant Bat. I have designed some headed notepaper and everything. Our logo is a giant bat, and our tagline is 'swooping down to kill you'. We haven't really progressed any further than these administrative details, but we've decided that alongside ourselves, *Poldark* actress Angharad Rees is the company's third director. I'm sure she'll be up for it.

In these moments of jollity, we are a parody of media players. We are actually just writers for hire. We're only as good as our last commission. Our last joke, even. That's a very vital way to live.

Once you're out in the marketplace, no longer suckled by a day-job, this vitality – sometimes indistinguishable from insecurity – becomes a way of life. After nine straight years in gainful nine-to-five employment, I've been out for two.

It was a long handover at *Q*. But by the autumn of 1997, by which time we were well stuck into the bacon-roll routine of the *Movie Club* and playing at TV presenters, I was free. The process of extricating myself from Sellotape-dispenser drudgery was decelerated by my desire to keep things amicable and open-ended with Emap. Having come this far, I had no desire to start making enemies now. And anyway, they had been good employers for four years, allowing me a long enough leash to drink two and a half pints of Pils every lunchtime, make stupid jokes about rival magazines at international awards ceremonies and damage some rare, irreplaceable shrubs.

It wasn't about the money, but it was. Because I had moved in steady increments up the Emap ladder, I'd only ever really enjoyed steady, incremental pay hikes. There is a sting in the tail of working for a matey, open-door, party-throwing company like Emap: you are, as an employee, expected to be *grateful* to work there. Hence, the wages are on the whole Dickensian. As the editor of a magazine, you have intimate knowledge of your staff's salaries. This means you not only know how little your friends are actually earning – which is an unnatural thing to know about your friends – but you also know how narrow the gap is between what they earn and what you earn. It quickly becomes apparent in salaried work that the whole house of cards would come tumbling down if the English weren't so secretive about how much they earn. I'm not saying you should shout your wage from the rooftops, simply that a little more *glasnost* on the subject would make it more difficult for corporations to underpay. I knew for a fact that, as editor of a magazine that made a staggering amount of clear profit a year and sold 215,000 copies a month, I was earning the same as a senior press officer at a major record company.

Knowledge is paranoia. Metro had a clearout of some old first-generation computers the year before I left. They were literally giving away Macs following a fifth-floor upgrade, so I took one home. On *my* wages, I was hardly in a position to turn down freebies. The computer turned out to have belonged to Barry McIlheney. I know this only because he hadn't bothered to clear his hard drive before relinquishing it, which was remiss of him – some might say dim. To punish my managing director for this lapse in security, I felt it only right to scroll through and read the documents he'd left on there. Nothing that earth-shattering, actually, but I enjoyed reading the letters he'd sent to senior publishing staff confirming their pay rises. They were all on a lot more money than me, and with some justification – they had more responsibility than me, they'd served more years at the company, many of them had not just run but launched hit magazines, and at least two had co-presented Live Aid – but still, in the grander scheme of things, they *weren't on that much*. In those documents, I saw my future: moving up the company ladder and seeing my salary rise by further steady increments, still expected to be grateful for the privilege of working at Emap, and never really earning *that much*. I was no bread-head, but I had given my life and an important part of my men's health to *Q* magazine, and I quite wanted to live in a house rather than a rented flat. Also, I had started to earn a bit of tele-vision money on the side. And television pays you what you're worth, if not a little bit more than what you're worth. Unlike magazine publishing, which is awash with anomalies and injus-tices, there are industry standards within TV for what, say, a writer should be paid for a half-hour script. In print, you could be paid anything between 18p and 50p per word for a feature, which really mounts up. Guess which magazine pays 18p?

I dropped my bombshell after the mysterious, decisive two-week flu, but promised Emap that I wouldn't desert my post until a suitable replacement had been found. A noble gesture, much appreciated by the fifth floor, which led to an agonising but self-imposed six-month notice period, as I proved difficult to replace. I didn't flatter myself that, like a rare shrub, I was irreplaceable – it was just the market. Not enough potential *Q* editors knocking about. Or perhaps the Dickensian salary put them off.

Eventually, they rustled up a man called David Davies, not the chief executive of the Football Association but a career smoothie from the senior editorial echelons of *Mixmag*, a happening rave magazine Emap had recently acquired for its portfolio, thus scuppering any plans Andrew Harrison had of launching *Techno for the Smaller Man*. David and I, who appeared to have little in common, were duly photographed shaking hands by *Music Week*, and although I sniffed back a tear when handing over the keys to the metallic-green Ford Escort, the retreat from executive power could not have come any sooner. It was Bill who wrote the following epigram in my leaving card: 'You only leave twice.'

Thus did the loyal and brilliant staff I had at least helped put together get a new me. As if to make his mark, the moment David Davies was through the door, he literally rearranged the deckchairs, moving all the desks into a large doughnut shape, perhaps inspired to do so by a conference awayday. I naturally hoped that Bill and John and Danny and Keith and Isabel and Kim and Claire and Louise would get on fine with their new editor, and I also hoped they would never like him as much as they liked me.

The next time I entered the unrecognisable *Q* office, it was to deliver on disk a 125-word review of Brian Eno's first solo album for four years, *The Drop*: 'Seventeen tracks of vari-ambient that are merely pretty without annotation … Nice, but inauspicious' – three stars. It didn't look much on the page, but it was auspicious. It was the work of the self-employed.

Before going in to see Clive in his office, which is situated in the middle of the open-plan first floor at Watchmaker Towers, Stuart and I hesitate. We could just knock and enter. After all, it is 2.00 p.m., the allotted time. But we don't. Partly because it's Clive James in there. But mostly because he might be asleep.

We are eventually spotted by his PA, who sits at a desk outside.

'Is it OK to go in?' Stuart stage-whispers.

'Let me just check,' she says.

She comes over and quietly raps on his door. Silence. She raps with a little more volume.

'Yes!' Clive calls.

She opens his door and pokes her head round. 'Stuart and Andrew are here.'

'Ah, come in, come in!' he booms.

Clive power-naps. This is a workplace skill I've only come across once before. John Peel does it. People who've worked with him at Radio 1 or *Home Truths* verify that, during the day, Peel will just sit on a comfy chair in the office, close his eyes and nod off. Just like that. He then awakes, perhaps twenty minutes later, refreshed and rested, and raring to go again. Clive actually has a camp bed in his office. I expect he just slips off his shoes and does what Peel does, for a fixed hour, every day. And then the afternoon can commence, with his multilingual brain firing on all cylinders.

He looks a little crumpled and squintier as we enter his private chamber. I once went to sleep during the day when I was editor of *Q*. I was having a particularly rough Friday, suffering the aftereffects of an all-office 'mad cider' blowout the night before. Around midday, I repaired to the toilet cubicles to clutch my head as per editor tradition, and was overcome with the urge to curl up on the really very clean floor and rest my head. I slept swiftly and soundly. Bill came in at one point and heard me snoring. He was, however, discreet enough to not mention it to the rest of the staff. About forty-five minutes later, I re-emerged, claiming to have been called up to the fifth floor. Gosh, how long ago all that seems now. Having a day job. Having responsibility.

Clive asks his PA to fetch us some coffee. He asks if we mind if he smokes. He knows neither of us minds. We confirm this and he lights up a cheroot.

We have come to know Clive's hideaway well over these past weeks. Part office, part study bedroom – perhaps at the

Sorbonne in the late sixties – it is piled high with books, as you'd expect for a polymath, but is sweetly personalised with photos cut from magazines and blu-tacked to the wall around his camp bed, many featuring vintage sex symbols like Sophia Loren and Gina Lollobrigida. There are also haikus, in Japanese. The good thing about being at such close quarters with a man so learned and enquiring is that there is literally no point trying to impress him. It would be like sitting around playing a new riff to Hendrix or attempting to tackle George Best in a kickabout. So you just don't bother. It actually makes for a relaxed atmosphere.

Clive once asked me idly if I'd read a particular book – *The Genius of the System: Hollywood Film Making In The Studio Era* by Thomas Schatz – and I had read it. I hope my excitement wasn't too apparent, but it was like shouting 'Snap!' in a card game.

'Have you read a book called *Genius of the System* …?'

'Yes! I bloody have! I have read a book called *Genius of the System*! I, Andrew Collins, have read a book that you, Clive James, have read! Have you ever been to Utrecht with the Boo Radleys?'

I'd actually only read half of it, but you're not telling me he hasn't speed-read a couple of these volumes of *The History of the Decline and Fall of the Roman Empire*.

Jamesian cheroot on the go, the three of us sit down and watch the next batch of tapes, once Stuart has got the video going – technology not being one of Clive's specialist subjects. We skip through endless clips harvested by the research team upstairs that may or may not inspire us to produce comedy gold. First, some bits of Eisenstein's 1944 Russian classic *Ivan the Terrible*, which tickle us as Ivan looks a lot like 350-pound Greek crooner Demis Roussos, which is one for the older viewers. It's a gift: silent footage begs hilarious subtitles. We make a note. Next, a curious grainy sequence from the 1920s of a Charleston woman dancing elastically with a chimpanzee.

'Liz Hurley and Hugh Grant!' Clive exclaims with school-boy glee.

I mark the sheet that came with the tape, too self-aware to suggest Princess Diana and Wayne Sleep. You don't mention Princess Diana in front of Clive James.

Do we know if Clive ever danced with his friend Diana? He loves to dance. At Watchmaker office parties it is the honour of one or two of the glamorous harem to join Clive in a tango. It is a shame that convention prevents Stuart and I from dancing with Clive James, because that, ultimately, is what we'd most like to do. And afterwards thank him for *being him.*

'This is the last one of these I'll do,' he mutters casually, *sotto voce,* as we are up in the production gallery watching some VT. Stuart is elsewhere, perhaps having a cigarette, so it's just me and Clive. And he's dropped a bombshell. What the freelance journalist in me might consider an exclusive.

'Really?' I say. Clive James giving up light entertainment television? It's like Alistair Cooke giving up *Letter From America* or the Queen giving up her Christmas Day speech.

'Yup. Go out while I'm on top,' he says. 'Before they stop asking me. These shows are just so much work.'

This is unarguable. A three-hour millennial ITV spectacular is tons of work. Never mind all those fumigated hours we've spent in his study bedroom going over tapes and fine-tuning gags about Lumière and Sacha Distel, we then made a rod for our own backs by writing in a musical number for the finale, borne largely out of one rather flimsy final conceit. Here's what Clive is going to read out for his final deskbound link tonight:

... But as time ran out towards the year 2000, a new golden age had begun: the age of Blair. Blair would lead the British people out of drudgery, misery and servi-tude, into a new Millennium where every family would have a 400-foot Ferris wheel and a dome of their own at the bottom of the garden. At the end of the Millennium and at the beginning of a new dawn, what could be more fitting than to meet the man with his name on the Blair era …

At which point, according to the script, *Lionel* Blair enters at the top of the stairs. He stands solemnly before his people and makes a statesmanlike speech:

'Nothing's impossible, I have found …'

At this point, the band will strike up.

And then we envisage Lionel Blair singing 'Pick Yourself Up', made famous by Fred Astaire and Ginger Rogers, and soft-shoeing it down the stairs, followed by all of the previous celebrity guests from the prizegiving bits, which will include – yes! – Christopher Lee, Helen Mirren, Felicity Kendal, Matthew Kelly, Margarita Pracatan, Leslie Phillips, Magnus Magnusson and token under-fifty, Tara Palmer-Tomkinson. Even though Watchmaker are dab hands at booking celebrity guests, this is still quite a tall order. But it's going to happen, and an appreciative studio audience is going to witness it happening. Before this evening is out, light entertainment will walk the earth. And Clive James will walk away.

On top.

We had no star guests in eighteen consecutive months of the *Movie Club*. It wasn't that kind of programme. We were 'offered' Woody Harrelson at one surreal stage, by a film PR who had either never stayed up late enough to watch the show, or thought that Harrelson's star power was so great we'd rearrange the format around him. But we simply didn't have the staff to accommodate him, and it would have meant him being made up by the fire exit. So we did the right thing and said no to Woody Harrelson. It remains a *Movie Club* badge of honour.

A Night of a Thousand Years hasn't booked Martin Kemp. That's this programme's dubious badge of honour. It has, though, booked pretty much everybody else. A more motley galaxy of stars you could not imagine, but the sheer number of these glittering people lined up and singing along to 'Pick Yourself Up' with Clive at their epicentre is a sight to behold. And I suppose if you're going to consign a millennium to the dustbin, you might as well do so with Sacha Distel and Lionel Blair. The real joy of being a writer, of being a backroom boy, is that you can type 'Lionel Blair' or 'Judith Hann' or 'Barry Venison' and it's someone else's job to rustle them up, in the flesh, which they do. There's something of the alchemist about it.

Because there's a wrap party when it's over, all the production staff are dressed smartly for the recording. No gardening jumpers tonight. This lends the night a fitting air of celebration, or perhaps the feel of a wake, depending on how much you know about Clive's sensational future plans. It's not actually New Year's Eve – New Year's Eve telly is traditionally filmed in early December – but there is still something cyclical and epoch-making in the air.

Though Stuart and I have both done TV studios before, it's cool being backstage at an ITV light entertainment show when you have such a large stake in its success. There are no actual passes or laminates; you just have to move about the warren and negotiate the endless cables, ramps and curtains leading to the studio floor with absolute self-assurance. We are fifth and sixth on the bill – with every right to loiter wherever we please. Without us, well, there would be no Ikea the Affordable gag.

A sense of relief overwrites the sense of climax. The appearance of the musical number means the studio recording is almost over, one that's dragged on way beyond sensible endurance for the audience. A three-hour spectacular runs for about two and a half hours flat, and that's without pick-ups and a fully choreographed musical number involving a 71-year-old Magnus Magnusson, a 75-year-old Leslie Phillips and a 77-year-old Christopher Lee. When I was fresh out of college, living in a garret and hungry for a cheap night out, I used to attend recordings of TV comedy shows – *Don't Miss Wax, Have I Got News For You, Alexei Sayle's Stuff, Whose Line Is It Anyway?* – and no matter how long they kept you in your seat, expected to laugh again at jokes you'd already laughed at, you never resented it. *Because it was free.* You got to see an elongated, live version of a TV show, complete with unbroadcastable fluffs and swearing, there was a warm-up comedian to keep you scurrilously amused while they reset and retook, and when it was on the telly, often months later, you could point at the screen and say, 'I was there!' I only hope these criteria held up tonight for the poor souls locked in studio one until midnight. They've got homes and we've got a party to go to.

After the last link is spoken and the gate checked for any hairs (it's a technical camera thing), Clive gets the all-clear in his ear, accompanied by the reassuring reveille of production staff high-fiving in the gallery. He removes his earpiece, beaming, stands up and applauds the audience for their patience and their warmth, while they applaud him, in that special way that audiences pulling on their coats and filing out of their seats applaud. This would be the moment to announce his retirement from television, the Howard Beale moment, but he wisely chooses not to. The audience are too busy thinking about their own bladders to care that they have just witnessed a three-hour version of history, as well as a three-hour version of *history*. Sorry. You work with Clive James, you start writing like him.

Everyone's too frazzled at the aftershow to do anything scandalous. Another tour of duty over. Glasses clink. Party dresses are admired. Ashes are pointlessly raked over. Andy is again free to muck about. The great man starts to eye up potential tango partners. It's already late, so I make my excuses and leave early, certain as I weave my way through the empty LWT corridors that I will never work in TV with Clive James again. *Clive James* will never work in TV with Clive James again.

He only leaves once.

Once outside the building in the brittle night air, having respectfully said *g'night* to the nightwatchmen, I stop for a moment to take in the view. It's an unexpectedly potent sight: King's Reach Tower reaches powerfully upwards before me, the Stamford Arms tucked into its armpit. We're just a few yards away from a huge and irreplaceable chunk of my past. There are even a few lights on. The industry inside that building grinds on without me, and has done for seven years now. Similarly, television will grind on without Clive James. Blimey, it's cold. Too cold for an epiphany. I get into my waiting cab. Because even writers get account cabs home on ITV spectaculars.

'I'm not a cab!' shrieks the man in the driver's seat.

'Sorry, mate,' I mutter, and climb back out, having violated a member of the public's car. 'But thank you for *being you.*'

13

Having Nothing to Say
to Mark Fowler

Go to folder '*Time Team*'. Open new document in First Draft
screenwriting software. Auto-format: '*EastEnders*'. It's probably
not quite what they meant by 'security', but on my Mac I have
renamed the '*EastEnders*' folder '*Time Team*', just to deter soap-
secret thieves. One of the other writers had their house burgled
and PC stolen, with details of a number of future storylines on
its hard drive, at which *EastEnders* high command sent out a
memo reminding us to save exclusively to disk and lock our
disks in a big safe. I couldn't be bothered to do this – who uses
disks any more? And what if one corrupts with all your work on
it? – so I have instead used the *Time Team* deception.

Blank screen. Check yellow story document. Take away
blankness using words.

```
EPISODE 32


SCENE 32/1. JACKSONS'. HALLWAY. INT. DAY LIGHT.
07.30


[WELLARD IS ACTING STRANGELY, WHIMPERING AND
SCRATCHING UP AT THE FRONT DOOR. JIM COMES OUT
INTO THE HALLWAY TO PLACATE HIM]
```

JIM: What's the matter with you, you daft hound?
I've taken you out once — what more do you want?

[WELLARD JUMPS UP JIM]

I can't help you, son. I don't know what you're
trying to say.

[THE SOUND OF BANGING FROM OUTSIDE AND GARRY
SHOUTING]

[SHOUTS] Ain't you heard of a doorbell?

'And the winner is … *Emmerdale*!'

Bloody *Emmerdale*? The table's going over.

Ah, the glittering 2001 Bafta awards. The TV Oscars, as they must be referred to by law. Working for *Radio Times*, as I now do (amongst other things), has its advantages. We're the main sponsor of the Bafta awards this year, and that means an entire table in the Great Room of the Grosvenor House Hotel, reserved for *RT* staff and associated dignitaries. It's all about hierarchies, as ever. At *Radio Times* my title is film editor, which, although in many ways a cosmetic post among those created to give the magazine's sections a 'personality' (hello!), puts me on the top table.

It's nice to be here – even though I've now had more hot dinners at Grosvenor House than I've had hot dinners. Actually, let's call them warm dinners. Catering simultaneously for 500 does tend to take the mouth-searing heat off your red onion and apple tartlet with Welsh goat's cheese and sun-blushed vine tomatoes, spiced confit of Norfolk duck with baked sweet potato and plum sauce, honey-roast carrots and parsnips with a rosemary-infused potato cake, or saffron risotto with a medley of baby vegetables and a cheese sauce – that's the vegetarian option.

Getting to the table first, as I always obsessive-compulsively do while the dress-suited stragglers hang back at the champagne reception, allows you to take in the lie of the land and even make last-minute seating changes before everyone else arrives. This is risky, as the seating plan will have been conceived with surgical precision by the head of your table, be they publisher, series producer or station controller. It's traditionally boy-girl-boy-girl, with guests *deliberately* seated between other guests they don't know, to encourage team-building and social pollination. Sometimes, it's easier to surrender to fate. Tonight, I've been seated between Dr Mark Porter, TV's medical heart-throb and *RT* columnist, and *somebody I don't know* from the office on my right. I hardly know anyone from the office, so this isn't difficult.

I refrain from talking shop to Dr Mark Porter, as he's not in surgery now and I'm sure he'd be uninterested in the book I've been reading about ameliorating your own asthma through breathing techniques, because if all of Britain's five million asthma sufferers tried it, the pharmaceutical industry would be brought to its knees and with it the conventional medical establishment. But who cares? He seems to be old friends with Alice Beer and she comes over for a chat at one point, which means *I have met Alice Beer.*

The *Radio Times* table is well placed, right under the famous nose of tonight's host, Angus Deayton, who, according to the newspapers, is being paid £50,000 to raise an eyebrow and read off an autocue. The sneering press coverage speaks mostly of the jealousy of journalists – who are an incredibly jealous lot, as I have discovered myself. If it is actually £50,000, I say he's worth every penny. You're not just paying for what he *does*, you're paying for what he's *done*. He's *Angus Deayton*. I've never been asked to host an awards ceremony outside of the cosy, in-house *Q* Awards. Stuart did an out-of-house gig once, for the Guild of Photocopier Salesmen or something, possibly in this very room, and he hated it. I believe the words 'never' and 'again' passed his blue lips as paramedics stretchered his ego from the podium.

Emmerdale winning best soap is a rare shock result, especially to those of us connected with *EastEnders*. I'm relieved not to be on the *EastEnders* table when the winner is announced. Nobody comes here to lose. You genuflect magnanimously and say, 'Maybe next year,' and applaud for the cameras as they pass between the tables, but you hate everybody connected with *Emmerdale* in that moment, as they have reduced what might have been a night of triumph and champagne-all-round into little more than a corporate jolly. Those farm-based bastards.

Good to see my old pal Graham Linehan onstage to collect Best Situation Comedy for *Black Books*, which he co-writes and directs. To think we used to work on *Select* together almost ten years ago. But time bends.

Graham could often be found in the Champ back then. It was he who legendarily ordered a cheeseburger once, despite grave forewarning, and was dismayed to be served up a dry, over-cooked disc of meat in a dry bap. Not being English, he complained to the bar staff about the evident lack of cheese. He was informed, as if perhaps he was from another century, that the cheese was on the *inside* of the burger. A disgusting thought, and, true enough, when Graham sliced into it, a trickle of bright orange pus seeped from its centre. We did warn him.

I also remember the time when I popped into the Champ on spec and found Graham on his own. I sat down with him, expecting the usual larks, but he told me with some embarrassment that he was meeting someone, and it was 'kind of a business meeting'. I duly moved to another seat with my Pils. And in came Alexei Sayle. That's who he was meeting. One of my comedy heroes – and one of Graham's, you could be sure of that. I tried not to gawp, or earwig.

This transpired to be a meeting about the sitcom that would

become *Paris*, which launched the comedy careers of Graham and his writing partner Arthur. Next stop: *Father Ted*, and all the accolades that came with it. And now he's picking up a Bafta. No more cheese-oozing burgers for *him*. I like the way these things turn out.

SONIA: [OOV] Granddad!

JIM: [FLUSTERED] Yes, love?

[IN THE KITCHEN, SONIA IS EATING BREAKFAST, GLANCING THROUGH A FOLDER AT THE SAME TIME. JIM ENTERS. WE CAN STILL HEAR WELLARD WHIMPERING IN THE BACKGROUND]

SONIA: [WITHOUT LOOKING UP] Got any plans tonight?

JIM: I'm going to Peggy's do, aren't I?

SONIA: Good — because I want the place to myself.

JIM: Not more studying.

SONIA: No — I want to pamper Jamie. Make up for being boring.

JIM: I'm sure he's been keeping himself amused.

After what feels like an age but may actually have been two, the ceremony is over, and the food consumed. The spiced poached pear with port wine sauce has been pushed around 500 plates. The ice bucket on the *RT* table has been cleared and refilled and almost cleared for a second time. What opulence. But no licence-fee-payer would deny us this feast, because we are TV.

We are *Morse* (*Radio Times* Readers' Award), we are *So Graham Norton* (Best Entertainment Programme or Series; Best Entertainment Performance), we are *Coronation Street* (Bafta Special Award), we are *Big Brother* (Best Innovation), we are Lynda LaPlante (Dennis Potter Writer's Award), we are Louis Theroux (Richard Dimbleby Award for Best Presenter), we are *The Naked Chef* (Best Feature), we are *Longitude* (Best Drama Serial; Best Actor, Michael Gambon), we are ... Dame Judi Dench (Best Actress). What mere mortal in this land would begrudge us a meal and a few drinks? We keep them amused.

I weave my way over to the *EastEnders* table. It's time to make myself known to exec producer John and the assorted cast members. It's exciting to see so many of the show's new stars here – Kat Slater! Mo Slater! Garry Hobbs! Martin Fowler! – at a point in their careers where *all this* must still seem terribly exciting, but Mark Fowler's the daddy. Not literally, obviously, not with the AIDS, but the elder statesman of the group. Mark's been on Albert Square since 1990.

Back in the days when Graham Linehan ate in the Champion, John was our producer on *Fantastic Voyage* at the old Radio Five. John *Yorke!* We thought he was nuts to give up a promising BBC radio producer's job to go and work as a script editor on *EastEnders*, but we were wrong: look at him now. Top dog.

John spots me and flushes with embarrassment on my behalf. One of the writers is coming over!

He gets up from the table to greet me. 'Andrew! What are *you* doing here?'

He doesn't mean, 'Who let *you* in?' by the way. It's a reflex question.

'I'm on the *Radio Times* table. Sorry about the ...'

'Ah well. It's nice for *Emmerdale* to win for a change. Let me introduce you. Have you met ... ?' He gestures towards the actors.

'No, never have.'

When you tell people from *outside* that you're an *EastEnders* scriptwriter, this is the first thing they ask you, without fail: 'Can you bring Dirty Den back?'

To which the answer is: no. Dirty Den is dead. He drowned in the canal in 1989 after being shot with a bunch of daffodils by someone from the Firm. Sharon identified his body after his signet ring turned up on a stall at Bridge Street Market. He is dead. He ain't never coming back.

The second question is: 'Which characters do you write for?'

To which you must patiently explain that individual writers don't write for individual characters. You are given individual episodes to write, like slices cut from the same never-ending dramatic salami. In other words, you write for *all* the characters. I'm not sure if this is a disappointing answer or not.

And the third question is: 'What are the actors like?'

To which the answer is: no idea. The writer's lot is a solitary one. You toil away at a hot computer, at home, and email each draft to the script editors. Then you go up to Elstree for script meetings before returning to your office to write the next draft. And when you've finally finished and the script's been signed off and distributed to the cast, you're as often as not straight onto the next one. As a result, there's never time to hang around the set while your episode is being shot. Ergo, you never get to meet the actors.

Until now, that is.

This is the conversation I had with Mal Young in his office at *Brookside* seven years ago.

'You should write for *Brookie*,' he said, over a cup of coffee in a *Brookie* mug. He'd just given me a tour of the set and we were chatting while we waited for my cab back to Lime Street.

'How can I write for *Brookie*?' I said, slightly bamboozled by the suggestion, out of the blue.

'Well, you watch *Brookie* ...'

This was true. I was addicted to the Liverpool soap, having watched it religiously since it began in 1982. I nodded.

'That's half the battle,' he said. 'If you watch soaps, you can write soap. And you're a writer.'

'I'm a journalist,' I corrected him.

'You still write.'

I shrugged. This was pie in the sky stuff. I wasn't here for a job, I was here to soak up the rays of Britain's most exciting soap at close range. As well as being features editor of *Q*, I looked after its new TV section, and as such had dispatched myself to the suburbs of Liverpool to research a short piece on the inexorable rise of *Brookside*. This was body-under-the-patio time. Everybody was talking about it. I'd never once considered writing for a soap. I was a music hack.

Many an untrained scriptwriter had found employment at *Brookside*: it was in many ways, and in tune with its own roots in the 1980s, like a YTS writing scheme. Even Mal himself had started out as an extra on the show, and now look at him: series producer, *grande fromage*, answerable only to – *hushed tones* – Phil Redmond himself. With such a high turnover of storylines, *Brookie* positively encouraged new and unqualified people to try out. I had once been an *NME* reader with a typewriter. Could I now become a *Brookie* viewer with a word processor?

No. I dismissed it. I lived in London for starters, and I had a full-time job for seconds.

My cab came, and I went south, with a *Brookside* plastic bag full of *Brookside* mugs, *Brookside* badges, *Brookside* bugs (remember them?) and *Brookside* car stickers. I didn't even have a car at that stage to stick them on. But these things change.

This is the conversation I had with Mal on the phone in the *Q* office in late 1996.

'How do you fancy writing for a new soap?'

Here we go again … 'What new soap?'

Mal had recently been poached – that thing I had never managed to do – by Pearson, a media conglomerate. This meant leaving his beloved Liverpool and coming to London, a pilgrimage it seems many of us must make eventually. As head of drama, Mal had been charged with developing a brand-new soap for Britain's soon-to-be-launched fifth terrestrial knob, Channel Five. Unlike the established *EastEnders* and *Coronation Street*, it would go five nights a week, Australian style. With a tight budget and a punishing turnover, they needed as many keen writers as they could get their hands on, and in the workshop spirit of *Brookie* wanted to start one or two out from scratch. Which is where I came in.

'But I'm the editor of *Q*,' I stated, for the record.

This time, Mal wasn't taking no for an answer. I was a soap fan. I could string a sentence together, I could easily learn the rules for setting out a script and I had weekends, didn't I?

'Here's the worst-case scenario,' he said. 'You write us a script. It's shit. We get someone else to rewrite it. You get paid a thousand quid. And we never ask you to write one again.'

Count me in!

I suspect part of me was already thinking ahead to a post-*Q* life, a life without share options and a company car, even though my poor, abused body had yet to bail out on me and speed that process up. I gave myself a couple of half-days off and attended early meetings at the programme's new studio base, which was out in the wilds of Middlesex, so it was just as well I had my Escort now. Here, around a big conference table, over Danish pastries and endless coffee from those huge pump-action urns, characters and stories were thrashed out, and it was just like … working on a soap! The appalling working title was *Running Wild*, which was wisely changed to *Family Affairs*. It was set in a fictional place called Charnham, which was sort of a bit like Maidenhead, and centred around one family, the Harts.

Mal gave me a sample script by a seasoned writer called Keith Temple from which I would copy the basic format: underline character name, stage directions in capitals enclosed within square brackets, all typed in one column down the right-hand side. I was commissioned to write episode number nineteen of *Family Affairs*, without any knowledge of what the characters looked like, as Mal and his team were still in the process of casting. The first piece of soap jargon I learned was the word 'ep', which means 'episode'. Also, a 'cliff' is a 'cliffhanger'. As you can see, it's mainly shortening existing terms, to save time.

It's important to note here that soap writers don't, as a rule, come up with the plots. This would be unworkable. For a 'continuing drama' to work, storylines must be plotted way in advance, the big ones – a murder, a pregnancy, a new family – sometimes by a calendar year. Hence the paranoia over security. Tabloids would exchange coin of the realm for future titbits. There are teams of people working full-time on storylines, and they are called storyliners. I don't know how you get to become a storyliner. It's an even more invisible job than writer, albeit one that wields a big stick.

The first episode – sorry, ep – of *Family Affairs* went out on Channel Five's launch night in March 1997. My first went out four weeks later. It had professional actors in it, with my words coming out of their mouths! One of them was Ken Farrington, who used to be Billy Walker on *Coronation Street* – how about that? And one of them was Annie Miles, who used to be Sue on *Brookside*, the one who got pushed off the scaffolding. Soap legends. Added to this new thrill, my name came up at the end of the opening credits.

Once I'd wrestled myself free of *Q*, writing soap actually took over as my main source of income, if not strictly my Technicolour dream job. Mal Young had turned out to be some kind of Liverpudlian soothsayer. So, the first chapter in my freelance life was characterised by drives out to Hayes in Middlesex, or trips up to Covent Garden to Channel Five's colourful HQ, for story meetings. Then it was back home to do the work. Due to the high turnover, the stories were given to you pre-chopped into scenes – all you had to do was provide the dialogue and hand back a script that looked like one of Keith Temple's. It proved an unbeatable apprenticeship in TV scriptwriting. Come the end of my two-and-a-half-year tenure at *Family Affairs*, I'd written thirty-two episodes of national terrestrial television, all of which – except one – went to air.

Let's not be coy about this: my last ep, number 637, was ceremoniously taken off me by my script editor and given to another writer to finish. It was like a maverick cop having his badge and gun taken away. As a result, they 'let me go' in the summer of 1999. Court-martialled by a soap. This will sound awfully convenient, of course, but I was ready to walk. A year before, due to unspectacular ratings, *Family Affairs* was taken over by a new production team, led by Brian Park, who'd earned himself the nickname 'Axeman' as exec producer at *Coronation Street*, largely for killing off Derek. I wasn't a big fan of the new regime, with their catchphrase 'Wouldn't it be *brilliant* if …?', even though they were clearly doing exactly what they'd been charged to do – raise the show's profile. They killed off the entire Hart family in a bizarre barge explosion ('Wouldn't it be *brilliant* if … everybody died?') and raised our profile for precisely a week. The viewing public can be cruel. For me, the rot set in from that explosion onward. Ridiculous new characters were introduced and ridiculous new storylines woven, and, I'll be honest, a lot of the joy went out of the job. There you go, I said it: the job.

Episodes 636 and 637 proved to be my last, as my lack of enthusiasm for the show had begun to rub off on the page. I made continuity errors that rather suggested I had stopped reading the story documents properly, and made the tactical mistake of providing ridiculous dialogue for the ridiculous characters, in the belief that they could carry it off. For the first time in two and a half years, a complete second draft was requested. This was followed by a brief letter from the series producer wishing me all the best in my future writing projects. That hurt.

Thankfully, in the year *Family Affairs* was launched, Mal was poached – Again! Think of his salary hikes! – by the BBC, who made him Head of Drama Series. I now had a friend at Television Centre. I started to wonder if perhaps he had been put on this earth to be my guardian angel, as he called me in and put me to work on two consecutive dramas in development at the BBC, one about a PR firm, called *Splash.com*, the other about an office romance, *Me Jane*. In both cases, 'development money' was forthcoming, which was a new concept to me. This helped pay for toner and disks, but mostly compensated me for my time – all those hours spent in meetings at the Beeb with script editors and producers and Mal, batting round ideas, moving towards 'script stage' and drinking an awful lot of that pump-action brown liquid, which may have been coffee, may have been tea, and in fact is known among hardened BBC employees as 'Uniquench'.

Nothing came of either project, but I was learning the ropes of the television writer: 10 per cent actual television writing, 90 per cent meetings. Then, in March 1999, I received two phonecalls in the same week – prompted, we may assume, by Mal. One from *EastEnders*, one from *Holby City*, both asking me to send in some samples of my work, with a view to 'trying out' on these long-running BBC soaps. I was knocked sideways. This would show *Family Affairs*.

```
[SONIA DETECTS SOMETHING IN JIM'S DELIVERY]

SONIA: [SUSPICIOUS] What's that supposed to mean?

[JIM BACKTRACKS — HE PICKS UP ON THE BANGING]

JIM: Is this a knock-knock joke? Because it isn't
very funny.
```

Big difference between *Family Affairs* and *EastEnders*? (I didn't get the gig at *Holby*, by the way.) About twelve weeks. Three months pass between first story meeting and transmission on *Family Affairs*; six months on *EastEnders*. It's the difference between working on a weekly music paper and a monthly magazine: Integrity Time. And in that time, you get to write a lot more drafts, sometimes four or five, but it can rise to six or seven if the pieces of the jigsaw don't fall together.

Big similarity? Both are situated way outside of London, one in Hayes to the west, the other at Elstree Studios in Borehamwood to the north, an hour's drive or a meandering suburban train ride either way.

On both programmes, a weighty story document contains all plotlines for a given month. On *EastEnders*, scene breakdowns are the writer's job, which gives more dramatic freedom and adds more pressure. But you're paid two and a half times as much per ep, which is only fair, as rather more people watch *EastEnders*. There are a lot more rules on *EastEnders* too, as it's been going for fifteen years and they kind of know what they're doing up there.

For instance, of the ep's twenty-six-minute running time, 19.5 minutes should be shot in studio and 6.5 minutes on the lot. Each week you 'inherit' three existing sets, to which you can add three of your own choosing, in consultation with the other writers and script editors working on your block of eps. To whit: 'I can live without the B&B, but I must have Pat and Roy's kitchen.' If Peggy leaves the Vic in scene two and appears at the launderette in scene four, make sure she's got enough time realistically to get there during scene three.

Oh, and you're not allowed to write phonetic 'Cockneyisms' – ain't, 'ere, dunno, darlin', innit – leave those to the actors. Equally, don't use exclamation marks too often; it only encourages the cast to over-act. Never start a line of dialogue with 'Listen' or 'Look', as the cast tend to put these tics in anyway and need no encouragement. The phrase 'Can I have a quiet word' is *banned*. As are phrases such as 'God knows' or 'Jesus Christ!' for reason of the Sunday afternoon omnibus.

Certain among the cast are well known for polishing their own dialogue, but this is a privilege well earned. Mike Reid would famously add his own choice phrases, such as the classic, 'What do you take me for? Some kind of pilchard?' How we all wish we'd written that particular line of poetry.

No trade names. Thus, Night Nurse becomes 'Night Cure' and Eurodisney becomes 'Theme Park Continental'. And if you want to invent the name of, say, a restaurant, it has first to be checked by a researcher so that it matches no such existing establishment anywhere in the country. I found out the hard way that the hair salon I was sending Dot to, Mario's, already existed somewhere, so I had to change it between drafts to Bernardo's, which didn't. So what started out as a tribute to my favourite computer game character, ended up being a tribute to my favourite Italian film director, Bertolucci. Whether high culture or low, the writer must amuse himself or herself by scoring these minor victories. I even managed to work in a line from *Casablanca* once – 'maybe not today, maybe not tomorrow, but soon' – and either nobody noticed, or nobody minded.

Trying out for *EastEnders* is a bit like applying for a university: every now and again, a certain number of new 'places' become available, and hopefuls must literally pass an entrance exam to be considered for one, which involves writing a full scene breakdown and half a dozen actual scenes of dialogue, based on a real *EastEnders* story document. Thankfully, you get to write it at home, and not in a gym in complete silence.

Anyway, thanks to the *Family Affairs* crash course, I passed the exam and earned my first proper commission, *EastEnders* episode 931. This was like leaving a redbrick university and winning a place at somewhere with dreaming spires and punting. And I couldn't have arrived at one without first passing through the other. I started taking away the blank screen by putting words on it in September 1999, and five months, four drafts, a lot of notes and a wide selection of Elstree catering biscuits later, my first ep of *EastEnders* was broadcast on BBC1 in January 2000. I sat down and watched it, along with around 16 million other people. If I did a good job, then none of them will have noticed – and that includes the actors, who simply measure how good a script is by how many lines they get in it, and how many of their best emotion faces they get to do as a result of those lines.

Another rule: each scene must end on a reaction. The difference between popular TV drama and, say, a film, is that scenes have this clear ending – the camera is held on the face of Dot or Jim or Garry or Dr Trueman as a kind of dramatic punctuation. Their facial reaction lasts for *just that bit too long*. This must be fun for the actor. As a writer, you put this:

```
[OUT ON DOT'S CONCERN]
```

Or:

```
[OUT ON PAT'S SUSPICION]
```

And June Brown or Pam St Clement get to do the relevant face. Characters in *EastEnders* exist in a constant state of suspicion and concern. It's rare that a scene goes out on Zoë's indifference, unless it is a cavalier indifference to something meaningful said or done by someone else where indifference is in itself a portent of later concern or suspicion.

Before ep 931 went out, I had already been commissioned to write ep 975. This is your reward. You're only as good as your last episode on *EastEnders*. Your satisfaction comes not from being recognised in the street or from winning awards, but from not being noticed. From getting an ep away by draft four and not racking up a draft six. From sitting on the south-bound train out of Borehamwood after a between-draft meeting with your script editor and having a couple of the seventy pages of your script free of notes. From not fucking up *EastEnders*.

John presents me to the tableful of *EastEnders* cast members, each one a decent mention in *Heat*, each one instantly recognisable to 16 million people – and, by the same token, possibly unrecognisable to 34 million people. Each one more famous as their character than as themselves.

'Everyone, this is Andrew Collins, one of our top writers!'

Kat and Mo and Garry and Martin all say hello. I grin and say hello back. I'm not one of *EastEnders*' top writers. I'm one of its writers, but it's sweet of John to big me up. Mark is already standing, so he comes over and we shake hands.

'All right, Mark,' I say.

Mercifully, he doesn't hear me, thanks to general awards-aftermath hubbub, which is just as well, as *he isn't called Mark*. He is the actor Todd Carty. He plays Mark. I am a writer on *EastEnders* who's just called one of its principal cast by their character name. I am no better than those schoolchildren who hang around the barrier at Elstree and shout out 'Steve!' at the actor Martin Kemp, as he goes past in his cab.

So, here we are, me and Todd Carty, man to man, in our dicky bows. He's in *EastEnders*. I write for *EastEnders*. We have so much in common. We're virtually workmates. I have written lines for this man to say. I wrote this line for him, and he said it:

'I know what everybody else thinks, but it's me who has to suffer all the side-effects.'

And this one:

'You can spend too long worrying about what other people will think. Whatever I decide, I want to do it for me.'

I even wrote this one:

'You're not supposed to keep those on in here. Affects the dialysis machines or something.'

I've put so many words into this man's mouth and yet I can't think of any to put into my own.

'I think I recognise your name from the front of the scripts,' says Todd.

'Yeah,' I say, by way of eloquent response.

'You see a lot of names though.'

'Yeah, of course.'

'Anyway, good to meet one of the writers! Keep up the good work.'

Mark – I mean, Todd – goes back to his seat. I make my excuses and head back to the *Radio Times* table, where the dynamic is so much easier to cope with. What else is a soap actor supposed to say to a writer? And what else is a soap writer supposed to say to an actor?

'I loved the way you delivered that line about the dialysis machines!'

'Was that one of yours? Classic line. I said it to Jeff, didn't I?'

'That's the one. I loved you as Tucker Jenkins, by the way!'

'Thanks. Do you know what – even though Mark Fowler is an established enough character to have his own distinctive "voice", a voice that the writers are expected to "find" in their writing, thus ideally making it impossible to distinguish one writer's dialogue from another, I would say, on points, that you know my voice better than all the other writers.'

'You're very kind. You can spend too long worrying about what other people will think.'

'Wait a minute … Are you writing this conversation?'

```
[JIM GOES BACK OUT INTO THE HALL. SONIA GETS UP
AND FOLLOWS. SHE IS WORRIED. WELLARD IS STILL
SCRATCHING AT THE DOOR. CHAOS]
```

SONIA: Granddad.

JIM: It's them Slaters, always airing their dirty
laundry in public. [TO WELLARD] Get down, you.

SONIA: What did you mean about Jamie?

JIM: [DISMISSIVE] Probably something and nothing.
You go and finish reading your essay.

I killed Nick Cotton's son, Ashley. I drained the brake fluid out of Mark Fowler's motorbike the night before. Ashley, in a fit of pique after an argument with Mark that I instigated in the Queen Vic, hopped on the bike and revved it up. It was me who arranged for the keys to be conveniently left in the ignition. That took some doing. Then off he roared, narrowly missing Dot, his own grandmother, outside the Vic, and smashed into the launderette, coming off the bike and landing in a heap on the road. It was, in *EastEnders* terms, quite a major stunt.

Even Dr Trueman couldn't save him.

I also killed Posh and Becks, which was less of a technical palaver. These were Billy Mitchell's goldfish, and a more potent demise, as I'd actually introduced Posh into *EastEnders* in the first place, when Billy moved onto the Square for the first time. There was a bit of business with a box he was carrying, trying to keep it level, but why? Ah, I see, he was carrying a fish tank. Becks was introduced in a later storyline – a present from Little Mo, I think – but I had the fun of killing them off. The Piscine Axeman!

These have been my *EastEnders* landmarks, the privileges of the job. In total, over the past two years, I have written eleven episodes of Britain's premier soap: that's six and a half hours of primetime television drama.

It is the hardest job I've ever had. More fulfilling and financially rewarding than running *Q*, and more arduous than collecting trolleys for Sainsbury's. And of all the theoretically interesting media jobs I've had since leaving college, it's the one that, aptly enough, everybody wants to talk about. A friend of my sister's in Northampton actually accused her of *lying* when she mentioned what her brother did. People who've lost touch with what I've been doing say they saw my name on the credits of an episode and assumed it was another Andrew Collins. It is the notch on the CV that truly raises eyebrows. How can *I* be writing *EastEnders*? That's 'other people', isn't it?

My thoughts exactly.

```
SONIA: [WORRIED] Tell me, Granddad.


[JIM ROLLS HIS EYES]


JIM: All right, but you won't like it.


[OUT ON SONIA, FEARING THE WORST]


[CUT TO:]
```

14

Getting Drunk with Doctor Who

The machine beeps. 'Hi, this is Quentin Tarantino …'

He pronounces it in the American way: *Quen'n*. A pause.

'Ah, I'm supposed to be talking to Andrew Collins?'

Another pause.

'Is he there? Are you there?'

At which, Quentin Tarantino, on the line from New York, starts dum-de-dumming on my answer machine.

'Dum-de-dum … mmm-mmmm-mmm … doo-do-doo …'

A big transatlantic sigh.

'No? OK, well, I was supposed to talk to Andrew Collins, but he's not there, so. G'bye.'

Click. Beep.

I have to get a mobile phone.

Doctor Who's not happy.

'You're late!' he booms, like a cosmic headmaster.

I am rendered almost mute and simper something about public transport – not something he need worry about. He's seated, like a silver-haired Buddha, on a chair in the resonant, high-ceilinged lobby of the five-star Langham Hotel – an establishment notable for having a red carpet that actually extends outside across the pavement and into waiting taxis – wrapped in overcoat and scarf, his hands resting on his not unimpressive belly. I tell him who I am. I know who he is and he knows it.

Enough formalities. He rises to his full 6ft 2in height and I follow as he sweeps into the Palm Court restaurant for coffee and biscuits. The waiter who shows us to our table is foreign, perhaps French, and as such may not know who the Doctor is. He might assume he is another of the hotel's great big luvvies.

I *was* slightly late, but you wouldn't think that five minutes would matter that much to a Time Lord.

The days stretch out. The weeks gape. Time lolls in a hammock. The life of a freelancer is one of constant surprises. Sometimes the phone rings. Sometimes it doesn't. Could go either way. Sometimes Quentin Tarantino rings and leaves me a snotty message, even though I had no idea he would be calling, so it was not my fault that I wasn't there.

I've got a mobile now – I didn't even have to pay for it because it came free in a Barclaycard offer – so that's twice the probability of a phone not ringing.

Just before I left *Q* and put the asphyxiating strictures of routine well and truly behind me, we moved out of the flat into our first house. So, in preparation for my new life, I set up a nice little upstairs office with an Ikea desk, a platoon of Billy bookcases and a John Lewis filing cabinet. All self-assembly, so I had something to fill my time with before the work started trickling in. I knew my computer *had* a modem, because Stuart, incidentally the first *Q* writer to 'get the Internet', showed me how to work it back at the flat once – but try as I might, I could not repeat the trick. To compensate I invested in a fax from Argos and signed up for BT Call Minder.

We had a bit of a computer-related 'legal' during my first flush of seniority at *Q* actually, when Stuart casually wrote that a certain pop-rapper was gay – in an album review, of all benign places. And because this rapper had enjoyed a sizeable trans-atlantic hit, his attorneys were quick to get in touch, pointing out that their client was *not* gay, and that we had damaged his professional standing as a rapper by saying he was. At which point, watching the bolted horse disappear over the horizon, we asked Stuart to name his source.

'I got it off the Internet,' he protested.

At this stage in late 1995, the net was still a novelty, rarely used as a research tool in the office and though we had email we never really fired up the email computer as the *Q* address wasn't even printed in the magazine. This was where we were at with cyberspace. And no matter how hard we searched, using Infoseek and AltaVista, we couldn't find the page Stuart had used while looking up salient facts about the heterosexual rapper. We learned a hard lesson that day: don't believe anything you read on the Internet. It was a jungle out there.

So, with what to fill the columns in my brand-new blue Guildhall Account Book?

The two long-running *Collins & Maconie* bankers dried up almost simultaneously, effectively calling last orders on the double act which had served us so well as an *entrée* into the audio-visual media. There were no obituaries and papers were not signed, but without our long-running radio and TV shows to bind us, it seemed wise to find our own projects. Giant Bat remained a sheet of headed notepaper, Angharad Rees never contacted us about her directorship.

Watchmaker had put a lucrative development deal on the table for us, which I would have jumped at, but its exclusivity clause was a problem for Stuart, as the Radio Five Live magazine show he now hosted, *The Treatment*, was to be piloted for a TV transfer. Thus, he couldn't sign, and we couldn't sign, and the large sum of money was unforthcoming. I can't pretend I quickly forgave him for that, but at least it stopped us relying on each other.

So, Stuart pushed on with the radio, the 'fell-walking sophisticate' persona he'd always used against my 'impressionable clod' opening doors for him at Radio 4, where he found himself bringing bluff but erudite regional charm to the likes of *Midweek* and *The Afternoon Shift*, and even Radio 3. He could soon be found sharing a tawny port and a *bon mot* with Professor Laurie Taylor and Libby Purves in the George. Meanwhile, I relied on scriptwriting to feed and shoe my figurative children. But intensive full days of writing dialogue for Jim and Dot leave many full days of nothing while your work is being marked. And what if my future did not lie in soap?

I had to keep my hand in with both journalism and radio, for fear of falling off the radar and ending up down a Borehamwood cul-de-sac.

So I did what any self-employed media handyman would do: I put myself about a bit. I said 'yes' to any job that came my way. As a result, these have been the most *various* times of my working life, and humbling, because no job is too small, and no job is too shit. If you run a finger down the 'incoming' column in my Guildhall Account Book you will see:

04.8.97	Pete Tong	gags	£150.00
19.11.97	Condé Nast	B Grape	£188.00
27.1.98	Somethin' Else	charts	£423.00
07.9.98	BBC North	The Loafers	£176.25
24.11.98	BMG	Sleeper biog	£235.00

This is my life. The life of an indecisive gentleman of the London-based media.

Am I a comedy writer? The Radio 1 DJ Pete Tong made me feel like one when he personally paid me to write him some humorous links when he hosted *Musik* magazine's inaugural dance awards: 'And now we come to Best British DJ – it seems short-sighted to single out a DJ of any nationality in these times of internationalism and world partying, but, hey, as anyone who's been to Ibiza will testify, the Brits are a race all on their own. Sometimes, at half five in the morning, literally *all on their own*.'

Am I a music journalist? Well, I still write bits and pieces for *Q* and *Select*. I also get the occasional byline in *Empire*, which sort of makes me a film journalist, except when Quentin Tarantino phones me and I'm not there, because I didn't know he'd be ringing. Then I'm a useless bastard.

Is it a comedown for an ex-editor to be reviewing Big Country reissues ('there's more to the windswept warriors than shortbread-tin singalongs'), and looking after *Q*'s half-page computer games section, and occasionally being dispatched to Chicago to get inside the minds of the Seahorses? I hope not. Because for an ex-editor, these trifles are shorn of greater responsibility and they actually feel like fun. I just wish that while I'd been the editor I'd raised *Q*'s freelance word-rate above 18p a word.

Writing for *GQ*, however, published by the glamorous, New York-based Condé Nast, represents a radical departure for me. Not in terms of what I might be writing for them or even what Condé Nast might be paying me. (It's 50p a word, since you ask. That's what fashion advertising does for a magazine.) No, what's different about this new professional relationship is that I don't actually like or read *GQ*. I've never been a men's magazine kind of man, and now that the more successful *Loaded* and *FHM* have dragged a publication that used to have Michael Heseltine and Michael Ignatieff on the cover down to their dollybird level, I am even less interested in what the former *Gentleman's Quarterly* has to tell me about my life.

When my Black Grape review appeared, I was supremely uncomfortable taking the magazine up to the till in WHSmith. In that instance I knew how those loyal old *Q* readers had felt when Danny put a naked Terence Trent D'Arby on the cover. They were embarrassed picking up a magazine with a nude man on the cover because they feared their heterosexuality would be compromised if anyone saw them, while I was embarrassed picking up a magazine with a nude lady on the cover because I feared my heterosexuality would be laddishly confirmed. I fought in the 1980s sexism wars under Colonel Ben Elton. And yet, when it comes down to brass tacks, I am quite happy to take *GQ*'s money. Does that make me a hypocrite? A gender traitor? A whore? No, it makes me self-employed.

Am I a radio broadcaster? Not in the sense I was when I worked on One FM. I now read out the computer game charts on independent local radio. It's quite a comedown. I am employed to read them out, by London's trendiest production company Somethin' Else, presumably because my voice is at least subliminally familiar to a certain slim strata of radio listener, and because I write about computer games for *Q*, which enables me confidently to annotate the titles as I read them out: '*Starfox*, the woodland-creature-based first-person space shoot-'em-up on the N64, is still at number two … '

It's not the most edifying job of my career. It's certainly not *Midweek*. The worst thing about it is not the professional shame, but the journey. The chart itself takes all of five minutes to record, but Somethin' Else are based in trendy Shoreditch in trendy East London, which is quite a hike from my base in South London, especially on a wet Thursday afternoon when it's the only thing I have to leave the house for. Five minutes of talking; two hours' travelling. Still, at least it gives me plenty of time in which to ponder the fruitlessness of my existence and to ask where it all went wrong.

Am I on television any more? Well, no, unless you count two appearances talking briefly about films on *The Loafers*, a comedic magazine show on BBC Choice presented by Steve Coogan's brother, Brendan, and a brassy woman called Gill. It's flattering to be invited on – you'll note that I'm very much still at the 'flattered' stage of media domination – and more importantly it opened my eyes to the legitimacy of these new BBC digital channels. *The Loafers* may be a tiny show watched by an audience in double figures, but it's housed at the mighty BBC

Manchester – they have a proper set and walkie-talkies and monitors – and I was made up to discover that I would be made up in a proper makeup room. I even had a dressing room, with key. It's certainly a world away from the *Movie Club* and its musty cupboard. But – and you'll have already spotted the flaw – it's in Manchester. So for my modest BBC appearance fee, I have to travel 400 miles there and back by rail, which certainly puts Shoreditch in perspective.

At least writing a two-page biog of the Britpop band Sleeper for their record company doesn't involve leaving the house. You know you've made it when record companies think your journalistic integrity can be bought by the yard: 'Sleeper have scaled the difficult third album hurdle with remarkable ease, developing, fine-tuning, learning and daring to grow up rather than squeeze into an unsuitable pair of trousers run up for them by the media.' I like Sleeper, but I love the fact that BMG Records pay better than Condé Nast, Pete Tong and BBC Choice.

A life of surprises. One or two of them pleasant, such as getting drunk with Doctor Who.

'I don't know why he's on the BBC!' rails Doctor Who, apropos of nothing, as he pours our coffee from the pot. 'He *negates* the news!'

He speaks of Huw Edwards, newly installed anchor of the revamped *Six O'Clock News*, and recipient of a George Clooney-influenced makeover for the occasion. 'What's the point of a fellow having a haircut which gets in the way of the news?'

This is the life. You get to take tea with Tom Baker when you write for the *Radio Times*. And *Radio Times* pay as much as Condé Nast, without the ideological crisis in WHSmith.

'Anyway, enough about Huw Edwards!'

We're actually here to reminisce about *Doctor Who*, as BBC2 are laying on a *Doctor Who Night* and he's hosting it. He's incredibly sanguine about the fame the Doctor has brought him, almost twenty years after handing over his sonic screwdriver to Peter Davison: 'Moving pictures confer a kind of immortality, and that's one of the wonderful things about being an actor: you live for ever. We are now in a time where the living are entertained largely by the dead.'

He relishes this last line, one I suspect he's delivered before, and takes a dramatic slurp of his coffee to punctuate it. I'm thirty-four years old. Some days, yes, I feel jaded and blasé as I sit down to write another draft of another episode of *EastEnders* or review another variant on *Street Fighter* for the half-page games section in the back of *Q*. But today, I feel like a boy again. I'm not just sipping my Palm Court coffee, I'm drinking in every word uttered by this living, sixty-five-year-old legend, who, as the Doctor, dominated so much of my childhood. Tom Baker remains the only Doctor I saw regenerate *into* and regenerate *from*. Our conversation – sorry, interview – covers everything from his early years at the National ('I knew Olivier quite well socially, and very jolly it was, too') to continued interest in him among *Doctor Who* fans ('They want to know the names of my cats, and what's my favourite flower – they're shocked when I say it's deadly nightshade!'), and after an hour, we have to call it a day. Biscuits consumed. Coffee drunk.

'What time is it?' he demands.

'About eleven,' I reply, calculating the hour from the fact that we've filled two thirty-minute cassettes for the *Radio Times*.

'They must be serving *drinks*!' he surmises, his face lit up like a child at Christmas, his boggly eyes alive. I imagine the staff of the Langham would have happily served him a *drink* when we first arrived, but you sense that, for Tom Baker, propriety dictates when and when not you may have a drink. At eleven, you may.

Stockholm's Globe Arena, the world's largest spherical building, or so they say, is usually filled with ice hockey. Tonight, it plays host to the MTV Europe Music Awards 2000, broadcast, or so

MTV say, to a potential global audience of one billion. The night of a thousand nominations is edging towards its close. Simon Blackwell and I are on standby, should anyone need us. We are the writers.

And then, at 21.24 Swedish time, it happens – precisely the sort of emergency we're on hand to deal with, like paramedics of the English language. Ricky Martin decides that he isn't going to co-present the Best Dance Act award with *American Beauty* star Thora Birch. This is our umpteenth such flounce in forty-eight hours. The first came at 12.15 yesterday when Sonique – exactly! – refused to present one with Kelis, because she doesn't like her hair. Then Jennifer Lopez requested that one of her limos be changed because it was the wrong colour. We overheard an MTV talent-masseuse on the phone say, 'Of course, of course, we'll send a dark-grey one.' Once he'd called off, he added, 'Or I could gouge her fucking eyeballs out. That might solve the problem.'

'Who's going to do it with her?' we ask.

'Thora's going to have to do it on her own,' replies the hyperventilating MTV go-between in a headset. I don't know her actual job title – most people at the MTV Awards in head-sets are just conduits between other people who do definable work. Many of them have the word 'talent' in their job title, and you usually have to ask one of them to ask another one of them to ask another one of them to get anything done. Lucky they're all linked by walkie-talkie.

The zero-hour Ricky Martin flounce is a shame, as one of the nice things about writing the MTV Europe Music Awards is devising Swiftian exchanges between the disparate celebrities who come on to present the big silver MTV logos …

SWEDISH ROCKER ANDREAS JOHNSON: Pop music has the power to unite all people of all races and all religions.

RENE FROM AQUA: Really? Are you sure?

ANDREAS JOHNSON: No, I just made it up for
something to say.

It's all in the flat Scandinavian delivery obviously. But there's no time to reflect. The go-between talks into her headset at another go-between, and confirms that Simon and I have been summoned to talk to Thora. We have been *summoned* a lot in the last two days, mostly by genial Wyclef Jean, event host, whose frantic creative energy means he keeps having 'ideas' about our lovingly honed links. There's something about a rapper shouting into the dark of the auditorium from the stage, 'Where are my *writers?*' that sounds like, 'Where are my *bitches?*' But now we must dash from the production office halfway round the circumference of the spherical Globe Arena to the VIP paddock. We are, along the way, relayed from one go-between to another like a baton, even though we have Blue Zone laminates, which actually get us *everywhere.* There is a protocol to be observed around the 'talent' within the MTV Universe which it would be wrong of us to question.

Last year, our first as sole scriptwriters for the MTV Awards and held at the Point in Dublin, Simon was *summoned* from the Portakabin we called home to deal with guest presenter Pierce Brosnan. He was 'concerned' with a reference to Sean Connery in the sparkling repartee we'd written for him. It's amazing how much more frightening it is when a go-between with the vapours tells you Pierce Brosnan is 'concerned' than if he told you himself. Here's how the impromptu script conference at the front of the stage went:

While Pierce himself skulked to one side, refusing to make eye contact with anyone else, his personal assistant spoke to the MTV talent go-between: 'Pierce has concerns about mentioning Sean Connery.'

The MTV go-between turned to Simon, who was standing right next to her, with a script and a pen in his hand for maximum professional crisis-side manner, and repeated, 'Pierce has concerns about mentioning Sean Connery.'

'OK, we'll take that line out,' said Simon. He even scribbled it out on the script to demonstrate how infinitely doable this was.

The MTV go-between turned back to Pierce Brosnan's assistant, who had heard what Simon had said, and reiterated, 'They can take the line out.'

Pierce Brosnan's assistant went over to Pierce in the corner and whispered something to him, which we must assume was, 'The writers say they can take that line out.' And he mumbled something back, which we must assume was, 'OK.' Pierce Brosnan's assistant walked back over to the MTV go-between and said, 'OK.'

The MTV go-between turned to Simon and said, 'OK.'

And then Simon came back to the Portakabin where I was still wrestling with a link for MTV presenter Edith Bowman, with a glazed look on his face. At which we skilfully deleted the Sean Connery line from the master script on the computer. Simon is usually found toiling satirically for Radio 4 comedies like *Dead Ringers* and *The News Huddlines* – as opposed to global comedies like this. While I'm more attuned to the trappings of the backstage *milieu*, its tour jackets and catering tickets and fruit platters, this circus of bollocks is still a world away from what I know.

In two years of doing this, Simon and I have become not just better composers of Swiftian exchanges between Alicia Silverstone and Gabbana out of Dolce & Gabbana, but better politicians and international diplomats. In Dublin, having prepared for host Ronan Keating a moderately irreverent intro for a certain rapper our producer said, 'You can't write that. He'll kill you.' At which we laughed. But she looked deadly serious and said, 'No, really, he will hire someone to murder you.' And we changed the line.

And there she is: Thora Birch. Much smaller in real life, as per the cliché, but luminous in her own, over-made-up kind of way. Simon and I shake hands with her, half-expecting our MTV go-between to do it for us, and try not to stare at her skin.

The Ricky Martin situation is explained to her in discreet terms that don't make him sound like a self-aggrandising Latino cock. Thora has already been moved once – she was originally down to co-present Best R&B Act with Dutch foot-baller Edgar Davids, but he's a no-show due to fog at Stockholm Airport. She is informed that Simon and I, who have taken to approaching celebrities with a Uriah Heep half-bow, will come up with something that she can say on her own.

'Write me something funny!' she squeaks, rather sweetly.

'We'll try!' we say, only too aware that we have mere minutes to perform this tall order. The MTV Europe Music Awards 2000 is barrelling towards its climax, after all, and script changes have to be conveyed to the woman who controls the autocue. This involves one or other of us leaving the sanctuary of back-stage and picking our way through the packed auditorium during a deafening Jennifer Lopez number, flashing the blue laminate at a series of security men to gain access to the scaf-folding tower shrouded in blackout curtains inside which the autocue lady sits. We wave the piece of new script at her, unable in the circumstances to communicate in speech, and she effort-lessly taps the changes into her computer, so that, as if by magic, when Wyclef introduces 'American beauty Thora Birch' and she nervously comes on, her new link will scroll up on a giant screen in front of her and she, an actress after all, will not have to think of anything.

'Hello, Sweden!'

It isn't funny. We didn't have time to come up with anything funny.

This is what we wrote earlier for Iron Maiden's Bruce Dickinson and willowy star of *The Beach* Virginie Ledoyen to say before presenting Best Rock Act:

```
BRUCE: Hello, Stockholm! I just want to say how
much I admire and respect this country for what
you've given the world.

VIRGINIE: The works of Strindberg, the genius of
Nobel and the sublime engineering of Volvo.

BRUCE: I was thinking more of the porn and the
vodka, but never mind.

VIRGINIE: Here are the nominees.
```

And this, tonight, from that very stage, in front of a potential one billion people, is what they actually say:

```
VIRGINIE: Hello, Sweden!

BRUCE: Hello, Sweden! Sweden totally rocks. It's a
great country for rock, it's a great country for
heavy metal, and here are the nominees.
```

Fuck 'em.

This is surely the most nailbiting and adrenalin-pumping a writer's life gets. It's all quite a buzz. You're invisible but, at the same time, indispensable. Darren from Savage Garden might have sent over notification, via his 'people', that he will *only* say the words, 'We are here to present the nominations for Best Hip Hop Act,' but without the lame Abba gags we had already prepared for him he'd have nothing to *reject*, and then where would his ego be? If you're going to see the words you have lovingly crafted rejected, then let it be by Heidi Klum and the Backstreet Boys. At least you'll have stories to tell your grand-children. And the catering's phenomenal.

'Where's the nearest pub?' demands Tom Baker of the Langham doorman in his top hat, white gloves and braid. We are in our scarves and coats and out on the red-carpeted pave-ment, pan-galactically thirsty now our work for the day is done and the minutes are ticking past eleven.

'Well, if you go down here,' the doorman explains, gesturing southwest with a gloved hand. 'Turn left, then cross the road …'

Tom looks impatient: too complicated by half.

'*Fuck* that!' he bellows, and turns on his heels, sweeping off in the opposite direction. I am sucked along in his wake. 'There must be somewhere a little closer.'

I suggest the George, which is only one street away and the staff there are more than acquainted with BBC luvvies.

'Lead on!' he shouts. I'm like Doctor Who's assistant.

Once inside the George, which is almost empty, the Doctor, unravelling his scarf, buys me a pint of lager and a pint of bitter for himself. In the seconds it takes for the jolly landlord to fetch his change, the Doctor glugs down his pint in one. Letting out a cartoon exhalation of satisfaction, he immediately orders a follow-up.

I once saw a famous TV weatherman drop into the George of a lunchtime, wearing a raincoat and carrying a plastic bag. He walked up to the bar, ordered a bottle of Special Brew, which I didn't even know they served, paid for it, poured it out into a glass, drank it down in short order without leaving the bar and walked, satisfied, out of the pub. A joyless-seeming act that must have lasted five minutes tops, it was like some kind of fix. I actually thought it was pretty cool, but I am a shallow indi-vidual sometimes.

The next round is mine. I wonder if I should actually get the Doctor two pints to my one, but it strikes me as presumptuous. If they sold jelly babies as bar snacks, I'd get some of those. This is surreal. I actually have a number of things that need writing at home this afternoon. There's a quiz about the 1990s for *Q* and a review of a Billy Wilder book for *Empire*, notable for the courteous way in which Wilder always refers to men: '*Mister* Fred MacMurray' and '*Mister* Jack Lemmon'. But it's not every day you get the chance to drink the middle of the day away with Doctor Who.

We down a number of pints, me always a pint behind him. We speak candidly of many things, including marriage, work, parenthood and sex, but it would be indiscreet of me to reveal any details, as our interview officially ended at eleven in the Palm Court restaurant of the Langham Hotel. We are off-duty now, the Doctor and I.

He rises to leave at midday, just as a few BBC stragglers are starting to drift in: *Mister* Tom Baker, ladies and gentlemen, running behind for his next appointment. Yes, in a final crowning glory, *he's* late. And I'm pie-eyed.

I doze off on the bus home to Streatham and wake up in Thornton Heath, forced to take another bus to get back to my house, whose mortgage is currently being paid for in what are known in the trade as dribs and drabs. I shan't be writing much of note this afternoon, that's for sure. It's been an indulgence that I shall put down to research and development.

I only wish I hadn't told Doctor Who my dark writer's secret.

My dark secret is this: I currently ghost-write a famous television personality's regular column in a well-known large-circulation publication. His name and his face appear at the top of the page. To the reader it will seem that the words of wit and wisdom which run underneath are his. And up to a point they are, in that he gives a rough approximation of the gist of them to me down the phone.

The drill is this: I have the famous television personality's mobile phone number, which I use to call him at a prearranged time on an allotted day, and he rattles off some thoughts off the top of his famous head on the relevant subject. There is something childishly exciting about having a famous person's mobile number, but I have not abused this trust. I scribble down his thoughts then transform this free-form dictation into a believable written column, which looks to all the world as if he wrote it. Ghost-writing is not a new practice in journalism, only to me.

The reason the famous television personality doesn't write the column himself is that a) he doesn't have the time, and b) he doesn't write for a living. He agreed to do the column for the publication on the strict proviso that he didn't have to write it, and that it would take up no more of his valuable time than a phonecall per column. He is, I imagine, paid handsomely for his name and his image and his time. I am paid less handsomely for my time, and to keep quiet about my name. It's a dirty job, and he's not going to do it.

Once I'd written his first column, I faxed it over to his office so that he could check and approve it. He said it was fine, and since then, I've not even bothered to run it past him. He trusts me to be him.

I think I have mastered his 'voice', and if he *did* write the column, I feel sure it would be a lot like the way I write it. Sometimes when I call him up he's en route somewhere and it's not especially convenient. On these occasions, ironically, I get to put more of myself into the column, which I enjoy. The less work he does, the more I do, and the more fun I can have. Once, when he was deeply busy, I pretty much told him what the column would be about, and he was grateful not to have to think about it. I talked him through it and put words into his mouth. We'd reached a sufficiently breezy routine, he felt confident that I wouldn't besmirch his good name – or his good picture.

This really is the bottom of the barrel, workwise. It's regular money for me, which all helps to pay the mortgage, I don't have to leave the house, and it means I am forging a relationship with this particular publication – one that I hope will lead to other work in the future – but it's ultimately humiliating writing 300 words that are credited to someone else.

Here we go then. Think of the money. Think of the career opportunities. It's ringing. Think of the long term.

'Hello?'

'Andrew Collins here.'

'Ah! It's that time again.'

'I'm afraid so.'

'It's a bit difficult actually. I'm in a shop.'

I try to imagine which sort of shop he'd be in. Not a pound shop, we may assume.

'I could call you back?'

'Nah, let's do this thing. What am I talking about this week?'

It is usually at this point that I wonder: what does he *know* about me? Does he think I'm some stringer? Work experience? The publishing equivalent of a shelf-stacker? Or does he know that I too was once on the television? That I once edited bigselling magazines? That I co-hosted Radio 1's coverage of the Brits for three years running? That I read out the computer game charts on independent local radio? Would it make a difference to our relationship if he did?

'Well,' I say. 'You've got a couple of choices …'

Haven't we all?

As the MTV Europe Music Awards 2000 reach their climax and Ricky Martin – who so *nearly* entered into the spirit of things and actually presented an award to someone else – sings 'She

Bangs' while dancing on top of a giant goldfish bowl full of women, Simon and I shake hands in the writers' room and make a vow never to do this again.

'Deal?'

'Deal.'

We should have seen sense last year, in Dublin, when The Edge came on to present one of the final awards with DJ Armand Van Helden. Van Helden gamely stuck to what was on the giant autocue and delivered a committed rendition of this witty one-liner: 'Don't push me 'cos I'm close to The Edge.'

After a ripple of recognition laughter from the young people of Dublin and a suitable pause, U2's guitarist went off-script and posed this profound question: 'Who *writes* this shit?'

We do, The Edge. We write this shit. We write this shit for a *living*.

15

Pissing Off Christina Ricci

Christina Ricci's not happy. But I will make her happy.

Having built a career on playing stroppy teens (she's twenty now but doesn't look it or act it), belligerent and offish are what you'd expect from her in the flesh, and in her defence, it is Sunday morning, and she is in a grey, wet London in November.

In the rest of the world's defence, she is also installed at the exceptionally grand and obsequious Dorchester Hotel, a heritage-kitsch magnet for visiting Americans with its heavy floral prints, Italian marble surfaces, endless laurel curlicues, plump velveteen tassels, ornate moulded cherubs, chintzy lamps, distressed wooden cabinets, four-poster pretence, irrelevant Japanese marquetry and, so it's said, the deepest baths in London. There are worse places in the world to find yourself on a Sunday morning, all expenses paid, especially when all you are expected to do is talk about your latest film to the European media.

Paul and I were ushered into her suite at the allotted time. It doesn't pay to be late – these junkets are run militarily: miss your slot and you risk losing your piece of Ricci. It's *not* her suite, it's the one block-booked by the film company, wherein interviews may be conducted in a controlled but conducive environment. The illusion is that you're being welcomed into Christina Ricci's room for a chat, when you are categorically not.

She wasn't here when we arrived, which gave us the grace

period in which to set up. Setting up involves making sure the BBC MiniDisc machine is working and moving the furniture so that Christina and I can sit beside one another on a couch and Paul can comfortably perch on the edge of a coffee table and move the mic between our mouths as we converse.

The door opened, and *let's-call-her* Jocasta the film PR did the introductions. Christina was in a dress-down V-neck jumper and had a skull-length, asymmetric, waxy black bob, which framed her world-beating moon face. We all shook hands. Christina has the handshake of a clingfilm parcel of pureed apple: noncom-mittal, perfunctory, *better* than you. There are people out there on Internet fansites who would die for the chance even to be in the same room as a Hollywood film star like Christina Ricci, never mind touch her apple-parcel hand. I was aware of this, as we moved towards the rearranged furniture.

You always assume that the film star doesn't know who you work for, even if they've been told. So you say, 'Hi, I'm Andrew. This is for the film programme that goes out every week on Radio 4, which is the BBC's speech station.'

'*O*-kaaay,' replies Christina, which means, 'Like I *give* a fuck. Let's get this over with.'

'This is Paul.'

'Hi.'

'He's in charge of the equipment. I'm not allowed to work the equipment, you see.'

This is my usual icebreaking little joke – based on truth, like all the best jokes – and if it doesn't raise even a grudging smile, we're in trouble. It doesn't. We are.

'Do you mind if we sit here?' I enquire, gesturing at the couch. 'So that Paul can sit there and pick us both up on the mic?'

'*O*-kaaay,' she replies, and we sit, much closer than she would like, and to be fair, much closer than I would like, as such prox-imity means she could, if she wished, read the questions on my sheet of paper. I always scrawl them, for this very reason.

We get comfortable, if that's not a contradiction in terms for a Hollywood movie star junket interview. Paul nods that the machine is working and off we go. Christina is not happy, but I will make her happy with the inordinate amount of research I've done and the intelligence of the prepared questions on my sheet of paper.

'Hello.'

That is my catchphrase. Hello. It's not much of one, I know, but it's the way I say it. I've been saying it for two years. If I'm perfectly honest, I copied the delivery off Mark Lawson, but if anyone here has noticed, they're too kind to say so. I like Mark Lawson. He's my new broadcasting hero. My new Clive James. It was he who championed me as a contributor to five-nights-a-week Radio 4 arts show *Front Row*.

'This week, the best film of 2002.'

Here I am, introducing *Back Row*, Radio 4's weekly film programme and sister of *Front Row*. It's January 2002, so you can see why my words are already so provocative. I can imagine some Tunbridge Wells-based Radio 4 listener spluttering, 'Did he just say best film of 2002? What the *blazes* ...?'

Cue: audio clip of film, in which, over Angelo Badalamenti's mellifluous, haunting score, a breathy female voice repeats the words, 'Mulholland Drive ... Mulholland Drive ... ' The music dips under my voice. It's very dramatic.

'And I don't just mean the best film of the last five days, I mean the best film *of the year.*'

'Dear BBC ... '

Mark Lawson used to like me and champion me, but I fear I've got a bit too big for my boots round the Radio 4 arts department, which he bestrides like an eggheaded colossus. Now that I host *Back Row*, I'm not allowed to contribute to *Front Row*. I must fend for myself.

That voice again: 'Mulholland Drive ...'

I love the production values on this programme. Stephen is very nifty with Sadie.

'*Mulholland Drive* will, in my opinion, be difficult to beat, because David Lynch's new film is simply a masterpiece. Set in a *noirish* Los Angeles it is almost a female amateur sleuth mystery, in that its two central characters, wannabe blonde starlet Betty and amnesiac vampish brunette Rita, seem to be on the trail of a crime. But, this being Lynch, little is as it first seems.'

Stephen, a softly spoken Welsh surfer, is the programme's third and current producer. Sadie is the editing software he and the other Radio 4 producers use. It's actually SADiE – Studio Audio Disk Editing. When I first started presenting *Back Row* two years ago, many of the producers here were still wielding razor blade and sticky tape, just like the Kangol-wearers used to at Radio 5. But the digitopia is here and the old, Chinagraph-pencil-scrawled tape machines with the bits of tape stuck to them like toilet-paper squares after a bad shave exist only as museum pieces. It's all done onscreen now.

'*Mulholland Drive* bears all the Lynchian hallmarks – dreams, theatre, sex, coffee, the highway, 1950s nostalgia, sinister demonic figures, Roy Orbison – and as such slots neatly into the director's canon, from *Eraserhead* and *Blue Velvet* to *Twin Peaks* and *Lost Highway*, but its genesis was entirely different. It was originally made as a pilot for a TV series for the American network ABC …'

When I was asked to record a pilot of a then-unnamed film programme to replace the departing *Talking Pictures*, I was up against a wish-list of tried and tested Radio 4 'names', none of whom was directly connected to the cinema. Whereas *I* had edited *Empire* for one issue. (Three issues!) I was the outside bet. The sleeper. What I like to think I brought to the table was a journalistic rigour – i.e. I wrote my own links. For whatever reason, I landed the gig, albeit with a six-month trial period built in.

'… It was rejected by ABC as too slow and too weird, which begs the question, had they perhaps commissioned the wrong David Lynch? Anyway, with the help of French funding, Lynch worked his open-ended pilot up into a free-standing, two-hour feature. It's important to note that he didn't just tack on an ending, he completely refigured it.'

I spoke to David Lynch, and I put it to him that in theory, turning a rejected TV pilot into a cinematic masterpiece should never have worked.

'*Andrew*, it shouldn't have worked.'

And there it is. The reason I do this job.

The voice of David Lynch, speaking 'down the line' from a studio in a *noirish* Los Angeles using my given name in his Pacific Northwest squawk. I recognise it as the age-old interviewee's trick of instant bonhomie signified by the use of the interviewer's name, but I'm not too cynical to enjoy the sound of it. Not yet.

Christina Ricci's new film is awful. *The Man Who Cried*, written and directed by Sally Potter, is a self-satisfied, cod-operatic chocolate-box period piece about a Russian Jewish émigré who falls in love with a gypsy, played by Johnny Depp, amongst other torrid but picturesque adventures across pre- and post-war Europe. It actually doesn't matter what the film's like; it's our excuse to meet and interview Christina Ricci for *Back Row*, and Christina Ricci has done some really interesting stuff, even if *The Man Who Cried* isn't among it.

So we dutifully plough through my polite questions about the new film, and Christina gets to parrot the lines about how Sally is 'an *emotional* director' and how she got 'creeped out' by the love scenes, and if it's not exactly going swimmingly, it's polite and usable. The signature *Back Row* interview runs at about five minutes – for which we calculate on needing twenty minutes of raw material to edit down on Sadie. Because we are the BBC, film companies usually stretch to twenty minutes, but they will occasionally take the piss and offer John Travolta for five, which we will turn down. That would be fine for *Newsbeat*, who only need two soundbites and they're done. But we are Radio 4, a speech station. With all this in mind, you soon get an ear for what is and isn't 'usable'.

The trick with the film-star interview is to know precisely when to get off the new film and onto more interesting matters, such as their *other* films – in other words the famous ones, which Radio 4 listeners might have seen. You interview Kevin Costner about *Thirteen Days*, you move onto *Dances With Wolves*; you interview Michael Caine about *The Cider House Rules*, you talk about *Get Carter*; you interview Woody Allen about *Curse of the Jade Scorpion*, you get onto *anything else*. Everybody understands that the film star has flown in to promote the new film, but equally, if that's all we spoke about, *Back Row* would be little more than a PR wing of the film industry, which it isn't. So, glancing at my sheet of questions, and having harvested enough usable stuff about *The Man Who Cried*, I'm pleased to spot my first tangential question coming up next.

'Would it be fair to say, do you think, that your face has been your fortune?' Good question.

Christina shifts, uncomfortably. 'My face?'

'Yes.'

Awkward pause.

'It's just the face I was born with.' She gives a nervous, snorting laugh, meaning: 'Next.'

I glance back at my sheet of questions and forge on: 'Tim Burton, who directed you in *Sleepy Hollow*, described you as "a cross between Bette Davis and Peter Lorre". How do you feel about that?'

She shifts again. 'I don't know what to say. Tim's just Tim.'

This line of questioning is going nowhere. It seemed like an interesting avenue when I was researching her, and I do sincerely think that her face has been her fortune, but it's clear there's little she can add to that observation. She's right: it's just the face she was born with. So I glance back at my sheet of questions.

'Ang Lee, who directed you in *The Ice Storm*, said that "the face is a reflection of the mind" and that "Christina may not know it, but that is her power" ...'

At which she interjects, properly pissed off now. 'Can we please stop talking about my face?'

The interview is cut short. Paul and I leave. I failed to make Christina Ricci happy on a wet Sunday morning, and she didn't use my given name.

So, what did I learn from the Christina Ricci incident? One important thing: don't take a sheet of questions into an interview. It's tempting, but it becomes a crutch. It hampers the flow of conversation – even though it's not really a conversation – it distracts you, it breaks eye contact, and it makes you ask Christina Ricci three questions in a row about her face, just because that's what's written there, when she clearly doesn't want to talk about her face.

I actually had two more quotes about her face on my sheet: one from Don Roos, director of *The Opposite of Sex* – 'I think she's very conventionally beautiful in a 1950s sort of way, like Natalie Wood or Marilyn Monroe' – and one from Risa Braman Garcia, who directed her in *200 Cigarettes* – 'She's a hybrid of Madonna and Elizabeth Taylor.' Imagine if I'd ploughed on with those. It could have ended in a fist-fight.

Nothing like learning on the job, of course; treating Hollywood players as one long collective training course. *Back Row* is the nicest job I've ever had. Never mind the constant parade of international superstars I can tell people I've met – Kevin Costner, Tom Hanks, Uma Thurman, Johnny Depp, Michael Caine, Julie Andrews, Ewan McGregor, Joan Plowright, John Mills, Sissy Spacek, Anthony Hopkins, Matt Damon,

Woody Allen – this job means I've gone legit. I am now a broad-caster, and no longer a bloke who talks on the radio. Radio 4 actually sent me for half a day's voice training, where I learned how to speak. It wasn't elocution as such – although it's unspo-ken that I must learn to enunciate properly and pick up my tees and aitches for Radio 4 – more about delivery.

When speaking on the radio, imagine you're reading a bedtime story to a child. This was the most profound and useful piece of advice I took away from that half-day: normal conver-sational speed means words get lost in the ether. Though bedtime-story delivery may sound unnaturally slow and patron-ising to your own ear, it will sound just right when it comes out of somebody's radio.

I still feel a bit like a competition winner. Radio 4 is 'other people', not me. It's James Naughtie and Melvyn Bragg and Laurie Taylor and Jenni Murray and Humphrey Lyttleton and the person who reads the Shipping Forecast. But I passed my six months' probation and I've been saying 'Hello' every Saturday teatime for two years. Some days I even feel like a film critic, something that never happened during my one issue (three issues!) of *Empire*.

Quite why it should matter I don't know, as it's just a hotel for American tourists, but I now treat the Dorchester as my own. I always put on long trousers for the occasion, even at the height of summer, regardless of the fact that American tourists pay no such heed to knee etiquette, and in return, the hotel staff treat me as, well, one of the constant parade of journalists sent to interview famous stars at the Dorchester.

Big difference between interviewing famous people for print and interviewing them for radio? You're in it. Questions can be rambling, abstruse and chatty in a print interview, as you can always neaten, indeed, reword them when you transcribe and write it up. In front of a microphone, what you say is what goes out on Radio 4, hence clear exposition like, 'Tim Burton, who directed you in *Sleepy Hollow* …' This improves your licks. Keeps you alert. Removes the ramble. You become a better interviewer as a result – which is handy, as I've never been a very good interviewer.

Considering I've been doing it since July 1988, when James Brown sent me to King's Cross to capture the innermost thoughts of the Heart Throbs, and that I've done it across continents and all branches of the entertainment industry, I never really cracked interviewing. Always too keen to be the band's friend or the interviewee's number one fan, I never really returned from a print interview with an exclusive, or a revelation, or even a quote that would work as a headline. Adrian at *Q* never returned without one. Phil Sutcliffe at *Q* never returned without a full confession. Dave Cavanagh would stay up all night with an interviewee to get the inside track if he had to. I once sat on Richey Manic's bed until he nodded off in front of me, but all I got from it was a slurred insult about Steve Lamacq. When I interviewed Paul McCartney, he expertly dropped a morsel into an otherwise perfunctory rehearsal of the same old affable same old about he and George Harrison quite fancying the Queen in the 1950s, but the tabloids never picked up on it.

What I can do, if I may be so bold, is make the interviewee feel uninterviewed. And now that I'm interviewing at least one film star or film director a week, this is a worthwhile string to my bow. The one thing you soon pick up about the art of interviewing Hollywood stars is the power of flattery. Sycophancy and adulation are the lubricants that keep the engine purring in Hollywood. Without them it would be just a lot of insecure actors and technicians, wandering about, lost. We in the British media like to think of ourselves as above all that bowing and scraping – leave it to the film company flunkies, PRs, stylists and assistants whose jobs depend on deference – but let me tell you, it works wonders. Flattery gets you everywhere.

I learned this the hard way. I interviewed Christian Bale for *American Psycho* – his *entrée* into grown-up movies and a pretty controversial choice with its quasi-pornographic violence to a Huey Lewis soundtrack – but I decided that, as a former child actor from Wales, he wouldn't require the preliminary gushing. He'll be surrounded by fawning yes-men and yes-women saying, '*Loved* the film!' He won't need another poor sap doing it.

I had actually *loved* the film but pulled back from saying so when we were introduced for fear of losing his respect. There are times when you must segregate yourself from the herd and establish your journalistic impartiality. So we shook hands, sat down, waited for the thumbs-up from the edge of the coffee table and conducted the interview. It was perfunctory and just about usable, but Bale never really relaxed into it, despite my best efforts at informal charm, and treated me, I felt, with chilly suspicion.

Once our allotted time was up, Bale and I stood, shook hands and did the après-interview small talk.

'That was great – thanks,' I said, pulling on my coat.

'No, I really enjoyed it,' he lied.

In that awkward limbo between getting up and leaving the room, while Paul packed the MiniDisc and microphone away, I threw this in, casually: 'I really liked the film, by the way.'

His expression completely changed. 'Really?'

'Yeah. I'm a big fan of the book, but I thought the film really captured the essence of it.'

He lit up and became animated for the first time. We chatted amiably and enthusiastically for a few moments, totally uncommitted to tape, and I realised my tactical error: *he actually needed to know that I loved the film.* He needed to know because *American Psycho*'s not everybody's cup of tea and he still thinks he might have made a terrible mistake, and it's not just ego-nourishment, he's truly insecure about its reception. This was the one occasion on which I should have said, '*Loved* the film!' the moment we shook hands. The interview would have been vastly improved as a result.

So, now I make certain to get in an early gush.

Such as with Hugh Grant, whom I interviewed for *About a Boy*, the appeal of which, I would argue, is almost entirely down to his immaculate comic timing. When I met him before the UK premiere, again on a Sunday, I asked, 'Is your immaculate comic timing natural or learned?'

His response: 'I like you very much indeed for saying that. I like you anyway. I liked you the moment you walked into the room' – which sounded very good coming out of a radio. He even delivered it with immaculate comic timing. I refrained from telling him that I'd provided quotes for a tabloid newspaper when he accidentally got sucked off by a prostitute.

Radio interviewing in fixed time slots teaches you timing. You really start to get a *feel* for twenty minutes. I'm not sure how much use this will be in real life, but it's a skill of sorts. Stephen and I have a little trick. If there's a controversial question to be asked, he'll tap my foot with his own at approximately fifteen minutes in, so that if the question causes offence – like the Ricci face enquiry – we'll have enough pig iron to go back to the office with. A good example of this was when I interviewed – yes – Jerry Bruckheimer. I know who he is now. How could I not? After his hellraising partner Don Simpson was found dead on the toilet in 1996, Bruckheimer's name took on a new cachet, as he continued to factory-farm huge blockbusters of a certain octane content like *Con Air*, *Enemy of the State* and *Armageddon*. I interviewed him for *Pearl Harbor*, one of the worst films of 2001, and the difficult question I wanted to put to him was this:

'At the press screening I attended, people were actually *laughing* at the romantic scenes. How do you feel about that?'

It was one of those questions that gave me a rush of blood to the head when I asked it. After all the soft soap and the flattery, this was journalism. This was confrontation. This was dangerous. This was a man who'd blown up Pearl Harbor. It might make him cry.

In the event, the expensively manicured *Mister* Jerry Bruckheimer smiled, remained calm and asked me a question in response:

'And how many of those people had paid to see the film?'

'Well, none of them,' I replied.

His expression said, 'Exactly.'

I suppose if the mood had gone sour, I could always have told him that we'd once been on a yacht together. But it's usually not worth trying to 'get in' with an actor, director or producer by using some tenuous common ground. I informed Alicia Silverstone, whom I interviewed for *Love's Labours Lost*, that I had written her speech for the MTV Europe Music Awards 1999 in Dublin. She was sweet about it, but clearly couldn't give a flying fuck, and had to rack her brains even to remember appearing at the MTV Europe Music Awards or ever being in Dublin. When I interviewed Morgan Freeman for the second time, I informed him that I had interviewed him before. He was so thrilled he blew out the interview and suggested we go out for dinner to discuss old times instead. No, he didn't. He couldn't give a flying fuck either. Flattery is one thing; ingratiation is another.

There are creative ways of flattering their delicate egos. One of them is to scan the interviews they've already done for the American media and locate the Obvious Question, the one they'll be sick to the back teeth of answering. Locate it and either skip past it, or else turn it on its head.

Case in point: Robert Redford, who was persuaded to give us an interview about *The Legend of Bagger Vance*, which he directed while he was at Pinewood Studios shooting something else. Now, *The Legend of Bagger Vance* is a handsomely shot but Disneyfied tale about a spectral golf caddy in 1930s Georgia, played by Will Smith, who brings downhome, magical wisdom to a bunch of white people on the occasion of a big golf tournament staged to save a club from closing down. The Obvious Question, one rehearsed by every hack in the United States, was this: 'What attracted you to make a film about golf.'

To which Redford would patiently respond, 'It's not about golf.'

It's a metaphor, you see. Vance is a ghost, not a real caddy – he's here to reconnect the white folk to the spirit within themselves, or some such bollocks. Anyway, it's no more about golf than *Invasion of the Body Snatchers* is about an invasion of the body snatchers.

So my opening gambit to Robert Redford at the start of our allotted thirty minutes, during which I was duty-bound to move off *Bagger Vance* and onto *Butch Cassidy and the Sundance Kid* and *Three Days of the Condor*, was this:

'OK, your new film. The first thing to say is that it's obviously not about golf.'

'I'm so glad you spotted that!' he declared.

And the interview progressed happily from there. He was unnecessarily flattered that I'd 'understood' his deep new movie and felt he had me pegged as a smart cookie from the BBC. And we got to talk about *The Sundance Kid*. I don't think I'm especially smart for being able to flatter a Hollywood icon like Robert Redford, I just think all the other journalists are dim for not doing so. I can't tell you how many times a film star or director has commented, 'Wow, you've really done your research!' after I've referred back to an earlier film of theirs, or come up with a salient fact about their work. They are only taken aback because experience suggests that nobody else who conducts radio or TV interviews has done any more prep than skim the production notes for the film they're in the Dorchester to talk about. It is a piece of piss to appear more knowledgeable and prepared than the person from *Newsbeat*.

I use this confidence trick to compensate for the fact that I'm not much of an interviewer. I have become, thanks to *Back*

Row, a world-class flatterer. And I never ask this: 'What makes you choose a film – is it the script or the director?' That's five minutes of unusable guff right there.

Let's push the boat out here and have a bit of sympathy for overpaid Hollywood stars. They're expected to sit in a suite at the Dorchester Hotel for an entire day, sometimes two or three, while journalists ranging from jaded to hypotensive are wheeled in and wheeled out to ask the same basic questions: What was it like working with …? How does it feel to be nominated for …? What was it like doing a love scene with …? To which they must respond with words of wit and wisdom, at all times flushed with enthusiasm for a film that they finished shooting eighteen months ago but which their contract dictates they must tirelessly promote, never with a sigh, never with sarcasm and never with a hint that they'd rather be doing something less boring instead.

I once did a roundtable with Keanu Reeves for *Devil's Advocate*, and even though there were ten of us round the table we hit a lull, until one enterprising hack piped up: 'This is a question I like to ask everyone I interview – what's your favourite fish?'

To which a bamboozled Keanu replied, 'What, to eat, or to look at?' Which was a reasonable enquiry, unlike the one just fired at him. In that instance, I forgave every vacuous thing Keanu Reeves might have said, and might say in the future. It's a brain-eating game. No wonder Dave Cavanagh once got up and walked out, a luxury not available to the Hollywood star.

So, in a sense, you've got to love Christina Ricci for allowing the mask to slip and making me feel the idiot I was. We filed her interview under 'U' for 'Unusable' alongside Sofia Coppola and István Szabó.

István Szabó is the Hungarian director of two acclaimed foreign-language films from the 1980s: the Oscar-winning

Mephisto and Oscar-nominated *Colonel Redl*, both starring Klaus Maria Brandauer. He came into Radio 4 to be interviewed about his latest English-language release, *Sunshine*, a 'Euro pudding' according to my producer. However, Szabó's command of the English language was rudimentary. Quite how he'd directed an opulent saga about three generations of Austro-Hungarian Jews with English actors like Ralph Fiennes, Rosemary Harris and Rachel Weisz I shall never know. Presumably through an interpreter. Anyway, our interview was stilted, unenlightening and awkward. Not István's fault. Or mine. Perhaps Magenta Devine's, as she'd been in to grill him beforehand and may have frightened the life out of him.

Sofia Coppola was nothing worse than a dull, self-conscious, monosyllabic interviewee – which was also a pity, as I *loved* her new film, *The Virgin Suicides* – but the blame for the interview's unusability lies squarely with me.

Here's a secret: film companies can get you brand new films on video. They'd always prefer the media to see them on a screen, at a media screening, in a screening room, and as such will even lay on personal screenings for Jonathan Ross. But in emergencies, such as the presenter of *Back Row* not being able to get to a screening before interviewing the director, there's usually a way of sending round a VHS copy, as long as you promise to bring it straight back, not tell anyone and not make copies to sell on a market stall. If a film or PR company tell you they *haven't* got it on VHS, they're lying. Even the newest and biggest blockbusters are put onto VHS to send out during the Academy Awards season, mainly for those members of the Academy too old or incontinent to get out to the theatre, and there's always a master copy. Thus did I get a handy video of Sofia Coppola's brand-new, unreleased film, *The Virgin Suicides*, couriered over to my house the night before interviewing her. Unfortunately it was a US video, and my machine would only play it back in black and white. It was still a fabulous piece of work: its images were as beautifully framed as photographs, the acting exquisite and its tone at once wistful and nihilistic – and it looked lovely in crisp monochrome.

The interview next day did not start out a classic. For a kick-off it took place in a large, frigid conference room in a boutique hotel – not exactly conducive to relaxed conversation, and no floral print furnishings to create a warm acoustic. Plus there was tension in the room because Sofia knew and I knew that the subject must arise of her derided eighteen-year-old turn in her dad's *The Godfather Part III*, which had put her off acting for life and effectively put her on the path to directing. *The Virgin Suicides* was her first feature film and this was her first major round of European interviews as a director. Not to talk about *The Godfather Part III* would be an act of Stalinist denial.

So, we did. She didn't have a lot to say on the subject ('It was hard'), but it created a vacuum into which any goodwill we'd generated looked like being sucked. And we hadn't generated a lot. So I reiterated that I *loved* her film by playing my trump card. Without a sheet of questions – never take in a sheet of questions! – you are wise to memorise at least four or five bankers. Good, solid, smart questions that will get you out of any hole and re-establish your authority and/or affability. This was mine:

'Watching *The Virgin Suicides* in black and white, it struck me how much your experience as a photographer feeds into your work as a director, as some of the shots are framed as exquisitely as single photographs. Was that conscious?'

See? It shows that I know she studied photography at college (research) and bestows added artistic resonance to her work (flattery). However, there is a major flaw to this question, and Sofia Coppola was quick to spot it.

'You've seen my film in black and white?'

Fuck. How could I be so stupid? I'd admitted seeing her film in a way she never intended it to be seen. I'd compromised her art. I back-pedalled wildly:

'I didn't see the *whole* film in black and white,' I snorted, trying to make light of it. 'I was just fiddling with the contrast knob before watching it and I saw the *beginning* in black and white. Don't worry, I rewound it and watched it again in colour.'

This was a lie – I had *only* seen *The Virgin Suicides* in black and white – but it was a lie worth telling to defuse the situation. And then I realised, like I was shot. Like I was shot with a diamond. A diamond bullet right through my forehead. And I thought: my God.

My crime was not watching her film in black and white, it was …

'You watched my film on TV?'

Producer Matthew, through imploring use of his eyes and the occasional involuntary squeak, was doing everything he could to communicate to me that I should probably stop talking now. The PR, *let's-call-him* Conor, sitting in on the interview at a respectful distance, was mouthing the Rosary.

I had no answer to her question. It didn't require one. She knew that I had watched her film on TV, *because I had told her*. The interview was cut short. I had failed to make Sofia Coppola happy and she hadn't used my given name.

But I *loved* her film.

'I *loved* your film!' I reminded her, as Matthew led me away. I bet Mark Lawson never did anything so stupid.

I have since seen *The Virgin Suicides* in colour. I loved it even more. But Sofia Coppola has moved on, and so have I.

16

Getting On Famously with Black Rebel Motorcycle Club

'So, there seems to be a real Anglophile edge to the music you make,' I observe, trying to get in with men so taciturn and unfriendly you'd think they were being feted by the British media solely in order to inconvenience them. 'There's certainly a lot of Jesus and Mary Chain in there. Is that conscious?'

Silence.

Actually, it's worse than silence. Silence is something you can work with in real life, but this is not real life, this is radio. This is live radio. There'll be no tinkering with Sadie after this. It's a black hole that threatens to engulf us all. A Black Rebel Motorcycle Club hole.

'That's a *good* thing,' I reassure them. 'We love the Mary Chain.' I think I speak for the whole country when I say that.

One of these grouchy fools – I think it's guitarist Peter, but it might be bassist Robert, they all have Jesus and Mary Chain hair – calls up every last drop of energy in his soul to form a response to my impertinence.

'Two songs,' he spits. 'We've got two songs.'

He doesn't mean Black Rebel Motorcycle Club only have two songs. He means they have two songs that might, in a court of law, be judged to sound like the Jesus and Mary Chain. Just two. Out of, like, fifteen or so, man. I realise in this hopeless, demoralising instance, of course, that the Jesus and Mary Chain are Scottish, so not emblematic of anybody's Anglophilia, but such semantics are not what's wrong here. What's wrong is that I've got a rock trio from Los Angeles who don't really want to be interviewed on the radio, and I'm interviewing them on the radio. Perhaps I should say, '*Love* your album!' because I do. I really do. Or at least I did until I met these ungrateful, monosyllabic, shoe-inspecting berks.

I am a DJ. I am what I play. Unless it's 'Young Girl' by Gary Puckett & The Union Gap.

Now this is a photocopier I can work with. Feel the arrogant, can-do vibration that greets the laying on of hands. It's located away from the main office, tucked behind a chest-height partition in the Hub, next to the buried treasure of the stationery cupboards. Not exactly secret, but secluded, away from passing trade.

The Hub is the unfortunate Newspeak name given to what is actually just a common 'goldfish bowl' area with glass walls where the fridge, kettle, sink and Kenco vending machine are situated, and where bands and visitors are plonked. It's not a *hub* – the main office is clearly the centre around which all activity revolves, unless they mean the hub of tea-making, sitting-around and wondering how to adjust the volume on the demonstration digital radio. That said, the hey-wow-look-at-us table football does attract interlopers from other floors, mostly over-caffeinated online tykes, although I once caught Dr Raj Persaud giving it some wrist action in a break between recording *All In the Mind* for Radio 4 down the corridor – a job which must put quite a strain on the wrist.

It's in a world of its own, humming and jack-knifing away; this is a photocopier that makes me glad to be back in an office after four dislocated years in freelance exile. It even staples documents together when they're done, if you're confident enough to address the possibilities of the touch-sensitive control panel and apply your surgeon's fingers. Daft, but playing the copier like Rick Wakeman always gives me a feeling of superiority. I'm sure other people in Broadcasting House know how to get the best out of a magnificent machine like this one, but anecdotal evidence suggests that people up here on the fifth floor mostly just thump the big green button and hope for the best – a methodology attested to by the endless wasted sheets of A4 and even A3 imprinted with half a corner of the original document blown up to ridiculous dimensions, or twenty unnecessary duplicates spewed out by accident.

Presenters don't photocopy. Presenters expect lesser mortals to photocopy things for them. Perhaps that's why I relish doing it so much. The presenters on 6 Music are either comedians, musicians or the kind of DJ who's worked his way up from Radio Shropshire. These people have no copier skills. There's a fella who works in our music news department who speaks, with no irony or self-awareness, of his 'skill set'. More blasted Newspeak to make my stomach turn, but if I had a skill set, it would include confident command of the photocopier. I don't mind claiming that for myself at this advanced stage of my working life.

If in real distress, you're meant to go to Sally. I rarely go to Sally. If toner is running low, replace it. If A4 tray is out of paper, fill it with some more paper. In case of paper jam, just follow the simple instructions – a case of opening a few flaps and turning a few knobs. Contrary to received folklore, paper jam's not the end of the world.

I've turned up with today's running order to duplicate before a show and the copier's just been left, jammed, as if for all eternity. You can picture the scene: some Xeroxing *naïf* has experienced a bad paper feed, stood there helpless as the machine ground to a halt with a deep mechanical sigh, kicked it a couple of times, pressed a few random buttons and then just walked away. Not only is that bad copier etiquette, like leaving the lid up, but oh look, there's Chris Martin.

For a young man so unremarkable of face and with no discernible hairstyle, he carries the unmistakable crackle of celebrity and importance with him. It must in many ways be dispiriting to be in his band: nobody's ever going to notice you unless you're stood in a line with Chris. Perhaps they like it that way, Jonny, Guy and Will. I've never met Chris before, but I've interviewed Jonny and Will, and they were great: effervescent, off-message and very funny. They seemed more than happy to be chatting on 6 Music – and perhaps chatting away from the magnetic field of Chris. It is, I think, the mark of a musician that they're happy to come onto 6 Music. We may be small, but we mean it, man.

Because of Coldplay's very public support of environmental causes, I prepared for my interview with Jonny and Will by logging on to Future Forests and buying myself a tree. I printed out my certificate, which certified that I, Andrew Collins, had planted a tree in the Coldplay forest, and I presented it to the drummer and guitarist of Coldplay while we were chatting on air. I expected them to be impressed, animated and grateful. Research. Flattery. They didn't *appear* to give a fuck. They were nice enough about my carbon-neutrality gesture, but especially bothered they were not. I surmised that this whole environment thing is really Chris's baby.

So now they're back, with their glorious leader in tow, and I'm interviewing them again. It is a mark of further greatness that a musician will come back onto 6 Music for a *second time*. Gary shows them through, offering tea or coffee from the Kenco machine, which, being a keen environmentalist, Chris refuses, requesting instead a water from the cooler. The others have coffee from the Kenco machine.

It really is a terrible, planet-hating monstrosity – and a fixture at the BBC – you slot in one of the supplied plastic-and-foil capsules and boiling water is forced through the pierced capsule, whereupon Kenco coffee, PG Tips, Earl Grey, a laughable imitation of cappuccino or Suchard drinking chocolate is miraculously produced, which dribbles out of the spout into your plastic cup. *Et voila*! The used plastic capsule – and I don't know about you but I find that coffee tastes so much more authentic out of a *capsule* – drops into a tray underneath, to be decanted into a bin when the tray is brimful with discarded plastic. Interestingly, if you just run boiling water through the machine, without slotting in a capsule, it still comes out brown. Nice.

Photocopying done, I respectfully close the lid, grab the stapled running orders, one for Frank, one for Gary, and dart back to the office to pick up my Coldplay questions and my water. It's a pre-rec, so we're in Studio 5F. The rule with speech on a music station is no more than four minutes. You eventually get a feel for four minutes. Another skill for my skill set.

One member of Black Rebel Motorcycle Club is actually gazing dreamily out of the window. Dreaming he wasn't here. Dreaming he wasn't the drummer in a band who are doing pretty well for themselves considering this is their first album. Top 25 in this country, and with two Top 40 singles taken from it so far, all from a band who can't get arrested in their native land. You'd think they'd be glad to be over here, smothered in appreciation and props, an *NME* cover, a three-page *Q* feature, a lead album review in the *Guardian* and a personal invite to support Oasis at the Albert Hall. Time to lap it all up, surely? No? OK, why not just piss everybody off and look out of the window instead.

'You're obviously doing well over here, and in Europe,' I proffer, still trying to butter them up, because it's my job. 'Is there anything you particularly miss about home?'

This time the dread silence is at least broken by sighing.

Harold Pinter would love Black Rebel Motorcycle Club. They understand the dramatic clout of a pause.

Like many things about 6 Music, which is only just over a year old, Studio 5F is a bit crap. Almost quaint. It works and everything, and all the pre-recorded shows on the network are done in here, but the hardware is pre-Gulf-War and the layout is all to cock, with the DJ desk facing a wall and the rest of the studio behind your back. This means your guests have to squeeze in down one side, on your left, while you contort your body so that you can keep an eye on the computer screens in front of you and your hands on the faders while maintaining eye contact and not going off-mic.

It's not ideal. But it's all we have, and we make do and mend here. In many ways, we're lucky to have this much dedicated equipment and office space of our own. Certainly the *Daily Mail* and other licence-fee-hating journals have a problem with how much of *your money* the BBC is ploughing into projects unavailable to the greater populace. And it's true, we are just a little digital radio station. It's why our little audience loves us, and why bands as big as Coldplay agree to come back and talk to us. Because we exist outside of the constraints and compromises of a huge national music network. We can sort of do what we like.

'Sorry about the studio!' you say. It's the standard opening gambit in 5F. I say it to Coldplay. They mutter that it's fine. They've seen worse radio studios than this in their time, probably in Eastern Europe. Will and Jonny sit obediently behind their tables, waiting for Chris, who's outside taking a call. He's the kind of rock star that when he takes a call, you can't help but wonder who he's talking to. A world leader perhaps? Bono? Nelly Furtado? G-w-y-n-e-t-h?

When he re-enters, he seems distracted.

'I won't answer any questions about my private life,' he states, bluntly, for the record.

'Hey, this is 6 Music!' I reassure him. 'We're not interested in *all that*!'

We *are*, obviously. *He's going out with a film star!* But I'm not about to jeopardise the station's relationship with Coldplay over a bit of tittle-tattle about his famous long-necked vegan ladyfriend.

*

I have given up everything for 6 Music and it feels good to devote myself to one cause after the past few years of professional promiscuity. Having mostly clambered aboard established, iconic institutions – *NME*, Radio 1, *Q*, *EastEnders*, *Radio Times* – when given the opportunity to join something on the ground floor I jumped at it. 6 Music is like *Family Affairs* all over again, except with more photocopying and Kirsty MacColl.

'Hi, Andrew, blast from the past: John Sugar here. Hope all is well. I'm currently engaged in something tremendously secretive at the Beeb called "Network Y", and I'd very much like to have a natter with you about it. Give me a bell. Manly hugs. John.'

This was the back end of 2001, the year I met Jerry Bruckheimer, killed Ashley Cotton and was made film editor of the *Radio Times*. John Sugar used to work at Wise Buddah. He produced the final, Sunday-afternoon, ejector-seat series of *Collins & Maconie's Hit Parade*, and gave it something of a pop spin, booking guests like Ant and Dec, Kylie Minogue and, well, Darren from Savage Garden, the less said about whom the better. John is an ebullient, sunny sort of bloke with no hair on the top of his head but a compensatory amount on his arms. One of life's cheerleaders, if it all went belly-up in the media he could be the inspirational coach of a young offenders' football team and take them to the top. Anyway, just like pretty much everybody else Stuart and I worked with in those early days of steam radio, John has resurfaced – a blast from the past – to improve our lives. I duly gave him a bell and met him in the Broadcasting House canteen for a natter.

'Network Y' was to become the embryonic BBC 6 Music, a brand-new digital radio station aimed at 25–44-year-olds with a music policy that falls squarely between Radio 1 and Radio 2. It seemed at that stage to be mainly John in a makeshift office with a couple of rock encyclopedias, calling people up. He was on a recruitment drive, and had already signed up Iron Maiden's Bruce Dickinson for the rock show, Brinsley Forde for reggae and Craig Charles for funk. It was starting to sound like Radio *Stella Street*.

John's plan for me was to host the network's *Desert Island Discs* rip-off, *My Life In CD*, a pre-recorded hour-long interview with a suitable musicianly type picking tunes that tell their life story. This sounded right up my alley and I certainly couldn't match his other signings for star power, so I accepted his offer kindly. I was paired with bear-like producer Frank, a well-spoken blues and reggae enthusiast who does an impeccable Basil Brush impression and gives everybody nicknames. We recorded three pilots: Glen Tilbrook, Courtney Pine and, for variety's sake, Radio 4 comedy-panel-game stalwart Linda Smith. Even though the station wasn't launching for another six months, we somehow convinced all three that their candid reminiscences would actually be broadcast, and weren't just practice. These early days were run on favours and promises and John's Wise Buddah contacts book.

I will genuinely *never* forget the day we committed to tape the delightful Linda Smith's life in CD. We recorded the pilot deep within an adjacent building to Broadcasting House in a studio so unprepossessing and bare that its very use signalled that no other studios were available, but hey, this was Network Y, whose licence had not at that stage even been signed off by Tessa Jowell (who blocked the launch of BBC3 for eleven months because she didn't like the look of it). When we emerged from the joke studio, flushed with the satisfaction of having made agreeable radio, reminiscing about Ian Dury and The Blockheads, rain-lashed holidays in the Isle of Wight and who Linda's favourite Monkee was, we were immediately called into a nearby office.

'Something's happened in New York.'

There we watched live news coverage of a plane crashing into the World Trade Center. The infant century took a new and horrifying shape.

*

Perhaps driven by the global war on terror and the shifting plates of geopolitical power, I decided to throw caution to the wind and asked John if I could in fact *not* host another pre-recorded hour-long interview show but instead train to be a proper DJ. It seemed the only realistic response to a post-September 11 world.

'John,' I began, over our next cup of canteen coffee, in the manner of a teenager who's about to ask his dad for some money, 'what are the chances of me doing some proper DJ-ing? With faders and everything?'

'Is that what you want?'

'Yeah,' I replied, with all the reckless abandon of the new epoch. 'It is.'

'Well, let me have a think …'

My *ad hoc* career in radio had up to that point largely existed in the pre-recorded netherworld, with the retake safety net taut beneath me at all times. Most of the satirical inserts Stuart and I provided for Mark Goodier were done in bulk and played out at the required time. Same with the *Hit Parade*. I was not a total stranger to live radio, having co-anchored the Brits and the Mercury for Radio 1, but even then we didn't spin the discs. I wanted to get my hands on a DJ desk and learn what all the buttons did, and because Network Y was still in gestation, like the war on terror, it seemed an opportune moment.

Also – and it would be disingenuous not to 'factor this in', as people who sound like they've been on a course all now seem to be saying – Stuart had raced ahead of me in terms of radio notches, landing *The Album Show* on Radio 1 after the *Hit Parade* folded, on which he drove the desk, and now he was being asked to deputise on Radio 2 for a wide selection of older men. He was fast becoming a proper DJ. I wasn't. I know, I know, *it's not a race,* but having entered showbiz as one half of a team, it felt oddly slack to have fallen so far behind Stuart.

As luck would have it, Tom Robinson – yes, *the* Tom Robinson, upstanding new-wave figurehead of 'Glad to be Gay' and '3-5-7-9 on a double white line' fame – was piloting for Network Y's three-hour drivetime show. His touring schedule made him unavailable for a fortnight, so John very kindly booked me in to record some trial shows in that time. Again working with Frank, I finally got my feet under a desk and went in for a day's disc jockey training with a fresh-faced young man called Chris Hawkins.

Chris actually *had* started out on Radio Shropshire, but like many of 6 Music's expanding roster of presenters and staff, came directly from Greater London Radio, closed down in 2000 due to lack of interest, despite wailing and gnashing of teeth by the small band of Londoners who loved its Triple-A music policy – that is, 'adult album alternative'. It was unsettling being trained by someone at least ten years younger than me, but hey, Chris certainly knew his way round the brand-new computerised playout system, whose futuristic name, Dalet, looked a bit like Dalek but sounded a bit like mallet.

We've all seen documentary footage of DJs at work behind their desks. It's all about cueing the needle up on a record, pushing faders and slamming in 'carts', in other words, the cartridges that contain the jingles and idents. Yeah, right, well get out of the 1970s, we don't do that shit any more. The records are now on computer. They're 'on Dalet'. These are loaded in before a show and your job is to fire them off, which, happily, still involves moving faders up and down. Moving faders up and down had become my ultimate prize. I had something to aim for and the quest already felt intoxicating.

Not every record is stored on the system, which is otherwise known as 'the core'. Pretty much everything Kirsty MacColl ever recorded is on the core, but only one Fall track, and no Wedding Present. Thus, Fall and Wedding Present tracks must be either ordered up from the BBC grams library, or more likely brought in from home like your gym kit. 6 Music is the kind of place where a lot of things come in from home. I already have a significant portion of my record collection permanently at the office, including my own core of disco compilations, as 6 Music doesn't play disco as a rule, and I do.

I got the job. Before Christmas 2001, John, in conference with Radio 2 management, whose task it was to oversee the birth of the BBC's first new radio station for twelve years, put together the launch schedule. Tom Robinson won the evening slot, arts siren Tracey MacLeod landed *My Life In CD* and I was gifted drivetime: 4 p.m. to 7 p.m. Which wouldn't be called drivetime as nobody had digital radios in cars and wouldn't be driving at that time. Instead, it was christened *Teatime*, which adds a touch of Northampton to the otherwise metropolitan set-up. Or so I like to think.

I was over the moon. I had *asked* if I could be a DJ, with faders and everything. Three months later, thanks to the patience of Frank and the experience of Chris Hawkins, they were telling me I could be one.

There's a moral in there: if you don't ask you don't get.

Neil James was a DJ, presumably still is. In the early 1990s, he was a new face at Radio 1. I don't know where he'd come from, very possibly Radio Shropshire, but at the time, like anyone with a foot in the door of national radio, he was delighted to get a few deputising jobs. One week, he was asked to sit in for Mark Goodier on the *Evening Session* – a nice showcase for his talents – and he was doing an interview with a band whose identity has been lost in the mists of time. They were chatting about 'Bobfest' at Madison Square Gardens, the tribute concert marking the thirtieth anniversary of Bob Dylan's first album and featuring Neil Young, Sinead O'Connor, Eddie Vedder and others. The nature of the tribute and the quality of the bill were discussed, and James summed up, in suitably grave tone, with the apocryphal words, 'What a shame Bob Dylan didn't live to see it.' At which one of the band respectfully informed him that Bob Dylan was alive and well. James looked pleadingly at his producer through the glass and said, 'Can we go again?'

But they couldn't 'go again'. It was live.

A story to haunt every budding DJ.

Nick, that's his name. He's the problem, I reckon. The weak link. He's not even American, he's from Devon – perhaps that's why he feels he has to try even harder than his two bandmates, trying to affect West Coast cool but only managing West Country rudeness.

I'm starting to long for the interrogative days of Ricci and Coppola. At least they had good reason to be huffy with me and made some effort to be polite in the initial stages of our relationship. It's all Black Rebel Motorcycle Club can do to look me in the eye and form sentences in response to my perfectly reasonable questions.

'Not really,' answers Peter or Robert, after what feels like minutes of time-bending dead air but is in fact only seconds.

'You don't miss *anything* about home?'

'The usual stuff,' he elucidates. That's it though. Enough detail.

'How does it feel to be feted by the British press?' I ask, patiently. What I really want to ask is, 'How long do you think you'll be feted by the British press if you behave like pilchards?'

The studios are in a different BBC building to the 6 Music office, thus every day, Monday to Friday, at about a quarter to *Teatime*, we march across the road with our heavily stickered programme box and our Wedding Present and disco CDs and our snacks, bidding a cheery hello to Penny and Gary on reception and flashing the BBC passes clipped to our belt hooks. This is Hallam Street, the tradesmen's entrance to Broadcasting House, where the dogged pack of autograph hunters lay in eternal wait, led by the one we call Roy Cropper because he looks a bit like Hayley's husband on *Coronation Street*. You have to admire their tenacity and forward planning. They're not *sad*, they don't hang around

Hallam Street all day. In fact, their huddled, expectant presence on the pavement indicates with barometric certainty that someone famous is in the building, be it Patrick Swayze, Peter Mandelson or Michael Crichton. Somehow they remain constantly abreast of the guest schedules of Jonathan Ross, Steve Wright, Sue Lawley etc. Dressed for all weathers and in constant internecine competition for the same calligraphic quarry, I half-hope that one day they'll bother me for my autograph.

As it is, I may walk freely past them twice a day, in and out, like clockwork, without being hassled. There are even postcards of the 6 Music DJs up by Penny's desk for easy identification, but still I do not merit a corner in the autograph hunter's book. It's a sobering situation, but I'm not here for the fame, I'm here for the faders.

Should I ever attract any unwanted attention at Hallam Street, I'll always have Frank and Gary. Both big lads, they look for all the world like my personal security, flanking me all the way past Penny to the lifts. Frank has given me the nickname 'Champ' – which I much prefer to College – and Gary is 'Hoss', a reference to *Bonanza*, which went off the air about ten years before Gary was born.

Small is beautiful, as German economist E.F. Schumacher famously noted, and 6 Music embodies that spirit. It may not have made me famous, like Rossy or Wrighty, but it has made me a DJ.

I had to give up *EastEnders*, of course, with a little sadness. John Yorke was very understanding, and very kindly left the door open for me, should this crazy DJ dream go belly-up. I also had to give up *Back Row* after two and a half years. I'd optimistically tried to combine *Back Row* and *Teatime*, but it was like having a wife and a mistress. Sparks flew. I became embroiled in a tug-of-love between Frank and Stephen. The mistress won and became my wife.

*

We had met Black Rebel Motorcycle Club in 6 Music reception and walked across to Hallam Street with them. They too were unmolested by Roy and his gang, which was probably just as well. I'm not sure how thrilled Black Rebel Motorcycle Club would have been about interacting with men in rainwear. En route, I did my best to buddy up with the band by demonstrating that I knew a bit about them and wasn't just some interchangeable DJ going through the motions.

'You had a bit of visa trouble, didn't you?' I asked Nick the drummer, who'd been unable to join the other two on a recent US jaunt for that very reason.

'Yeah,' he said, visibly tensing. 'Let's talk about that, shall we?' He put his arm around me in a manner that can only be described as aggressive. Where were Frank and Gary when I needed them to protect me? 'Let's talk about that *for the whole of the interview!*'

He squeezed my shoulders. Hard. I tried to shrug him off.

'Don't worry,' I said, laughing nervously. 'I'm not going to ask you about the visa in the interview. We're not interested in *all that!*'

I bet Steve Wright never had this problem with Michael Crichton.

The handover. It's a fine old radio tradition. One DJ finishes; another one begins; they exchange a *bon mot* or two through the glass as Studio A takes up the slack from Studio B, creating a family atmosphere with a bit of gentle sparring and a baton exchanged. There's a golden rule in music radio that I've learned: never say goodbye. The end of you is merely the start of someone else. The network rolls ever onwards. To bid your audience farewell rather suggests that you are more important than the next broadcaster, which, even if you are Phill Jupitus, you are not. Jupitus, formerly Porky the Poet, is the most famous DJ on 6 Music and is the first one mentioned in any piece about us in *Media Guardian*, and the first one selected for any advertising for the station. Roy and co will have secured the signature of Phill Jupitus on day one.

The handover ritual has worked for years, on networks great and small, a schtick wittily mastered by Terry Wogan and whoever precedes or succeeds him, currently Sarah Kennedy and Ken Bruce. However, as previously established, 6 Music is a little radio station. We only have one 'live' studio. This makes smooth handovers with urbane chit-chat pretty much impossible. The second your last record is cued up and fired off, your programme team must hurriedly gather up your stuff – the stapled paperwork, the Wedding Present CDs, the stickered box, the used mugs, coats and hats – log off and vacate the cramped premises, so that an identical programme team can rush in and do the reverse. It's like the changeover between shows at a small, shared theatre at the Edinburgh Fringe. The most antisocial act a 6 Music DJ can commit is to end on a short record, like 'The United States of Whatever' or anything by the Ramones or Wire, thereby increasing the sense of panic.

For me, the slapstick handover is the essence of 6 Music: amateurish and messy, but tolerated and fun. We've been doing it this way for eighteen months and it suits us. There's a webcam in 5G, albeit, in true 6 Music style, not one that provides a continual feed to the website but one that 'takes a picture' every five minutes – so only the eagle-eyed online listener is going to glimpse the Whitehall farce. I actually wouldn't have it any other way.

It's a big day today. For the first time in 6 Music's short history, we're going to find out how many people listen to our little station and watch us on our little webcam.

'Well, thanks for that.' I exhale deeply as we play in the last Black Rebel Motorcycle Club track, 'Love Spreads', and the band get up to leave. Relief spreads. They can't get out of the studio quick enough. Only Peter – or is it Robert? – actually makes eye contact as we wave them out. I dearly hope that Nick gets his visa. Their plugger is waiting, like an expectant father outside a delivery room, ready to gather up his charges, wipe their noses, flatter their egos and deliver them to the next port of call in their bid for media saturation. I suppose you might call it a total-lack-of-charm offensive.

The single sounds great. I *love* their single, and I shan't let their uncommunicative, shifty, juvenile behaviour in 5F colour my judgement. They say you should never meet your heroes, but that's rubbish. I've met Woody Allen, Robert Altman, Gene Hackman, Robert Smith, P.J. O'Rourke, Clive James and The Farm, and they all turned out to be tremendous individuals. Perhaps you should just never meet Black Rebel Motorcycle Club.

While the interview played out on 6 Music, I actually had messages of sympathy coming in from listeners.

Rajar is short for Radio Joint Audience Research, the official body who get out there and tot up national radio listenership by asking some people to note down which radio stations they listen to and for how long – *in a diary*. Yes, a diary. In an electronic synapse-crackling digitopia such as the one in which we operate, this may strike the uninitiated as a shit system. But you've got to have one and it's the only one we've got. There are advantages: it means that if you get a disappointing quarterly Rajar figure, you can blame the system. Kelvin MacKenzie, chief exec of the Wireless Group, who operate the elegant TalkSport, has made whingeing about Rajar his vocation in much the same way that Martin Luther King devoted himself to the civil rights movement and Chris Martin does to Fair Trade bananas.

I feel there should be a drum roll here …

According to our first Rajar since launching in a blaze of Phill Jupitus in March 2002, we have a modest weekly audience of 154,000 listeners. Faces around the office are blank. Is that good or bad? To put it into perspective, BBC7, which plays repeats of old episodes of *The Navy Lark*, gets an audience of 236,000. Worse, arch enemy Emap's branded 'jukebox' stations, *Q*, *Kerrang!* and *Smash Hits*, draw 553,000, 864,000 and

– fuck! – 953,000 respectively, without even going to the bother of having DJs, or competitions, or handovers, or features with punning titles like 6 Musings or Ruff Riff, or timechecks, or interviews with bands you've never heard of called Obi or Lincoln or JT Mouse; just jingles to remind you which branded station you're listening to. This is all potentially rather depressing. Even John Sugar is having trouble talking it up. There is much mention of 'a respectable start' and 'something to build on'. We're already looking towards the next quarter.

I've worked on magazines read by more people than listen to 6 Music. I suspect more cab drivers, bar staff and students watched *Collins & Maconie's Movie Club* at 1.40 a.m. than listen to 6 Music. We're only beating Radio Cornwall by a couple of thousand. But hold your horses! We're only eighteen months old. If we were a baby, we'd only just be taking our first steps. And we've had Coldplay in the back of our cab *twice*. And Radiohead. And Paul Weller. And the Monkees. And Sam out of Sam and Dave. And Obi and Lincoln and JT Mouse. And what other radio station would bother to stage Goth Week? Or a week dedicated to the pop-cultural importance of Woking, Guildford and Croydon called The Surrey State of Music? OK, so our Punk Weekend had to be cancelled because the Queen Mother died and we, like all other BBC stations, had to switch to 'appropriate music' from the special obituary box in the studio, but we try.

What's important is that I've got an office job again, which has put some much-needed shape back into my working life, like a wire coat hanger. It has given me access to a magnificent photocopier. I clock on and clock off and brave the autograph hunters and exchange merry banter with Penny and Gary on security, because, after studio engineers, it's always good to get in with security. What's more, I find myself fighting for a cause.

This time next quarter, we could have 155,000 listeners.*

* We did.

17

Eating Coronation Chicken
with Doctor Who

'Walk down Stockwell Road and if you're coming from Brixton Tube it's on the right, opposite the wine bar.'

These are my directions to Colony 34.

'It is a small cul-de-sac, and you feel as if you're walking into a small council estate. Which indeed you are. As you go further in, it bends to the left and at the very end, through a blue gateway, is the studio.'

Colony 34 is an Earth colony in the distant future. There are over two hundred colonies in this region of space, grouped together on five habitable worlds. This particular planet is home to Colonies 15 to 68.

'It has a huge blue metal shutter. The person-sized door will most probably be ajar so give it a tug.'

As with any place that humans go, there is wealth and there is poverty; some have done well in their brave new world, others struggle to survive.

'Our studio is as far back inside as you can go – just wander through the long corridor and you'll find the green room at the end.'

It is day five of the June scorcher and day three of Wimbledon when I get to be in an episode of *Doctor Who*.

I leave early, so as to beat the stated 10 a.m. start time and get to the green room before all the actors. I feel, in many ways, like an interloper, a fraud, that competition winner again. Still, if I can fit through a person-sized door, it would be silly not to try it. I'm going to be in *Doctor Who*, a claim with which I have actually been boring friends and colleagues ever since I received the call-up – and I'm not one to announce my career successes from the rooftops. The sentence I have been over-using of late usually begins, 'You'll never guess what … ?' And they never do. How could they?

The original telephone conversation between Gary Russell, head honcho of Big Finish productions and provider of the convoluted directions, and my voiceover agent Annette, went something like this:

'Would Andrew like to be in an audio episode of *Doctor Who*?'

'Hahahahahahahahahahahaaaaa!'

The subsequent conversation between Annette and myself went something like this:

'Would you like to be in an audio episode of *Doctor Who*?'

'Hahahahahahahahahahahaaaaa!'

It's not a question that needs answering, is it? The money, Annette assured me, was small, 'but they'll give you lunch'.

I needed no further buttering. I would have happily made lunch, packed it into Tupperware tubs and served it to them in exchange for this golden, once-in-a-lifetime opportunity. I am going to be in an audio adventure of *Doctor Who*. If I'd been asked a year ago, pre-Eccleston, I would still have leaped at the chance to become a footnote in *Who* history, but the Doctor has re-entered popular culture in such a profound way in 2005, thanks to Russell T. Davies, the franchise now carries a brand-new cachet. *Doctor Who* is cool again, and I am to be a footnote in its history.

Know this: I was cast in a Big Finish *Doctor Who* audio adventure because they needed a radio presenter to play a radio presenter, albeit a futuristic one. I will be treading in the self-mocking footsteps of Tony Blackburn, who played a DJ in an audio adventure called *The Rapture*, episode thirty-six, released in September 2002, the chief difference being he played himself and I am to become Drew Shahan, a cross between Jeremy Paxman, Nicky Campbell and James Whale, or at least, that's how I intend to play him.

Play him! I know. I can talk it down as much as I like, but today I am to be an ac-tor. I will use my interpretative and performing skills to bring words on a page to dramatic life. Perhaps my agents will have to start listing me on their website under 'actors'. (Perhaps not.)

I did play a hospital radio DJ called Andrew in the Radio 5 comedy *Fantastic Voyage*, which was clearly quite a stretch, so I do have a modest footnote of form in the acting game, I tell myself. That said, my episode of *Doctor Who* is no comedy. It is presented as a radio broadcast, with the Seventh Doctor, Sylvester McCoy, and perky assistant Ace, Sophie Aldred, involved in a kind of peasant uprising and being interviewed by roving reporters from futuristic radio station Live 34.

I must assume I was considered for the part because of my day job at 6 Music, itself once a futuristic radio station, now part of the furniture. In this, once again, one chunk leads to another chunk. It may be haphazard, but my career does seem to follow this rule. I am often asked to speak to groups of students and tell them how I got where I am today. This is handy for me, as I'd quite like to find out myself. But there can be no dispute over this particular career synapse: 6 Music led to *Doctor Who*.

I received the script a week ago. At seventy-six pages long it's a dense read with some hefty speeches, not least for anchorman Drew. Thankfully most of my part is in the style of a live rolling-news radio broadcaster: 'In the last two hours an explosion has rocked the Colony's First City. Government sources are claiming that the blast was deliberate ...'

I'm hoping I can manage it. There's a bit towards the end where I have to react to the fact that 'financial and editorial control' of the station has been taken over by 'a state-appointed body' and there are a few dot-dot-dots in the script to suggest hesitation. My big moment of drama comes when roving reporter Charlotte turns up in the studio, where I have become a puppet of the state, and tells me to get up off my knees. She then takes over. Drew is proven to be weak. It's a lot to ask.

More bamboozling is the thought of *ac*-ting opposite Sylvester McCoy and Sophie Aldred, who have fifty years' experience between them. I'm a confident performer, but I'm in bad shape. For them it's a full-time job. I ponder the pitfalls as I cross the threshold of the studio. Will the other thespians resent me for taking a job that ought to have gone to an Equity member?

My plan worked anyway. There's nobody here. At all. I found the cul-de-sac on the council estate, tried the door, which was indeed person-sized and ajar, and in I came. When you're a freelance media all-rounder, you enter a lot of strange buildings, clutching a lot of directions on pieces of paper and are on guard constantly for fear of being challenged. I wander down the long corridor and find what must be the green room at the end. It's empty, although the jug kettle's still warm. It's a modest set-up, made claustrophobic by the air-conditioning ducts which dominate the ceiling of the green room and kitchenette. But there are fruit bowls on the tables containing fun-sized chocolate bars and Wotsits, and a travel Connect Four, which is welcoming. The studio itself comprises three soundproof booths, which face the control room and here's a large, friendly-looking fellow who, if he isn't an engineer, ought to become one.

'You here for the record?'

'I am,' I say.

He extends his hand. 'Toby. I'm the engineer. Gary will be here soon.'

I know what Gary looks like as he's been on *Doctor Who Confidential* – BBC3 companion show to BBC1's main event. It's possible that my own unfettered ramblings on *Confidential* have identified me as a fan and put me in frame for Drew Shahan. Every little helps. Gary, compact and camp, used to be a child actor – you may or may not remember him as Dick in *The Famous Five* on ITV in the late 1970s – but in adult life has allowed *Doctor Who* to engulf him, as *Doctor Who* is wont to do, editing the official magazine, writing novels, penning the comic strip that ran briefly in the *Radio Times* in the mid-1990s and moving to Big Finish full-time, where he writes, directs and produces, a regular can-do sort of guy. I identify with that.

Toby re-boils the kettle and explains the drill: thanks to military planning they record a whole sixty-minute episode in one day. By dividing up the forty-three scenes and grouping them around which actors are required for each batch, Gary can call his cast at staggered intervals throughout this intensive day. For example, the 10 a.m. call requires the presence of *Mister* McCoy, Ms Aldred, Bill Hoyland, a veteran thesp who plays the baddie, and an Australian actress called Zehra who plays Charlotte the reporter. And me. Let's not forget me.

Suitably calmed by Toby, I start to get a *Doctor Who* space-station vibe from the oppressive overhead ducting. The atmosphere zings to life with the arrival of Gary and, hot on his heels, 'Sylv', as he is rather camply called by those who know him. He's a small man, and wearing sandals, but he is the Doctor and I think I just about manage to suppress any visible signs of fanboy excitement at meeting him. As Drew Shahan, I will later be on my knees, but that's *ac*-ting.

One of Gary's other jobs, beyond directing and producing, is making sure the actors are happy. He is very good at this, perhaps because he's been on the receiving end. Gary knows Sylv, and Sylv knows Gary, and when Bill arrives, it turns out that Sylv knows Bill and they swap thespian war stories, as well as holiday plans – Sylv is off boating on the Aegean before jetting to Australia for a *Doctor Who* convention appearance with Colin Baker and Katy Manning. Sylv is just back from a six-month tour of *Arsenic and Old Lace*. Bill went to the opening night. Bill has just landed a small part in the next Woody Allen film although he hasn't met him yet.

I have met Woody Allen, but keep this to myself, as interviewing him for the radio is categorically not as impressive as being cast in one of his films – also I'm spectating here. I'm not really a part of this luvviedom, as much as I yearn to be. Ah, here come the two writers. I'll talk to them.

Perhaps my fortieth year is a time for firsts. In October, I appeared as a pundit on *Newsnight Review*. In the same month, I had my first ever piece published in *Sight & Sound*. These personal milestones were linked. I had always been a fan of both august institutions, but never considered myself a candidate for either. However, something about reaching the big four-oh had reshuffled my ambition cards.

So I asked the producer of *Newsnight Review* if I could be on the programme. And I asked the editor of *Sight & Sound* if I could write a piece for the magazine. I was, after all, only a DJ because I'd asked if I could be one, a technique that had first worked for me in 1988 when I'd asked if I could review a film for Gavin Martin. The worst that could happen was Gavin saying no and laughing me out of the editorial half of the *NME* office, or John Sugar saying no and laughing me out of the BBC canteen. Equally, with the cloak of protection offered by email, both Tanya Hudson, series producer, and Nick James, editor, could say no and laugh me out of their inboxes. They didn't have to go to that much trouble – they could simply ignore me, the way busy people are empowered to do. So I sent them both an email. A begging letter.

It's life-affirming to put your ego on the end of a hook and cast it into unknown waters. It's so much easier to carry on with what you're already doing and keep your head down. Mark time. Watch the clock. Count the pennies. But life would be intolerable if we knew everything. Sending an email is hardly jumping out of a plane or putting your house keys on red at the roulette wheel, but if I was the sort of tosser who used the phrase 'comfort zone' then that would be precisely what it takes you out of. And if you don't ask we know what doesn't happen.

Still imprinted on my mind is this incident from back in 1992 when Karen transferred a call to the features desk at the *NME* from someone I'd never heard of called Tania Branigan. She must have caught me at a weak moment.

'Hello,' said Tania Branigan, confidently. 'Are you doing a cover story on the Manic Street Preachers when their album comes out?'

'Yes, I imagine we will be,' I answered. 'Why?'

'I should write it.'

This threw me. 'What do you mean?'

'I mean, I should write the cover story.'

'And who are you again?'

'My name's Tania Branigan.'

At which I believe I adopted something of a patronising tone. 'Well, let me explain how these things work. If we do a feature on a band, I'll commission one of my feature writers to write it.'

'That's boring,' she said. 'You should get me to do it. I'm sixteen and I'm a big fan of the band and I could write it from the point of view of a fan.'

'I'd have to see some examples of your work before I could commission you, and blah, blah, blah live reviews blah, blah, blah.'

I gave her the brush-off but I really liked Tania's spirit. She was only sixteen. When I was sixteen my ambition was to save up enough Sainsbury's money to buy the new Cure album. I certainly wasn't phoning the *NME* and demanding I write the next Cure cover story. Tania and I arranged to meet up at a Frank & Walters gig at Sheffield University and while the

support band were on – somebody Philip Hall had been banging on about called Radiohead – we sat in the bar and I gave
her what I hoped was some practical advice for breaking into
the music press: use short sentences, make them active not
passive, don't pull your punches, avoid use of the word 'I'. It
was the first time I had ever imparted any professional wisdom.
Looking back, I wish I'd had the guts to commission her to
write the Manics cover story. I was too hidebound by tradition
to take a risk. For all I know, it might have gone down in the
annals of rock journalism. I never heard from Tania again. You
can imagine the feeling of paternal pride I got when her byline
started cropping up in the *Guardian*. She is now a political
correspondent at the paper. If you don't ask, even if you don't
get at the time, you might get later.

Anyway, whether through embarrassment or politeness or
something else, *Newsnight Review* producer Tanya, whom I knew
vaguely from her time on *Front Row*, and Nick, who'd once asked
me to contribute to a *Sight & Sound* industry poll, both answered
my begging email in the affirmative. I had to wait my turn for a
slot in both cases, but sheer strategic neediness had worked out.

The same thing happened to Stuart at the end of 2000,
around the same age as I am now, when, out of the blue, he
decided that he wanted to appear at the Edinburgh Fringe.
Having been up there as a journalist, pundit and even TV
presenter on a number of occasions, he reasoned that this
might be his only chance to cross the line in the sawdust before
he got too old and sensible. He invited me and Quantick to join
him on this potentially hazardous excursion into live comedy,
and *Lloyd Cole Knew My Father* was the result; a self-effacing,
scripted, three-way reminiscence about our time as music journalists at the *NME*, which we performed before an audience at
4 p.m. in a cellar at the Pleasance every day for eight days in
August 2001. It was like a really expensive eight-day holiday in
Scotland with added stress and paranoia.

Lloyd Cole proved a positive experience, best remembered by those at the festival for Quantick having to be winched off the top of Arthur's Seat by mountain rescue after he scaled the famous 823-ft hill in 'slippy shoes' and was unable to get back down again. This provided an excellent injection of publicity for our show, mid-run. Steve Coogan came to see it, although no offers of work from his production company Baby Cow were forthcoming. But we did 'transfer' to London, if that doesn't sound too grand, with three nights at the ICA. We also performed the show in a room above a pub at the Cathedral Arts Festival in Belfast and at a private party thrown by our old employers Mark Ellen and David Hepworth at a sushi bar. Stuart and David made tits of themselves reading extracts out of context on Ned Sherrin's *Loose Ends*, Radio 2 commissioned us to turn it into a six-part series and, to top it all, in 2003 Lloyd Cole got involved.

I'd just interviewed him for *Teatime*. As a lifelong fan it was a genuine thrill to meet him again, having done so only once before, in 1991, at Soho's famous Bar Italia for the *NME*, during which he recommended Raymond Carver, who then became one of my favourite American writers. If you're going to get a reading list off a pop singer, get one off Lloyd Cole. Anyway, as we were doing our goodbyes in 5G, he dropped a quiet bombshell in that endearing Buxton-to-New-York accent of his:

'Listen, I'm doing a solo gig at the Bloomsbury in London next month and I haven't got a support act. Do you fancy rounding up Maconie and Quantick and doing twenty minutes?'

'Are you serious?'

'Yeah, why not?'

Thus it was that Stuart, David and I supported Lloyd Cole at a gig in front of people. Unannounced, we just marched onto the stage at a packed Bloomsbury Theatre and, after a short apology for what they were about to receive, performed about a third of our Edinburgh show, including the bit where I put on a curly wig and leather jacket and pretend to be Lou Reed. Nerve-racking it most certainly was, but in the spirit of pre-midlife-crisis firsts, it was right up there. Stuart could retire to the Lakes happy.

I don't think I was much cop on *Newsnight Review*. I had my hair cut specially and did my best with the Robert Frank photography exhibition, the Sam Taylor-Wood photography exhibition (that's too many photography exhibitions, isn't it?), *Ghosting* by Jennie Erdal and *Finding Neverland*, but I never quite found my mojo, and no sparks flew between myself, Paul Morley and Another Woman. It was a big tick meeting Kirsty Wark, and the aftershow buffet was magnificent, but I was no good, and here's how I know I was no good, even though they said I *was* good: I've never been invited back.

That was getting on for a year ago. I can take a hint.

The piece on Gene Hackman, my all-time favourite American film actor since I was fifteen, ran in the November issue of *Sight & Sound*. It had been edited and laid out beautifully, like a dream, and I read it back countless times, as if perhaps next time I opened the magazine, it wouldn't be there, or it would be but written by another person, someone who *usually* writes for *Sight & Sound*. Like *Newsnight Review*, it was a personal landmark. And yet one that came and went. I have written nothing for them since.

Again, I can take a hint.

We set to work, standing at our quarantined music stands with our scripts propped like we were in *The Archers*, gesticulating wildly with our hands even though it's audio. It's hot in those glass cases. Perhaps this is where we started paying for our little piece of fame … in sweat.

It's amazing how quickly you fall into luvviedom. Once you're thrown together in a small space with other performers it becomes instinctive to support one another. That's clearly where 'You were marvellous, darling' comes from. It's not a bad thing. Actors are not bad people. They're insecure, but that's because they're self-employed and live in a world where people with no more skill than the ability to bare their breasts in a Jacuzzi can become celebrities, and where DJs with little acting experience can get acting jobs. In this regard, I can say that appearing in *Doctor Who* has changed me. Acting – even pretending to act, which is probably a tautology – concentrates your mind so much that acting becomes the whole world while you're doing it. Even in a hot booth in Stockwell. Especially in a hot booth in Stockwell.

The two writers have travelled all the way from the West Midlands to be here, and can you blame them? The thrill of seeing your words appear out of the mouths of professional actors, even icons, is one that repeat-fee money can't buy. James is an actor himself, and something of a luvvy, while Andrew is the quieter, more writerly one, who protectively disallowed his eight-year-old daughter from watching the recent, Victorian-set episode 'The Unquiet Dead' – scripted by *The League of Gentlemen*'s Mark Gatiss – for fear of sending her behind the sofa.

The buffet lunch is magnificent. Salad and coronation chicken and prawns and avocados and fresh fruit. I feel silly for packing my own. I almost tell my Tom Baker anecdote over food ('Fuck that!') – after all, I am now eating coronation chicken with Doctor Who! – but decide against it. The Tom Baker anecdote is only interesting if you're on the outside. These people are on the inside. One of them *is* Doctor Who. The others are professional actors who probably like a drink themselves.

After lunch, the second shift arrives: first, Sophie Aldred, who turns out to be a real earth mother and lovely. She has a new baby with her, clamped semi-permanently to her breast, as maternity leave is not an option for the self-employed. She proudly reveals that she breast-fed her previous child whilst in the booth being Ace, with the microphone up. Now that's juggling. Next are Ann Bryson, former Philadelphia Cheese girl (I bet she loves still being thumbnailed by that), and Duncan Wisbey; I share an agent with both of them. Duncan trumps my quiet persona by sucking on an ice lolly and blending almost totally into the background.

'Philip Olivier can't make it,' sighs Gary after taking a call.

This puts a crimp in the military planning. Yes, Philip Olivier who played Tinhead on *Brookside* until they took it off the air, and recently turned gay icon with his rippling musculature on Olympic-based reality show *The Games*, which he won. Tinhead plays the Doctor's companion Hex in the audios, but sadly won't be with us today because he's changed agents, and the outgoing one, possibly in a fit of pique, didn't tell him about the *Who* job. He'll come down in two days' time for pick-ups. I have no scenes with Hex and don't have to come back, which is a shame, as I'd like to meet him. All his scenes are with Charlotte the roving reporter, so Zehra draws the short straw – or the long one, as they'll have to pay her for another day's work at Equity rates. Zehra sounds more like a Doctor Who character than an actor.

Drew is in the can by three o'clock. My actorly confidence was buoyed each time Gary didn't say, 'Can we do that again?' through my cans. I've had a snapshot taken with the Doctor and Ace up against the blue door, so I am free to leave the council estate of dreams. I bid this happy band of travelling players farewell, all too aware that I'll never be called back to appear in another episode of *Doctor Who*. I've already been in one more episode than I'd ever have dared dream when I was watching 'The Ark in Space', aged ten, and memorising the intricacies of the plot for possible future use in *Doctor Who Confidential*.

As when I left the stage to sporting applause at the Bloomsbury, unclipped my mic on the *Newsnight* sofa and reached the end of my Gene Hackman piece, I'm quite sad to leave it all behind. But I wish them all well in their acting careers. They really *were* marvellous, darling.

18

Going On after Garry Bushell

'Take a seat and I'll tell her you're here.'

Who doesn't feel like Rupert Pupkin when they are asked to wait in reception? Reception is the great showbiz leveller. We are all schmucks in reception for the length of the lifetime it takes for someone to come and fetch us, whereupon, taken into the bowels of the building, we may become king for a night.

'Thanks very much.'

I've started throwing in 'thanks very much' instead of 'thanks'. It's a nice touch, I think. I hope it doesn't come across as insincere. There's enough insincerity in the media. I put down my suicide bomber's rucksack, take off my coat and sink down into this caricature of a sofa in a reception that looks as though it's just been decorated and might, in fact, be dismantled at any moment, perhaps dressed only for a TV prank show. I'm perspiring noticeably but not through nerves about the audition, simply through overactive sweat glands. Sweating has never actually prevented me from doing my job, but it does have a habit of making me glisten on arrival in reception. It's unseasonably warm for November and I have walked at a lick from Vauxhall Station to ensure arrival at the appointed time.

A glamorous young woman enters. She has the look of an elongated, less chipmunky Cat Deeley in a spangly top and heavy makeup – her skin unembarrassed by even a thin film of perspiration. I know she's here for the same audition as me because I hear her parrot the same name at the reception desk.

A girl who's not the receptionist comes through with a plastic cup of water for me and is asked to decant another for the glamorous woman who's not Cat Deeley. What's it like being that girl? She's on the bottom rung of the media ladder – dispensing and carrying cups of spring water from the kitchenette for people attending an audition – but she may well be filled with hope and dreams, and you can't legislate for that. It would be wrong to feel sorry for her.

'Thanks very much.'

I suck the spring water down greedily, hoping to lower my body temperature before the audition. The girl who fetched the water, *let's-call-her* Aquarius, is at a constant audition. She's auditioning for a spot on the next rung up. The glamorous, dry-skinned woman comes over and sits beside me, taking off her jacket. She perches on rather than sinks into the sofa and thus retains poise and elegance. She's checking her makeup in a compact and plumping up her hair. She's making me feel hot and frumpy. Should I be checking myself in a mirror? What would I do about it if I didn't like what I saw? Is a forty-year-old man employed for his looks? Surely if I get the job it will be on reputation, CV, experience. My face has never been my fortune, even with my new teeth.

Experience. I'll be honest, I haven't done that many auditions. When Stuart and I first sought representation from the peerless Kate, our agent, she sent us along to a casting for some new TV idents, I think for Midland Bank, as it was still called in those more innocent, less globalised times. We were required to act out famous scenes from films, *Braveheart* being one of them ('You'll never take away our *freedom!*'), the rest I've blanked from memory. These were then to be animated so that it looked like two goldfish were acting them out in a bowl. The goldfish bowl turned out to be an apt metaphor.

We were terrible. Really self-conscious and stiff, although the producer and the director and 'the client' and all the other people behind the camera assessing us from outside of the bowl said we were *great*. They are obliged to say this. *You were marvellous, darling*. They will have said it to all the other hopefuls, including, out of interest, the comedian Ben Moor, whom we recognised in reception, and Andrew Lincoln, or Egg off TV's *This Life*. Both of whom might well have *been* great. We will never know. I remember glimpsing the finished goldfish idents before big films on ITV with a what-might-have-been sigh and never being able to work out whose voices they were. Not mine and not Stuart's, that's for sure.

As ever with Stuart, it was enjoyable just to do the audition, to put ourselves up for something new. We came out of that poky office in Soho on quite a high, not because we were any good, but because you do get a little hysterical when you find yourself in surreal positions, like acting out *Braveheart* as fish. My friend Dave Keech and I were asked by female fashion students to catwalk-model some of their clothes when we were at Nene College. We gamely changed into what turned out to be a blue-catsuit-woollen-jockstrap-and-ballet-shoe ensemble in a store cupboard and found ourselves helpless with laughter, unable to stand, let alone prance. Same brand of hysteria.

It is the mark of a top agent that within minutes of the non-binding showbiz kiss of non-contractual partnership, you find yourself called for an audition for a national television spot. Whether you're successful or not, you must put yourself about a bit. Get in the race. Have your name on a few clipboards.

Sympathise with the hardworking agent of a client who doesn't actually know what he wants to do. Kate asked me if I would like to try out for this presenter's job because it was about films and she knows that this weak part of me does want to get back into presenting and most weeks I know a bit about films. As I had nothing to lose but a further sliver of my dignity,

I said yes. Which is why I'm lost in this sofa and wondering if Cat Deeley is with me or against me.

'I think we're here for the same thing,' I pipe up, taking a sip from the plastic cup Aquarius kindly dispensed for me.

'The film thing?' she asks.

We tell each other our names. I shake her hand, which is long and slender and weak. I am reminded of my old drinking buddy Tom Baker's line as the salty sea dog in that episode of *Blackadder*: 'You have a *woman's* hand!'

It's not uncommon to attend auditions without knowing quite what you're auditioning for. The company whose reception this is initially told Kate that I was up for co-presenter of a movie review show for Sky. Actually, we've been slightly hood-winked. It's for a movie review show for a tiny new commercial channel that will be available to Sky subscribers. See what they did there with their clever wording?

When you are waiting in reception for someone you've never met, you reflexively sit to attention every time anyone comes through. This could be them. It could be *the person*, or at the very least someone who's come to fetch you and take you *to* the person. No, they've walked straight past. This could be them. No. And so it goes. Cat and I are waiting for *let's-call-her* Morag. She's the producer of the film thing.

Eventually, after two-thirds of a cup of water, Morag, *the person*, comes through, bundling out another couple of audi-tionees with maximum bonhomie (shit, *he* looks young), and fixes us in her gaze, at which we both jump up and put on our please-employ-me smiles. It's not so far away from the indignity of *On the Waterfront*, when jobs on a banana boat are handed out at the 8 a.m. shape-up, and only the privileged few get to work.

Morag greets us warmly, shaking my hand. Her handshake is much firmer than Cat's, but then she's a producer. She and Cat, or so it seems, go *way* back. They air-kiss. That's because Cat's been recalled – callback being the first glimmer of hope for any auditionee. This is her second bite of the cherry. Whether, strate-gically, this is a good thing for me, I'm unsure. Have they sort-of-half-decided on her and are now looking for a male to match? And if so, does that give me any kind of advantage, or does it just mean that it's quicker to find a female presenter who's 'easy on the eye' – to use the unsavoury post-sexist vernacular – than a male one? I can say with my hand on my heart that I have no problems with being forty. I'm fine about it. But today, here, begging for work on a film thing at the shape-up, and paired with a long woman in her twenties, I feel a little old for the part.

We are led up some stairs, through some offices staffed by actors employed to look like they're actually working here by whoever's making this TV prank show, down a corridor, and into a studio. En route, Morag chats about the channel with a casual air that suggests I ought to know exactly what kind of channel it is. Turns out it's funded by the exhibitors, that is, the cinema chains, so even though we'll have *total* freedom to say what we like about the films we'll be reviewing, we can't be too negative, as it's all about getting people out to the cinema. In other words: we will have *partial* freedom. After previous dalliances in this area at *Empire* and on *Back Row*, this really is a PR wing of the film business! It's at this stage that I am overcome with a pleas-ing, Zen-like state of calm: I don't really want this job.

It will be just my luck if I actually get it.

I've done my homework. I was told to prepare for a couple of current films, and I have my opinions ready: *Revolver*, impen-etrable, better than *Swept Away* (haven't actually seen *Revolver* or *Swept Away*); *Flightplan*, gloomy, exciting, Sean Bean very hand-some as the pilot (have seen *Flightplan*). No time to rehearse – within seconds, Cat and I have had wires threaded through our tops, a ticklish, impertinent procedure that makes you feel silly and awkward the first time you experience it, but never again thereafter. With lapel microphones clipped to our non-existent lapels and battery packs placed in back pockets, we're set.

Morag places us on our marks – the ubiquitous gaffer-tape crosses on the floor. We face diagonally across each other at a camera each, fitted with a scrolling autocue. None of your desks or swivel chairs; it's one of those cheap-and-cheerful standing-up programmes. What to do with my hands? With just seconds to centre ourselves and get into character, the cameras roll and I'm reading the autocue: 'Hi, I'm Andrew Collins and welcome to *let's-call-it Movies R Us*! This week, we're going to be taking a look at the new Guy Ritchie thriller …'

I must say, and forgive this lapse in modesty, I'm pretty good at reading. I can read. It was in my skill set long before I began looking for work. The words flash up, I read them. I gesticulate with my hands and hold them clasped when not. The improvised two-way 'movie review', which calls upon Cat and I to appear all matey and not speak over one another, goes well enough. She accidentally reads out one of my links, but there's no time for retakes; move on, bang, it's all over.

Our mics are unclipped and unthreaded from our tops and the battery packs removed with the lightning speed and efficiency of a Grand Prix pit-stop.

'Sorry, I read one of your links,' says Cat.

'Ah, it's not a problem,' I shrug. It's a film thing for a channel that's paid for by the cinema chains whose audience must be in the hundreds. Paris is burning, New Orleans is a wasteland, the Middle East's in turmoil, people in London still think they're going to get blown up on public transport and I'm forty years old.

Despite the conveyor-belt nature of the audition, there's just time for some small talk while Morag ushers us out past the next hopeful pair. Having turned it on for the cameras, our audition committed to a hard drive somewhere, this is our chance to glad-hand and schmooze and increase our chances of being remembered when they narrow the field down even further. Guess what? It was *great*. We were *really good. Thanks for coming down. Thanks for having us down.* Cat chats to Morag about another project she *might* be doing, then Morag turns to me.

Smiling sincerely, she says: 'I'm glad you could do this. I'm a big fan of your talking head work.'

At which my life is reduced to a pea.

I'm a big fan of your talking head work?

MY TALKING HEAD WORK?

I am forty years old. I don't know what I want to do or be. But, hey, I'll always have my *talking head work.*

It's not the fact that a TV producer likes my talking head work that bothers me. After all, I have done a spot of talking head work. Rather, it's that she might know me for my talking head work above all other work and perhaps – who knows? – for nothing else. It's like being a Philadelphia Cheese girl. Seventeen years in the media and I'm a talking head. My head talks.

There's nothing ignoble about it – 'talking head' is a television term that dates back to the 1960s and means, usually, a witness, commentator or expert (that word again), framed in a fixed medium shot by the director so that just the head and shoulders are visible. The head talks not *into* the camera – that would be presenting, which pays better – but just off to one side. This subtle effect is achieved by strategic positioning of the unseen interviewer, who will in fact usually be a researcher or producer. The moment the interviewer is seen on camera it's an interview, and you are no longer a talking head, but an interviewee, which pays worse. On average, for a standard clips show, a talking head session takes an hour, longer if they're really wringing you out. Remember to include the question in your answer:

Unseen researcher: 'What was it that made *Love Thy Neighbour* so contentious?'

Talking head: 'What made *Love Thy Neighbour* so contentious was the use of words like "sambo" and "nig-nog".'

I like to think of my *talking head work* as a nice little sideline, an easy way for me to get my face on the telly, hopefully say something pithy or witty or authoritative enough to make the edit, and generally stay in the loop. I certainly never intended to be defined by it. Or even complimented on it. After all, it's just constructing sentences with your mouth, looking at a researcher and trying to make the man holding the boom laugh.

Looking wistfully back over my career, I'd say my head's been talking since I was at *Q*. As the editor of a music magazine, it's assumed you know a bit about music, and, in truth, I do know *a bit* about music. I can do you Christmas number ones. I can do you Britpop (which I invented). I can do you politics in pop. These days I can do you a number on why downloading is killing the music industry. And there was a time when I could do you the Spice Girls, and did, on more than one occasion, very much trading on my special relationship with the girls forged during a five-minute chat in a Radio 1 Portakabin at the Brits in 1997 and a twenty-minute interview in a dressing room at *Top of the Pops* during the filming of *Spiceworld*.

In fact, it was one of my numerous Spice Girls talking head jobs, *Solo Spice*, shot in a photographer's studio in East London against a white background, that convinced me finally to get my wonky teeth fixed. The director used one locked camera and one hand-held so that in the finished programme each traditional head shot came with an arty inset containing an almost surgical close-up. One of these featured just my teeth. My giant, wonky, gappy National Health teeth. Viewing the finished programme was too much to bear. I phoned a number found in *Heat* about celebrity dental work and never looked back. The expensive cosmetic dentist who eventually performed the miracles in my mouth had grinning photos of happy customers Rolf Harris and Elvis Costello up on his mantelpiece. Not quite *Heat* material. The upshot is that my talking head work can be divided into Old and New Teeth.

I appeared on a documentary about Mott the Hoople, shot in a noisy upstairs room of a pub in Westbourne Park. True, there are people out there who know more about Mott the Hoople than I – they might even have seen them play a gig – but I own some Mott albums, I've read Ian Hunter's book *Diary of a Rock'n'Roll Star*, I can name all the band members (Hunter, Mick Ralphs, Verden Allen, Peter 'Overend' Watts and Dale 'Buffin' Griffin), and I can quote lines from 'All the Way From Memphis'. Plus, they asked, and there's the key.

Because I'm also pinned as some kind of movie buff, due to my connections with *Empire*, *Radio Times* and *Back Row*, I'm also asked to talk about the movies, which doubles my 'expertise' at a stroke. Throw in television – as *anybody* is qualified to talk about television – and you're looking at an accidental all-rounder. There are an awful lot of *Top 100* and *50 Greatest* countdowns, and nearly all of them are about pop music, television or the movies. And even though telly always seems close to running out of them, having sliced the cultural cake so many times the format is now a plate of crumbs, those much-derided countdowns make giftwrapped schedule-filling repeats for bank holidays and digital channels. Nostalgia may not be what it used to be, but the archive clips show is the gift that goes on giving.

The most extreme example of perpetuity is Sky One's *The Pop Years*, a self-explanatory strand on which I did a couple of turns: one year from the recent past per show, a running buffet of music clips intercut with various pop stars, TV presenters and actors from Sky footballing soap *Dream Team* reminiscing about East 17, Frankie Goes To Hollywood and Reel 2 Real Featuring The Mad Stuntman ('I like to move it, move it'). The talking head footage was filmed in a suite in the Grosvenor House Hotel. The producer was Ric Blaxill, who'd been at Radio One at the same time as Stuart and me, and had appeared in his capacity as *Top of the Pops* producer on the *Hit Parade*, so there were touchstones with my former lives.

It was a lot of fun to do, and for once, I wasn't on after Garry Bushell, as is usually the case with these gigs. I was actually on after Pete Tong. Due to the general lack of incisive comment and cultural contextualisation from the cast of *Dream Team*, a great deal of what I said on the day was used in the finished programmes. This was gratifying the first time they were aired in 2001. And it was gratifying the second time. And the third. But *The Pop Years* is still playing to this very day, a veritable *Mousetrap* of clips shows. Now that Sky One has spawned Sky Two and Sky Three, barely a week goes by without my Old Teeth appearing on telly in front of the swirling fondant colours and the big logo, making a pithy comment about Boyzone.

It's like being frozen in television carbonite, stuck in a perpetual loop, condemned to say the same things about the same pop records for ever. And that, ladies and gentlemen, is my *talking head work*.

Let's blow this myth: talking heads don't get paid every time the programme is shown. It's a one-off sign-your-life-away deal. The 'release form' is the Faustian piece of paper that must always change hands after you've spoken. Jimmy Carr or Zoe Ball or whoever else links the clips will get a repeat fee, but me and Paul Morley and Jaci Stephen and Terry Alderton and Paul Gambaccini and Garry Bushell and that bloke from the *Daily Sport* are owned in perpetuity by whichever wackily named TV production company gathered us all together and expected us to talk. So it's not exactly a living. But it is a line of work. And one talking head job inevitably leads to another. If you put on a decent enough show for *The 100 Greatest Tearjerkers*, you'll find yourself called up for *The 100 Greatest War Films*, and so on. Provide enough usable material for *Generation Jedi* and you'll end up on the long-list for *When Comedy Changed Forever*. And so it goes.

At least for the latter I was interviewed in a cheese shop in Pimlico, which was an experience. It's usually a cheesy bar. The serial talking head gets to see the interiors of an awful lot of nightclubs during the day, favoured clips-show setting for reasons of gauche décor and good depth of field. There's no way on earth I'd ever willingly enter the Purple nightclub in the grounds of Chelsea Football Club during opening hours with its red leather banquettes, mauve drapes and permanently adhesive floor, and yet I've crossed its alarming threshold *twice* in daylight, once for ITV's *Best Ever Bond* and once for an authored documentary about race on television which, to the best of my knowledge, has still never aired on Channel 4.

If your head talks in a disagreeable nightclub and nobody sees it, did it really talk at all?

Another myth: Stuart Maconie has not appeared on that many nostalgic clips shows. It just *feels* as though he has. This is one of the defining misconceptions of our solo work. The truth is, in common with the likes of Peter Kay and Johnny Vegas and Paul Morley and Wayne Hemingway, he tends to give good head, if you'll pardon the expression, and thus winds up all over any programme he participates in. Some poor sap might sit in the chair in the nightclub for an hour and only provide one usable soundbite. But not Stuart. From the initial hour's worth of pithy reminiscence he supplied for the show that started the cycle, *I Love the 70s*, he obviously struck gold with effortless regularity. They asked him back to top up later editions, which is why his shirt changed mid-series. The series ran for ten weeks. He was on every week, talking about a lot of things. That was his crime.

He repeated the trick with *I Love the 80s*. I was on that one – I went on after Louis Theroux – but I only ended up on *1980*, *1981* and *1982*. Stuart had a higher strike rate. The die was cast.

The ultimate backhanded compliment is to be asked on to a *Top 100* when the programme's almost shot and edited. Instead of being sent the full century from which to pick the items you wish to talk about, they're down to about eight that nobody else has said anything decent about. 'Have you got anything to say about *The Last of the Mohicans*, *Breaker Morant* and *Europa, Europa?*' they'll ask. And you'll say, 'Not really. I've got a lot of opinions about *Saving Private Ryan* and *The Great Escape?*' And they'll sigh. The compliment is that you're considered a safe enough pair of hands to help them grout those last few gaps. But it also means you're cleaning up somebody else's mess and all the good ones have been taken. Yes, I've performed this task on many an occasion. It's providing head by the yard; talking to order. The ultimate talking head sin – the one that would have you drummed out of the guild if there was one – is to comment on something you haven't seen and don't care about.

The best kind of clips show is the one where you are genuinely there to offer your own take, or your own memory, or your own half-baked sociological theory. The worst kind trades in 'moments', where pundits simply *describe* what the audience is about to see. That's what they really mean by a media commentator. Once, and only once, did I commentate on a clip that meant nothing to me. It was for *The Top 100 TV Treats 2003*.

'What about … ?'

'I never saw it.'

'Was it on the clips tape we sent you?'

'Yeah, but I never saw it at the time. I don't have any context.'

'Can you just describe it?'

'I don't really like to talk about stuff I haven't seen.'

'But it was on the tape.'

'Yeah, but …'

'Pleeeeeease.'

'I suppose I could say …'

'Thanks, we really appreciate it.'

And I did, and they used it, and I felt dirty when it went out. You must have standards. You must have principles. You must say no. They don't own you. If your head wasn't in front of their camera talking, they'd have nothing. Dead air. A pile of bricks and no mortar.

As soon as Stuart picked up his unwarranted reputation for being the bloke on all the nostalgia shows – in other words, erroneously, a man who couldn't say no, a man with no principles – he stopped doing them. It was quite difficult for him to say no. But he did.

I didn't. I said yes. While Stuart took the heat, I quietly got on with it and did the ones he didn't do. After *I Love the 80s*, when he retired, I did *I Love the 90s*. Then I did *The Pop Years*. Then I did *I Love the Muppets*. Then I did *Britain's Favourite Sitcoms, Britain's Best EastEnder, Top 100 TV Treats 2003, Top 100 Pop Videos, Top 100 Christmas TV Moments, Top 100 Tearjerkers, Top 100 War Films, Top 100 Scary Moments, Top 100 Children's Shows, Top 100 Movie Stars, Top Rated TV, Greatest Ever Disaster Movies, Greatest Ever 80s Movies, Greatest Ever Family Films, BBC Review of the Year 2004, Top 100 TV Moments 2004, Top 100 TV Moments 2005, Shameful Secrets* (can't even remember what that was), *Celebrity Naked Ambition* (wish I'd never done that one), *The Rules of Political Correctness, 25 Years of Smash Hits, Best Ever Bond, Spice: Girls On Film, Solo Spice, Generation Jedi, When Comedy Changed Forever, The Ultimate Sitcom, The Story Of Light Entertainment, 40 Years Of Fuck, Doctor Who Confidential,* and *Top Ten Cops* and *The Sounds of '69*, which I invisibly wrote the links for but didn't appear on. I even did *I Love the 60s*, which was only seen on the BBC website. It should also be stated for the record that I gave an hour of nostalgia gold to the makers of *I Love the Muppets* but they didn't use one single second of it. Fortunately I'm not bitter about it.

When very funny journalists or TV critics like to belittle what is a very popular form, they usually say, ha ha, what next? *The Top 100 Top 100 Clips Shows?* Or else they'll witheringly describe them as 'the sort of programme where Z-list celebrities reminisce about Space Hoppers'. This is pretty rich, as most of the people on these shows are journalists and TV critics. For as long as there are clips shows, there will be people who are willing to go on them, from every strata of the 'celebrity' spectrum. Not least Garry Bushell, and whoever's always on after him.

In the green room before what will turn out to be my only ever appearance on *Newsnight Review*, I compare notes with Paul Morley, who, like me, started out on the *NME* and has reached the same giddy heights. He was one of the reasons why I wanted to be a music journalist in the first place. And he just *asked* if he could be one, too. We have a lot in common, although I suspect Paul doesn't idolise me.

'Did you do *The Top 100 Christmas TV Moments*?' he asks me, over a piece of chicken satay on a stick.

'Yep, just done that one,' I reply. We're like two old gentlemen in a private club.

'I was going to say no,' he points out. 'But then they told me it was going out on Christmas Day! You've got to be on the telly on Christmas Day.'

'Exactly!'

We clink beer bottles, and try to focus our minds on the photographs of Robert Frank.

So this is what happens to people who start out in the music press. They do a bit of telly and a bit of radio and a bit of the other, and they end up in green rooms picking at licence-fee buffets and swapping stories, until a runner comes and fetches them.

There are worse ways to supplement a living, I suppose. And I don't know about you, but I really like Paul Morley's talking head work.

EPILOGUE

What *Am* I?

It's a normal day. Actually, no, it's not. What is a normal day? My ritualistic boarding of the Victoria train from the usual spot on the usual platform at Redhill station no longer applies, although I'm certain a trolley service of drinks and light refreshments is still available and that the train is formed of *eight* coaches.

Since embarking upon my journey to discover what I am almost two years ago, I've moved house again. We're back in London now. Consequently, my train journey is foreshortened to the point where I sometimes don't even bother to take *Bury my Heart at Wounded Knee* out of my suicide bomber's rucksack. This short hop also leaves practically no time for morbid contemplation of my obituary. Perhaps they'll just put me down as 'handyman'.

I'm forty-one, as planned. I'm still a career hyphenate, no nearer to specialising or settling into a groove or finding my brand. It's coming up to Christmas, although the snow that marked my fortieth birthday – and indeed my birth day – is looking unlikely in the unseasonable circumstances. Climate change may be speeding up, but my search for identity is still plodding along at the same old lick. My brother-in-law's sister's son will be eleven. I may or may not bump into him at a family buffet this year, as they tend to start doing their own thing at that age, steering clear of the adults. If I do, he may well have recently seen me on a clips show. I notice they've been repeating *The Pop Years* on Sky Three again with my Old Teeth. Would he still want to know *what I am?* Or would he have started worrying about more important things, like GCSE options and hair gel?

The Old Teeth are gone, but I am still around. It's been a busy year, keeping up the radio work while seeing a six-part sitcom through to fruition. BBC1 are threatening to commission a second series, which would at least add shape to next year, if not actually the stability I used to think I'd hanker after in my forties. But there are no guarantees and, after all, it's just freelance work, not a job for life.

Who really knows what they want to do when they grow up? That would be like seeing the end of the film first. It's not the final 'station-stop' that counts but the getting there. It's what you *do* that matters, not what you *are*.

The train pulls into Waterloo. I've barely had time for even a moderate spell of introspection. I'll work it out on the way home.

The lift descends to the ground floor of Broadcasting House. Hallam Street reception, my usual point of entry and exit, is cramped and functional compared to the Eric Gill majesty of main reception, but that's closed for refurbishment. You never know who you might bump into at Hallam Street reception. I met Johnny Vegas here while waiting for the lift the other week. We had that moment of uncertain recognition you get when two people who have never met but have seen each other on the telly make eye contact. In that split-second of social confusion, he cracked first.

'All right,' he said, with a bonhomie to suggest we were old friends.

'All right,' I said back.

I know my place. I am not even a tenth as famous as Johnny Vegas. He's probably on his way up to be interviewed by Steve Wright, I thought. I just work here. His warmth was gratifying.

'I love 6 Music!' he exclaimed.

'Cheers,' I replied, at least confident now that he had actually identified me. 'It's a good place to work.'

Further pleasantries were exchanged about 6 Music. It's always nice to discover a famous fan of the network. I wanted to tell him how much I admire what he does, but because he's so much more famous than me, the act of doing so would have reduced me to a fan. It's OK for Johnny Vegas to compliment me about my job, because I'm smaller than he is.

'Keep up the good work!' he said, as the *ping* of the arriving lift beckoned him into the bowels of the building.

I thanked him. 'Good to see you,' I said, meaning, 'It was good to see you for the first time,' rather than, 'It was good to see you again.'

What a nice man.

As I step out of the lift today, a gaggle of BBC folk are waiting to get in, including Paul Gambaccini. Now this confusion is remarkably common: *I have no idea whether I've met Paul Gambaccini or not.* I feel that I must have, on some past radio show, talking head job or other, but I can't say for certain. I adopt the safety tactic of the *general smile* – the one that can be interpreted as vague cheer if indeed we have never met and Gambo doesn't know who I am, or as a smile of unobtrusive greeting and broadcaster solidarity in case we have met and he does know who I am. That way, if he says hello, I won't have been rude.

He doesn't say hello. He merely adopts the *general smile* too, and squeezes into the lift I have just vacated. The comings and goings of entertainment folk.

Negotiating the automatic security barriers, I exchange a few cheery words with Penny as I sweep through; she's busy signing in some visitors with guitars, probably coming in for a Hub session. I'm out of the building, on my way to Wise Buddah, where I'm to record some links for a Radio 4 documentary. Always nice to do a bit of work at Wise Buddah, both for its historical connotations and the fact that it's only round the corner.

I stride out onto the pavement, calling out, 'See you later!' to Penny, without looking back. It feels good to treat this place like a hotel. I'm sure Lord Reith wouldn't mind.

Then someone calls out my name.

'Andrew!'

It's Roy Cropper. He approaches me from his regular pitch on the pavement with autograph book and pen held out.

'Would you sign this, please?' he asks, politely but firmly.

'Really? Of course!' I trill.

Rather than the impenetrable signature I put on cheques and release forms, I affect the more personable and curly-wurly 'Andrew' with the marker pen, simultaneously trying and failing to decipher the autographs already on the page, with whom I am to share this significant corner of showbiz legitimacy.

It feels very different from the first time it happened, when the young man at the 1994 Radio 1 Roadshow disconsolately and mechanically asked me and Stuart to sign his book. He didn't know who we were. It meant nothing to him. But Roy knows who I am. What, I ask myself, have I done to merit this sudden elevation from schmuck to celebrity? Why today? I have walked past him for *years* without eliciting a second glance. Surely it's not because of a chance viewing of *The Pop Years* on Sky Three? I have no answer.

One of his cohorts asks me to sign his book, too, and I do, again with pleasure (although it's not as thrilling as Roy asking me, as this second chap's following his lead).

That's it. The rest of the pack don't trouble me. As I walk away, with an undisguised spring in my step, I overhear one of them mutter to Roy, 'Who was that?'

'Andrew Collins,' he replies, and presumably then goes on to explain who I am.

Good luck with that.

*

It was while idly putting my name into search engines – and anyone in any corner of the media who hasn't done that is a disgrace to the profession – that I discovered I had my own entry on the Internet Movie Database, bereft of biographical annotation at that stage but with a mostly accurate CV, including a raft of barely remembered appearances under 'Self'.

There are nine people on the database called Andrew Collins; four actors, a director, a cinematographer, a designer and a 'miscellaneous crew' who turns out to be a supervising animator on Disney films – ironically the very job, as a child, I dreamed of growing up to do. Inexplicably, the director, whose sole credit is *The World's Greatest Goals: Vol 2*, is listed as 'Andrew Collins I', and the actor who played a character called Jarett in four episodes of US soap *The Bold and the Beautiful* is 'Andrew Collins II'. I feel like the Prisoner telling you this, but I am 'Andrew Collins III'.

There's only one Stuart Maconie, but there are nine of me. That's humbling for a start, although two of the actors only have one credit – Andrew Collins VII played 'Black Newspaper Man' in American football drama *Remember the Titans* (2000) and Andrew Collins VI was 'RAF Officer' in an episode of *Hi-De-Hi!* (1986). These are extras, aren't they? Or supporting players, as they prefer to be known. I hope they were as thrilled as me to find themselves IMDb-listed.

But the question remains: *what* am I?

Actually, I know what I am, and there's no shame in it. I am a pie chart. A constantly evolving diagrammatic pastry, with variously shaded slices etched into the crusts.

I'm a husband, a son, a brother, a nephew, an uncle, a tenant, a bird watcher, a London Transport photocard holder, an asthmatic, a blogger, a subscriber to the *New Yorker*, proud sponsor of a guide dog puppy called Fliss, and, as of July 2006, an Honorary Fellow of the University of Northampton – which,

I've since discovered, doesn't get me a table at either of Northampton's decent restaurants or allow me to drive geese through the Grosvenor Centre on public holidays. I'm quite happy to be defined by any of those things. The combination may even help to paint a fuller picture. But if you insist that I am defined by my job, I'm still a DJ, author, scriptwriter and film editor of the *Radio Times*, just as I was when I was forty and wracked with identity issues. I am also, I might add, available for public appearances, student seminars, consultation work, and a very nice slide show. But there's plenty of time to tame the pie and fill the obituary pages. After all, I don't intend to die today, or for another thirty-nine years at least.

Tomorrow? Well, who knows? And frankly, who would *want* to know?

Perhaps Utrecht.